MIRRORS OF AMERICAN CULTURE

children's fiction series in the twentieth century

by
PAUL DEANE

The Scarecrow Press, Inc.
Metuchen, N.J., & London
1991

The author gratefully acknowledges permission to reprint excerpts from the following:

"Black Characters in Children's Fiction Series Since 1968," by Paul Deane, in *The Journal of Negro Education*, v. 58, no. 2 (Spring 1989), pp. 153-162. Reprinted by permission of *The Journal of Negro Education*.

"A Century of Xenophobia in Fiction Series for Young People," by Paul Deane, in *Journal of Youth Services in Libraries*, v. 3 (Winter 1990), pp. 117-127; copyright © 1990 ALA. Reprinted by permission of the American Library Association.

"The Persistence of Uncle Tom: An Examination of the Image of the Negro in Children's Fiction Series," by Paul Deane, in *The Journal of Negro Education*, v. 37, no. 2 (Spring 1968), pp. 140-145. Reprinted by permission of *The Journal of Negro Education*.

British Library Cataloguing-in-Publication data available

Library of Congress Cataloging-in-Publication Data

Deane, Paul, 1928–
    Mirrors of American culture : children's fiction series in the twentieth century / Paul Deane.
       p. cm.
    Includes bibliographical references and index.
    ISBN 0-8108-2460-4 (alk. paper)
    1. Children's stories, American—History and criticism.
2. Children—United States—Books and reading—History—20th century. 3. Serialized fiction—United States—History and criticism. 4. Children's literature in series—History and criticism. 5. American fiction—20th century—History and criticism.
6. United States—Civilization—20th century.
I. Title.
PS374.C454D4   1991
813'.5099282—dc20   91-30998

Copyright © 1991 by Paul Deane
Manufactured in the United States of America

Printed on acid-free paper

*For Phyllis
and for Shaun and Christopher,
who read many of these books as they grew up and
who graciously allowed me the use of their library*

CONTENTS

Preface   vii

PART I: THE SERIES IN PERSPECTIVE

1. The Case of the Children's Fiction Series; or, Definition, History, and Problems of Analysis   3
2. "Not to Be Circulated": Criticism and Censorship of Series   16
3. What Do Jane and Johnny Read—By Choice? Children's Taste and Motives in Reading   30
4. Passport to Enjoyment: Style and Technique of the Series   48

PART II: ATTITUDES, BELIEFS, VALUES

    General Introduction   69
5. Family Life and Relationships   71
    Parental Image   71
    Images of Family Life   74
    Man-Woman, Husband-Wife, Father-Mother Relationships   85
    The Good Life   92
6. Extra-Family Relationships   97
    External Judgment of Persons   97
    Judgments of Race and Nationality   104
7. Miscellaneous Aspects of Life and Society   128
    Economic Concerns   128
    The Cycle of Life   135
      Romance   135
      Birth   139
      Physical Impairments   139
      Education   142

Death	145
Images of Social Institutions	146
Science, Scientists, and Technology	146
Law Enforcement Officers	154
War and the Military	158
Religion	162
Attitudes Toward the United States and Travel	166
Nature and Animals	168
Violence	176
8 Recommended and Unacceptable Elements	188
Justice	188
Optimism	189
Traits of Character	190
Reason vs. Emotion	190
Honor	193
Good Sportsmanship	194
Kindness	196
Pluck, Fortitude, and "Sissiness"	197
Afterword	201
Bibliography	205
Secondary Sources	205
The Series	219
Index	249

PREFACE

WRITING IN 1974, EXACTLY three-quarters of a century after the first appearance of the Rover Boys, J. Frederick MacDonald noted that "there exists no systematic and inclusive investigation of the hundreds of fictional series" (534). To date he is still correct. There is no full and comprehensive examination of the best-selling, most popular, most influential type of children's reading. Studies have been done of some aspects of some series. Many, if not most, of those in article form can be found in the Bibliography of the present work; they average approximately three per year since 1899. Full-length consideration has been given to specific areas, for instance, K. J. Stang's *Series Books for the American Girl: 1910-1940*, though only three decades of the twentieth century are covered and boys' books are omitted. J. K. Rosenberg in *Young People's Literature in Series* looked at an even smaller period, 1973-1975, and included nonfiction and publishers series as well as fiction.

Thus, one of the most fruitful sources of knowledge about the United States and its citizens, their attitudes, prejudices, values, and institutions has gone largely untapped. The study at hand attempts to remedy this lack. It examines, first, the position of children's series fiction in America since 1899, the year that series as we know them today actually began. The term "position" involves such elements as their historical development, the nature of critical opinion directed against them, attempts at censorship, and reasons for their success with juvenile readers from the points of view of taste, psychological motivation, and style. Then it will consider in detail the values, attitudes, and ideals which the books contain, giving attention to areas such as home and family life, personal relations, and social institutions.

Obviously, the primary source of information is the books themselves, and here two major problems arise. One is the enormous number of series and of individual volumes within them: to speak of thousands of series would not be far-fetched (the Stratemeyer Syndicate alone produced more than 800), and an average of between thirty and forty books within each seems a reasonable estimate. Several lifetimes would be required to cover them all, even if the second problem, that of availability, were not present: virtually all of them are no longer in print and most have been discarded or turned to dust. Choices of what books to include are sometimes voluntary, but often dictated by this latter condition and by the fact that until the 1970's, most public libraries refused to include them in their collections. While they have begun to do so now, they stock the most readily available ones—Nancy Drew, the Hardy Boys, and the Bobbsey and Sweet Valley Twins. A library with a complete collection even of these would be hard to find.

Where series such as these have been continued in print since their initial appearance, I have read them all. The Rover Boys and the original Tom Swift books show up at rummage sales of various kinds, and I have been able to read a majority of these "cornerstone" series. Secondhand bookstores within the past decade have become aware of the nostalgic value of these books, and one can find a few through this source. The difficulty, though, is not insurmountable. While there is an amazing range of scene and subject within a given series, most duplicate one another, and series on the same theme (for example, nursing and mystery) use many of the same devices and very similar titles. I have tried, therefore, to take several series dealing with home and family life, with Boy Scouts, with school, with travel, covering as much of the 1899–1989 period as possible in order to get comparisons and, if they exist, contrasts.

In general, I allowed the material to dictate to me. Originally, I had a format that seemed promising, but as far as possible, I read without preconceptions. Often my original ideas changed, disappeared, or reversed. This condition has been true especially since the 1960's. I have talked with many people closely involved with children's literature—teachers, library workers, critics; I have surveyed by questionnaires both children and adults. A few positions emerged: nostalgic pleasure, largely reinforced if not created by the passage of time; outright disgust; the feeling that series are good incentives for other reading, and a directly opposite view. My own approach was dispassionate,

Preface

though it has become less so about books published in the last decade, and my reaction to the new Hardy Boys Casefiles is negative.

To the books I brought thirty-six years of experience as a teacher of writing and as a critic of American civilization. Many of the books I enjoyed in and for themselves; many I finished with utter contempt. The bulk of criticism is negative, untenable, and meager. Literally none of it is based on the amount of material involved here, and it is often polemical, narrow, and unfounded because it is unsupported, at least in print, by evidence. I have tried to be fair and to base my reactions upon statistical evidence drawn from more than 1,000 volumes. I have ignored "official" and traditional points of view.

As noted, the series have received little specific study or criticism. That which exists is reflected in the first three chapters. The material in the final five chapters, drawn almost entirely from primary sources, has scarcely been treated at all. Even efforts to do so in the last decade and a half are based generally on a small number of books. In no case is their view comprehensive. The list of series titles included in the Bibliography ends with 1989. Since new volumes in series currently being written (e.g., Sweet Valley High) appear at the rate of about one a month, no list of them can remain up to date for long.

PAUL DEANE
Bentley College
Waltham, Mass.

PART I:
THE SERIES IN PERSPECTIVE

1 THE CASE OF THE CHILDREN'S FICTION SERIES; OR, DEFINITION, HISTORY, AND PROBLEMS OF ANALYSIS

THE TERMS "CHILDREN'S BOOKS" and "juvenile literature" are, like many generalizations, ambiguous. In colonial America *The New England Primer* was used by the Puritans with the instruction of children in mind. The work was a direct attempt to teach and encourage religious and moral values and thus was an educational and ecclesiastical tool. Should the *Primer* be considered "children's literature"? Is the fact that children will make use of a book the determining factor? Sister Monica Kiefer studied "hundreds of tiny volumes written especially for children and for their training" to discover "the changing status of the child in the colonial and national periods as it is revealed in juvenile literature" (1). Her sources were didactic textbooks—guides for children and parents—and not books that children could be expected to choose for themselves.

The most extensive attempt to trace the history and development of literature for children is *A Critical History of Children's Literature* by Cornelia Meigs, Anne Thaxter Eaton, Elizabeth Nesbitt, and Ruth Hall Viguers. In his introduction to this work, Henry Steele Commager raises an important issue, the theme in fact of the entire *History*: there is no dividing line, he claims, between books for adults and books for children. He mentions various authors who recognized that young people were entitled to enter the world of imagination: Scott, Thackeray, Dickens; before he is through he has included Franklin's *Autobiography*, *Walden*, *Moby-Dick*, Poe, and Cooper—writers and works that were "taken over" by children, though he admits that they were "written without children in mind" (viii). In fact a large part of the entire book is concerned with writing that was not done for children to read themselves. Virtually everything that Cornelia Meigs considers children's literature through 1840 is material that children have "taken over" (she goes back to the Anglo-Saxon Chronicles, for example); only in her coverage of poets and in her examination of Peter Parley and the Rollo books does she deal with writing specifically done for young people.

One faces a twofold problem, hence: to state a definition of children's books that will indicate the scope and terms of the present study of the children's fiction series and to observe these books in the context of the twentieth century. Although since 1900 fewer books were simply appropriated by children and more were written directly for them, the line is still a fine one. Elizabeth Nesbitt's treatment of the 1890–1920 period, for instance, includes Kipling, Stevenson, and Jack London's *Call of the Wild*. In this major critical work and other historical analyses of juvenile literature, series are identified only by the series name; individual titles and their contents are not discussed. There is no evaluation of series books in any but the most general and abstract terms.

This latter fact is most important in that the fiction series are almost the only books that have been consistently produced for the consumption of children themselves. The majority of others are aimed predominantly at adult tastes, since publishers realize that adults will buy them. The *Horn Book* leaflet, *Thirty Twentieth Century Children's Books Every Adult Should Know*, reveals the idea clearly: the average price for the thirty books listed was $3.25. Though the pamphlet is undated, it was issued before 1965, when the price was a stiff one for children to pay.

The children's books to be discussed here are limited to volumes issued in series. "Fiction series" refers to books written by one author (either an actual person using his or her own name or a pseudonym, or a syndicate, such as that of Edward Stratemeyer, producing books under the name of a single nonexistent author), involving the same major characters—heroes, friends, parents, villains—in a successive series of actions, scenes, and situations, each complete in itself but continuing the adventures of the major characters. Thus the many books by Thornton W. Burgess about such animals as Longlegs the Heron do not qualify, because while many of the same characters appear from book to book, there are no central, common

Definition, History & Problems of Analysis 5

characters who appear invariably in the same relationship. Series books are sold at minimum prices and can be bought by children themselves. A quarter century ago, the chief contemporary series—Tom Swift, Jr., Nancy Drew, the Hardy Boys, and Chip Hilton—were priced at $1.25, but discounted widely by chain, drug, and department stores, they sold for as little as $.29, a trifle compared with $3.25 for the *Thirty Twentieth Century Children's Books Every Adult Should Know*. In the updating and rewriting of such series in the past decade, the books now list for between $2.25 and $3.95, reflecting the inflation of the intervening years; however, since the "good" (that is, acceptable) children's books, such as the Caldecott winners and the like, list for an average of $12, the relative gap between them and the series is still maintained. Cost, as Lewis Terman (86) and Polly Ann Scott (3147) have pointed out, is a major factor in the widespread reading of series. Finally, the series are designed for and written to be read by children; it is not expected that adults will read such books to children, and consequently little or no opportunity for adult supervision or expurgation exists.

We can safely assume that in the realm of children's literature, series are the most widely read books—how widely is impossible to calculate, since they are traded and loaned extensively by children. Surveys of trends in children's literature are, therefore, misleading, since they do not include the series. For the past two decades, many public libraries have included some series in their collections, but beyond statements such as, "Kids love them," or the fact that the rate of borrowing requires frequent replacement of entire series, exact information about their popularity is unavailable.

One further limitation should be made. Until the 1970's, the fiction series were aimed at children between eight and twelve in grades three to six. With the appearance in the 1980's of such "new" series as the Nancy Drew Files and the Hardy Boys Casefiles, efforts have been made by publishers to extend the upper limits to perhaps fifteen, while the New Bobbsey Twins Series could probably be managed by an adept second grader.

As a background for the twentieth century, let us survey briefly the general state of juvenile literature before 1900. "The only literary diversion recommended for children before the

American Revolution was the reading of stories of a purely religious nature or tales of a didactic or moral character. . . . Books that provided entertainment or that stimulated the child's imagination . . . were looked upon as vain and worldly" (Kiefer 4). Sister Monica Kiefer's excellent study of early children's reading concluded that no real attempt was made in America to give children reading material suitable for their age and level of development. While the element of religion in books for young people did wane with the decline of Puritanism, about the middle of the eighteenth century it was replaced by "practical books of moral construction" (Kiefer 11).

No significant change occurred through the Civil War. Jacob Abbott's Rollo began to appear in the 1830's. Filled with moral dicta and instruction in correct behavior, the Rollo books covered a wide range of areas: *Rollo Learning to Read*, *Rollo Learning to Talk*, and so on, through Rollo's attempts to work and play. In 1840 Abbott took Rollo abroad in Rollo's Travels, and thereafter followed him to Paris, Scotland, and other exotic locales, thereby beginning a series tradition that still persists. Although the author assured readers in the "Notice" which prefaced *Rollo's Travels* that "no direct effort to convey moral instruction" would be made, he hastened to add that reading the book would "exert a considerable influence of a salutary character, upon the mind of the child"; among other things, Rollo's "docility" and "sweetness" would be exhibited.

Sarah Law Kennerly in her study of literary publications in the Confederate States of America found their contents mediocre in style, sentimental or moralistic in tone, reflecting stern attitudes toward the intellectual, moral, and religious training of children (6). On the other hand, Anne Thaxter Eaton in *A Critical History of Children's Literature* (Meigs et al.) found instruction as the main objective of juvenile books weakening in the latter nineteenth century. She noted the appearance of family life as a major aspect of children's reading: *Little Women* and *Little Men* are books about young people having good times together, enjoying warmth and security with understanding elders. The theme of filial obedience, however, was often present.

When *St. Nicholas: A Magazine for Boys and Girls* began in 1873, its editorial policy was stated by Mary Mapes Dodge as editor (all italics are mine):

1. To give *clean,* genuine fun for children of all ages.
2. To give them *examples* of the *finest types* of boyhood and girlhood.
3. To *inspire* them with a *fine appreciation* of pictorial art.
4. To *cultivate* the imagination in *profitable* directions.
5. To foster a love of country, home, nature, truth, beauty, sincerity.
6. To *prepare* boys and girls for life as it is.
7. To *stimulate* their ambitions—but along normally progressive lines.
8. To keep pace with a fast-moving world in all its activities.
9. To give reading matter which every *parent* may pass to his children unhesitatingly.

Most interesting to note, in view of such statements, is Eaton's suggestion that "with *St. Nicholas* didacticism as a chief theme in reading for children fled away forever" (Meigs et al. 7). Clearly every aspect of editorial policy intended to inculcate desirable attitudes.

Nevertheless, six years before the appearance of *St. Nicholas*, the real revolution had begun with the publication in 1867 of Martha Finley's *Elsie Dinsmore*. Elsie's life and adventures were to be chronicled for the next thirty-eight years, a period in which the ground was broken and the foundation laid for a new kind of writing for children: not only new in purpose, but new in form—the Elsie books were the first actual series for children. As Janet E. Brown observed,

> The old Sunday School had been dissolved; the publishers' desire to guide the young into paths of rectitude was second only to their not unnatural desire to make a profit.... The conscientiously moral story ... ceased to sell. Meanwhile there had been some earnest work on the part of enterprising editors to provide material both saleable and suitable for children.... It was as though there had been a slow discarding of the sober and confining garments of Victorianism, and a robust rebellion against didacticism, moral exhortation, and forthright instruction appeared. Juvenile literature had risen above patter and prudery and had come into its own. (126–127)

The revolution did not occur fully overnight, however; Janet Brown devotes the third of her five-chapter analysis of the Elsie series to a discussion of the religious views and didactic qualities of the books, in the course of it referring to Martha Finley's "narrowness, her rigidity, her unbending austerity" in books where "good was a positive virtue and the opposite of evil" (77). One is not certain that instruction as a main objective of children's literature has ever disappeared implicitly, but it was undoubtedly weakening explicitly in the latter 1800's.

Certainly, Horatio Alger's unfailing confidence in thrift, industry, cheerfulness, and providential intervention represents a continuation of the moral-didactic-instructional strain. Expressed in well over a hundred volumes beginning in the same year as the Elsie Dinsmore books, these elements were presented by Alger in stories that were exciting, adventure-filled, and interesting to young readers despite their platitudes. The same is true of the remaining member of what Dora Smith called "the immortal four": Oliver Optic, in his "116 cloth and paper volumes filled with drunken youths at sea who gambled," and Harry Castlemon's books about the Civil War (5).

Thus, a very cursory examination of the main lines of children's literature before 1900 reveals a gradual lessening of concern for the direct teaching of moral values and an increasing interest in entertainment for its own sake. This trend is paralleled by the history of American literature in general.

In the last decade of the nineteenth century, the average number of children's books published each year was 403.6; this figure included new books as well as new editions ("Juvenile Books During Twenty-Eight Years" 39). By 1910, as Dora Smith has shown (1) the didactic element was dying quickly and swashbuckling tales about Indians, sailors, and wild animals were taking its place; stories of normal children playing, studying, or traveling were increasing in popularity. Apparently as the aspect of entertainment increased, so did sales, for the average number of children's books published each year from 1900 to 1910 was 548 ("Juvenile Books" 39). How much of the increase was due to series books is impossible to say, since no compiler of figures classifies his data. The Rover Boys Series was available from 1899 and the Motor Boys Series from 1906. The Stratemeyer Syndicate began issuing the series that would make the greatest impact—Tom Swift and the Bobbsey Twins—both during the first decade of the twentieth century. (Total sales of thirty million are claimed for Tom Swift alone from 1910 to 1941, an average of a million a year.) During the next decade, the average yearly total of children's books jumped to 664, and the century of the series book was fully underway. Mary Eakins estimates that by the 1950's, the figure had almost doubled, reaching 1,113 a year for all books written specifically for children (51).

Such figures show only that the publication of children's books increased during the twentieth century. They do qualify the claim of Professor Jane Hannigan (when teaching courses in children's literature at Simmons College, Boston, in 1965) that the reason for the great popularity of series in the early years of the century was that nothing else was available; clearly a good deal else was available. Perhaps the reason for their popularity lies elsewhere.

Comparisons of series with other types of children's reading are suggestive. Elizabeth Nesbitt (in Meigs et al., *A Critical History of Children's Literature*) lists the main lines and chief writers of juvenile literature in the 1890–1920 period: Howard Pyle (stories of knights and medieval adventure), fairy tales, books about the United States, Kipling, Beatrix Potter (stories for the very young), Kenneth Grahame (also fairy tales and animal stories), fantasy, romance and actuality (including Thomas Nelson Page, Jack London, and Kate Douglas Wiggin), biography and history, picture books, and poetry (poetry has the largest bibliography of any chapter in the section, though children do not willingly choose to read poetry). None of these categories bears any relation to the fiction series except that of romance and actuality, and the authors discussed in that area, with the possible exception of Wiggin, do not involve themselves with subject matter in any major way similar to that of series. Again, if these were the chief things available for children to read, the series offered something quite different. Furthermore, five of the eleven categories (fairy tales, picture books, poetry, Potter, and Grahame), possibly more, are outside the reading tastes of children from eight to twelve. Ruth Viguers (also in Meigs et al., *A Critical History*) draws similar categories for the 1920–1950 period: folktale collections, modern fairy tales, poetry, sea stories, tales with historical backgrounds, stories of everyday life, regional stories, romantic adventures in other lands, history, science and inventions, and picture books. Of her dozen subject areas, only four are found also in series: stories of the sea, everyday life, foreign romances, and science and inventions.

One is compelled to conclude that the series are popular, not because other kinds of reading matter are unavailable, but because they offer children a kind of reading that other children's books do not. Despite the existence of many books other than series, the series have been consistently the best-sellers of the children's field. In 1974 Peter Soderbergh estimated that the Rover Boys Series (which began in 1899), the Bobbsey Twins (1904), the Motor Boys (1906), Tom Swift (1910), the Hardy Boys (1927), and Nancy Drew (1930) have together accounted for 125 million sales (865). In the 1970's, he added, Nancy Drew sold 1.5 million copies a year, the Hardy Boys another million, and the Bobbsey Twins 250,000; "Nancy Drew is the most popular juvenile book in France" (870). C. L. Biemiller wrote in 1973 that "the big days of the Tom Swifts, the Merriwells, the Rover Boys and the Hardys and all those nurse heroines are supposed to be over" (62), but five years later, Jean Mercier believed that Nancy Drew and the Hardy Boys alone averaged well over a million copies a year. Between these two, in 1975 an article in *School Library Journal* estimated that the Bobbsey Twins had sold more than 160 million copies, Nancy Drew more than 60 million and had been translated into twelve languages (not including efforts to translate them into Japanese) and were sold in seventeen countries ("Orange, N.J. Honors Nancy Drew" 10). Even if we recognize the obvious differences in sales numbers, the figures are phenomenal.

When one tries to find some pattern in the publishing of children's books after 1900, one faces several hurdles. For one thing, critics and commentators are given to establishing periods of publication and assigning descriptive titles to them; there is very little agreement, however, on what the limits and designations should be. Elizabeth Nesbitt, for example, sets 1890–1920 as a distinct period, while Dora Smith feels that the 1910–1925 period is a unit; Smith calls the period from 1925 to 1940 "the Golden Age," while Ruth Viguers places "Childhood's Golden Era" between 1920 and 1950.

Definition, History & Problems of Analysis   11

Another difficulty is represented by Viguers's description of trends and types in this latter period. The subject fields in her list show that very few kinds of literature are not included, a fact basically true of the entire *Critical History*: each of its sections is a list, first, of all major kinds of literature produced in the period covered; then a few "critical" statements are made about what the editors feel are significant examples of each type. Periods discussed differ from one another only slightly, and in reality the result is not a history so much as a list of preferences. Dora Smith does virtually the same thing. There is in print no study which shows, for instance, that a given decade is the age of aviation stories. Perhaps it is not possible to do so, though both World War I and II produced war series and Sputnik revived Tom Swift. It would be revealing if we could establish as a frame of reference a pattern of the development of juvenile literature in the twentieth century and plot the various series against it; we might be able to show parallel or divergent happenings. Such cannot be done, though, since the major critics of children's literature have merely listed for any period of time every imaginable type of book, and every imaginable type of book appears to some extent in every period of time. Until someone does a critical study of children's books other than those in series, categorizes more rigidly, and tries to account for the appearance of various classes of books, there is no background against which to test the series—which remain apart and distinct unto themselves.

Furthermore, this kind of analysis cannot really be done for the series either. Or if it can, to do so would be fruitless. First, similar series with almost identical material appear at different times: e.g., the Grace Harlowe college series begins in the teens, the Marjorie Dean college series in the twenties, and the Beverly Gray college series in the thirties—all taking their heroines in four volumes through four years of college. Second, in several series the same situations and highly similar titles appear: e.g., *The Bobbsey Twins in the Country*, *Bunny Brown and His Sister Sue on Grandpa's Farm*, *Honey Bunch: Her First Days on a Farm*, and *The Happy Hollisters at Pony Hill Farm* (the first two appeared in the teens, the third in the twenties, and the last in the fifties). Also comparable are *Sue Barton, Student Nurse* (1936) and *Cherry Ames, Student Nurse* (1944), *Sue Barton,*

Senior Nurse (1937) and *Cherry Ames, Senior Nurse* (1944). Time is not an element of importance in the series.

The last statement is not so outrageous as it sounds. An article from 1918 titled "Juvenile Books During Twenty-Eight Years" claimed a close connection between current events and the series. Pointing to the discovery of the North Pole in 1909 and the South Pole in 1911, to progress in airplanes and automobiles, it argued that such events had stimulated the writers of semiscientific juveniles to produce "the flood of books for boys and girls in series after series known as the Automobile Boys, the Motor Boys, the Rover Boys, the Aeroplane Boys, the Submarine Boys . . . and many other titles suggestive of the changing times in which we live" (39).

It can be demonstrated, however, that the connection is chiefly titular. To be sure, the series about the Rover Boys (i.e., those who rove) probably does reflect an interest in exploration and discovery, yet anyone who knows the series well realizes that it could have been—and likely was—written with no knowledge at all of specific locales. The titles are *On the Ocean, In the Mountains, In the Jungle*; even *In New York* contains no description whatever that could possibly distinguish New York from Chicago, Philadelphia, or London. The 1985 Hardy Boys entry *Revenge of the Desert Phantom* occurs in the same Africa that was written about in the 1929 *Don Sturdy in Lion Land*, one which their authors had never visited. It is true that the Boy Scout movement, which began in 1910, spawned a rash of series about scouting (Payson's first volume appeared the following year). But again, a reader of any of the several scouting series sees immediately that the connection between the movement and the series exists only in titles: one could change *The Boy Scouts in the Rockies* to *The Rover Boys in the Mountains*, or both to *The Outdoor Boys in the Blue Ridge Mountains* and no one would know the difference. The same is true of World War I: *Uncle Sam's Boys with Pershing's Troops at the Front* (1919) is the same book as *The Boy Scouts on Belgian Battlefields* (1915). *The Camp Fire Mystery* (1982), which could be subtitled *The Bobbsey Twins in New Mexico*, also might have occurred in Montana or Arizona, and except for a diagram describing how to build a bluebird nesting house, it has only the barest connection to the Camp Fire Movement. Ruth Viguers claims in *A*

Definition, History & Problems of Analysis 13

Critical History that the Lindbergh flight of 1927 touched off many aviation stories; the date seems quite late, since Tom Swift had built an airship in 1910; even then there was a lag, for the Wright Brothers first flew successfully in 1904. Perhaps there is a connection between Wilbur Wright's winning the Michelin Cup in France for a seventy-seven mile flight on December 31, 1909, but one would hesitate to make it.

The world of the series is an abstract one. As will be detailed later, the values, ideals, and attitudes, even with some very recent innovations, remain unchanged essentially in the series from 1900 to the present. The Rover Boys Series ran from 1899 to 1925; the boys grew up, married, and became parents, but neither they nor their world nor their ideas changed a jot. The Bobbsey Twins are more than three-quarters of a century old; they have aged from four and eight to six and twelve (a difficult difference to understand), but otherwise they are the same children: their world and perception of it, their relationships, their conversation (while updated periodically), are practically indistinguishable from first to last. Also unchanged are critical objections to the series, the psychological and literary motives of their readers, the way those motives are satisfied, their style and format. They do indeed reveal a great deal about the American mind, but not, it should be noted well, in the superficial sense that they reflect current events.

An additional fact of importance to a discussion of the children's fiction series and one which corroborates the preceding arguments is the existence of syndicates for the production of those books. The most important was formed by Edward Stratemeyer in 1903. Using at least thirteen different names including his own, Stratemeyer produced more than eight hundred books for children in various series "with machine-like regularity about places where [he and his staff of writers] had never been" (Shanklin 588). Under the name of Stratemeyer, he wrote the Old Glory Series, Pan-American Series, Soldiers of Fortune Series, Colonial Series, Mexican War Series, Dave Porter Series, and others. As Arthur Winfield, he wrote the Rover Boys; as Victor Appleton, the Tom Swift books and those about Don Sturdy; as Laura Lee Hope, the Bobbsey Twins; and under other pseudonyms, the Motor Boys, Bomba, Ruth Fielding, and more. Some of these works he wrote himself, while for others, he devised plots, conceived titles, added finishing touches, and generally superintended those that he did not personally create. Estimates are that he wrote 160 juveniles as Winfield, Appleton, and so forth, and created plots for about 700 more, as well as writing 50 as himself.

Roger Garis, son of Howard Garis, author of the Uncle Wiggily stories, claimed in 1964 that "Stratemeyer conceived most of the titles, and suggested many of the basic plots. My father—and later on, my mother, my sister, and I—wrote the original books. After the books were written, we turned them over to Stratemeyer, and he had them published by various firms—mostly Grosset and Dunlap—paying us flat sums for the books" (Garis 65). Further, he claimed that his mother wrote the Bobbsey Twins, his father, Tom Swift, while he himself wrote the Outboard Boys. Edna Yost wrote that later the Garis family began its own syndicate ("Who Writes?" 1598).

Stratemeyer's daughter, Harriet Adams, inherited the syndicate and ran it until her death in 1982. There never was a Victor Appleton, she stated, but a "writing factory . . . a whole stable of writers" ("Chip Off the Old Block" 66). After her father's death in 1930, Adams took charge, her particular interest being the Nancy Drew books, which she began writing with the fourth title, *Mystery at Lilac Inn* (1930). In 1954, she spoke of the Tom Swift, Jr., Series, saying that a "battery of specialists goes over everything to eradicate the slightest error"; the battery included experts on jets, rockets, physics, and television ("Chip" 66).

Although Grosset and Dunlap had published the original Nancy Drew, Hardy Boys, Tom Swift, and Bobbsey Twins books, in 1979 the Stratemeyer Syndicate decided to do business with Simon and Schuster instead, and the latter firm began issuing new titles in these series with no break in the numbering of volumes. Grosset and Dunlap sued the Syndicate for breach of contract; Simon and Schuster countersued, and Grosset and Dunlap ultimately lost the case, retaining, however, the right to publish the "original" series, which in effect ended in 1979. In that year, for example, Grosset and Dunlap brought out *The Thirteenth Pearl*, number 56 in the Nancy Drew Series, while Simon and Schuster published *The Triple Hoax*, number 57. Since then, Simon and Schuster, using its own "syndicate," has

Definition, History & Problems of Analysis   15

been producing entries in these series at the rate of about one a month.

The existence of syndicates for the production of the children's fiction series is further evidence that these books do not represent the peculiar opinions, prejudices, and philosophies of particular people, but those of groups, of publishing houses, of committees, to whom profit is the chief consideration. That there is little change or variation in the books is quite understandable: attention has been and is being given to the production of books that will satisfy the perceived wishes, needs, and attitudes of young readers. In this way, they are excellent indicators of what the mind of America is like at any given period. Peter Soderbergh refers to "an awareness of the books' usefulness as a mirror of our former selves" (870). They are also useful as mirrors of our present selves.

2 "NOT TO BE CIRCULATED": CRITICISM AND CENSORSHIP OF SERIES

TO EXAMINE THE KIND OF criticism directed at series books and to make some judgment about the nature and validity of it is most productive. In doing so, one becomes aware of consistent features. First, the series have received a great deal of general attention, most of it negative. Second, when series books are mentioned, they are lumped together under the title of the entire series, while individual books, with a handful of exceptions, are rarely mentioned. Third, the criticism has overall been phrased in general, abstract, and meaningless terms. The language and elements of this criticism have changed hardly at all since 1900—the same arguments, the same terms, the same reasoning are to be found again and again and so hardened that in 1974 Peter Soderbergh could divide all of it into "Classical" and "Developmental" (870). The conclusion, almost inescapable, is that the critics, librarians, and occasional teachers who have tried to discredit the series either have not read them and are simply reiterating views which have "always" been held, or have not read them critically or in sufficient numbers to make their comments sound. The work of proponents is scarcely better. While it is not the purpose here to champion the cause of the series or defend their contents and techniques, it must be noted that almost no person or organization has presented arguments which a basic course in logic would not reject as unfounded and inconclusive.

Before 1890 public libraries in the United States gave practically no recognition to children, nor had they developed services especially devoted to children. By 1900 library work with young people had become a "vital and permanent part of the whole library development in the United States" (Meigs et al.,

A Critical History 419). The year 1900 saw also the formation of the Section for Children's Librarians of the American Library Association, which in 1941 became the Children's Library Association of the Division of Libraries for Children and Young People and which stated fundamental aims and objectives and established methods of work. As Elizabeth Nesbitt says, "They evolved criteria for the selection and use of children's books which are eternally valid" (Meigs et al. 421). In this statement lies a main objection to the bulk of critical writing about juvenile literature, namely its tendency to generalization and abstraction. To assume any principle of criticism to be "eternally valid" indicates great temerity, as does the application of criteria developed a half-century earlier to books of the present.

Despite a movement for the evaluation of children's literature by the turn of the century, an informed and constructive criticism of juvenile books was still lacking twenty years later. Reviewers often dismissed a work as a mere children's book, ignored the child's point of view, and condemned the work for not doing what the reviewer thought it should (Meigs et al. 421). The beginning of real criticism of juvenile literature is generally assumed to be Anne Carroll Moore's review of *A Little Boy Lost* by W. H. Hudson, published in *The Bookman*, November 1918. Six years later Moore began editing the children's page of the *New York Herald Tribune*, a section called "The Three Owls." In 1924 also the *Horn Book* appeared, the first periodical devoted to children's reading (two years later its name became the *Horn Book Magazine*). *The Saturday Review of Literature* began a book page for children in 1927/1928, and the *New York Times Book Review* started a page called "Books for Young People" in 1930. Since then, reviewing of juvenile literature has been a recognized aspect of journalism.

What precisely has this criticism been like? Without singling out one source as most influential, we may begin to frame an answer by examining the terms published by the *Horn Book Magazine*, since it has consistently stated its aims and position. In *Fanfare . . . 1958–1962* it offered an "Honor List of Children's Books" issued in those years which "have values that make them worthwhile." The Introduction by editor Ruth Hill Viguers stated such values: "qualities of fineness and permanence," "distinction in writing and illustration," "sincerity," "joy in the writing," "experiences worth reliving," "lift young people above mediocrity," and "give children wings." The section written by Viguers for *A Critical History of Children's Literature* contains similar language: the "mass-produced books" of 1940–1950 did little "to build up resistance to cheapness and mediocrity by developing a critical imagination and the appreciation of good drawing, good writing, and genuine humor" (Meigs et al. 442). Earlier she had spoken of "a beautiful book which, though entirely in black and white, had lightness and gaiety" (436). Surely such words as "fineness," "sincerity," and "beautiful" have no objective standards of definition and can have only subjective meaning to their user, as can "give children wings."

Ruth Viguers is by no means alone in the use of such terms. Clara Hunt similarly refused to define what she meant in 1910 by "strong, high literature," "the highest, purest ideals," or "the weak standards of the empty-headed" ("Good Taste" 679–80). M. A. Carringer felt in 1912 that the subject matter of children's books should be "clean and wholesome" and that they should be written in "pure, simple, elegant language" (166). In 1921 Irene Bowman objected that series did not have "a high literary excellence" (212). Robb White felt that characters could be "bad, but with ordinary amounts of right instincts" (37). In the same way, Elizabeth Johnson did not specify what she meant in 1929 by "good books," but since her article, only two pages long, contains ten errors in grammar and punctuation, one doubts the ability of such a critic to judge writing as good or bad (679). Writing in the same year, Lillian Herron Mitchell evidently felt that her readers would know, perhaps instinctively, what "good books" and "right diction" were, since she did not define the terms; she pronounced the series "worthless," but did not explain why, and added that, "after all, librarians know that the best test of a good child's book is whether a literary-minded adult will enjoy it or not. By a literary-minded adult I mean one who appreciates the worthwhile in literature" (580). In 1939, Robb White, in *The Saturday Review of Literature*, believed that a good child's book was "well and sincerely written" (9).

This lack of adequately explained terms is a major aspect of the criticism of series books, and of children's books in general. Another weakness is the kind of argument used. Ernest Ayres, defending items on the libraries' "Not to Be Circulated" list of series and other books, asked, "Would any book of absolutely no value have lived as long as Elsie Dinsmore?" (528). Richard Smyers argued in the same vein: "Can something be steadily printed for sixty-four years, in seventeen languages, and be 'just a piece of trash'?" (190). It would be easy to show that quality and longevity are not necessarily connected. Irene Bowman objected to series on the grounds that a child gets "the same ideas presented again and again, often in an identical setting," so that after he or she has read the first volume, the child can sail through the rest "without mental effort . . . exactly what makes the reading of the series so delightful to the child" (42). In fact most series are notable for variety in settings, while her second theory is challenged by psychologists and sociologists, as Chapter 3 will show. Lillian Mitchell felt that the Nick Carter series had a place on the library shelf because "it is a type which illustrates a phase in the literature of our country"—a rather vague statement—although she admitted, "I do not know Nick Carter except by hearsay" (580). Such an admission of an unfounded belief makes everything else she says questionable. When, as noted earlier, she claims that the best test of a child's book is whether an adult would like it, she is on dubious ground. Yet the *Horn Book Magazine* believes the same thing: its list of thirty twentieth-century children's books every adult should know notes that these books "have interested college students to such an extent that they 'forgot' they were 'reading children's books.'" C. S. Lewis concurred that "no work of imagination is really worth reading at ten which is not equally (and often far more) worth reading at the age of fifty" (quoted in Wallace 116). The point would seem to be whether children enjoyed them, since presumably they were not written for college students or adults.

In 1965, Ruth Viguers condemned series books as "merely commercial ventures [whose] easy availability has, in fact, done harm in keeping children from discovering books that have lasting values" (Letter). Results of a survey to prove the truth of her allegation will be presented in a later chapter, but her idea is a classic one in the criticism of the series. A most revealing example of critical "logic" is Pearl Ward's survey of the reading of her class in children's literature at Los Angeles State College. No series books appeared in the resulting answers, a fact which she felt to be significant. However, the replies were to be signed, they were to be judged on writing, "intelligent responsibility, maturity," and they had to be presented orally before the class. In such circumstances, to express admiration for Nancy Drew, knowing the general critic-teacher-librarian feeling against series books, would have required great courage indeed (680–684).

Logical fallacies and generalizations are common in juvenile criticism. Margaret Beckman, for example, claims that librarians' standards "are based on an intensive study of all children's literature (both good and bad) at library school" (4612). This sweeping assertion, obviously impossible in reality, is followed by another: "There are only six to eight years in which a child can read *as a child*, and there are so many wonderful books to be read that he will never have time to read them all. To waste those few precious years reading the less than worthwhile is really a crime" (4613). To imagine that one has to read furiously because his childhood reading period is running out is a most curious notion. Generalization is also seen in Lewis Terman, who violently objects to series; he cites one case of a boy who read all the Alger and Tom Swift books and did nothing except wish for a fortune to drop into his lap. Such is Terman's only example of a deleterious effect from series reading: the boy was only twelve and the case is undocumented (78).

A most flagrant example of equivocation is found in Lillian Hollowell's discussion of children's series. She begins by condemning as sentimental, unscientific, hackneyed, and uninspiring the early-twentieth-century *fiction* series; then she quotes the *American College Dictionary* definition of series and concludes that such current series as Landmark Books, the Childhood of Famous Americans, and the Messner Shelf of Biography for Young People are much superior—realistic, factual, and done by experts in their fields. The problem is that she is no longer talking about the same thing. These latter books are publishers' series, not fiction, yet she equates the Uncle Wiggily books and these by way of a tortured definition (736).

Phyllis Fenner introduces another kind of weakness. "Have you ever tried to convince a boy who has read fifty-two Tom Swift books, and still loves them, that they are trash?" (542). It is impossible to find that more than 37 titles in the first series about Tom Swift were published, 15 fewer than the figure claimed by Fenner, a fact which challenges her accuracy and her knowledge in general. Lucy Kinlock is guilty of the same excess, claiming 112 books about the Rover Boys, when only 30 ever appeared (10). Another example of inaccurate information occurs in John Sisk's article on the Rover Boys. Sisk gives the author of the original Tom Swift series as Lester Chadwick instead of Victor Appleton and later affirms that Victor Appleton II "knows more about science than his progenitor and writes better prose" (143). Apparently he did not know as late as 1959 that a syndicate wrote the Tom Swift books and that no Victor Appleton II, or Victor Appleton I, for that matter, existed.

One final type of argument is worth noting. Bernice Wiederman explains that libraries do not buy Tom Swift because "boys can get them anyway," an amazing justification for a library's failing to carry a particular book. She further affirms that time will decide whether a book is worth keeping, indicating that *Huckleberry Finn*, *Tom Sawyer*, and *Moby-Dick* "proved their character after initial rejection" (680). Hereby she admits her own inability to judge a worthwhile book. At the risk of seeming to carp, her article misspells Melville's name as Hermann, omits an apostrophe for possession, has four comma splices, one run-on sentence, omits a comma before a direct quotation and a question mark at the end of an interrogative sentence—something of a record in an article of one page.

Thus the validity of the criticism of children's fiction series, notable for general vagueness of language, lack of defined terminology, a tendency to generalization and subjective opinion based often on traditional assumptions, is open to question. With these weaknesses in mind, let us examine the principal objections to series.

"The chief professional criticism, taught in our seminars, the library schools, is that all series are bad" (Golumb 137). While dissenters can be found, the bulk of critics subscribe to this point of view. Their feeling is expressed in ten categories.

1. That the series books are badly written is widely accepted. Lucy Kinlock, for example, spoke of "the ungrammatical commonplaces of the Bobbsey Twins" (11), in an article containing three grammatical errors. Josette Frank found "their language crude" (77). Terman believed that they had no regard

for literary style (77), while Ruth Viguers in a letter to Paul Deane added that "they have no trace of literary style." As noted earlier, such terms as "badly written," "crude," and "literary style" are defined by none of these people.

2. The unreality of characters is a frequent charge, as by Fenner (542) and Frank (77). Lucy Kinlock defined "a harmful book" as one whose "characters have no living equivalent," a situation found "particularly in series books ... where the vocabulary is so limited and the characters so repeated, that after acquiring one set of words and getting to know one set of people, the reader may go through as many as fifty books without having to use his mind or imagination again" (10). John Sisk spoke of the "motiveless" series characters (145), and Hollowell denounced "the unnatural pseudo-heroes of some Boy Scout stories" (736).

3. Plots of series books are viewed similarly. "Their plots are impossible" (Frank 77), containing "impossible, unreal adventures" (Terman 77) that move with "intoxicating speed" (Frank 76). The "over-excitement of the plots" was condemned by Phyllis Fenner (542). Dorothy Dodd criticized them as "sensational" (in Gardner and Ramsey 18), a charge which Gardner and Ramsey supported. In this respect, the most contradictory comment is that of Lucy Kinlock, who, finding the series sensational in plots on her page 9, one page later declared, "These books lack color and vitality of any kind." The most strongly worded objection is that of Clara Hunt: to her, the books are unrealistic affairs in which boys in knee pants capture crooks and make airplanes and submarines. They are depraved books, because they are lies which "drug the imagination or send it off into an opium dream ... a psychological whiskey-drinking that makes the victim unresponsive to wholesome natural tonics and begets a flabby craving for artificial kicks" ("The Child" 490).

4. Frequent charges of sentimentality are leveled at series. Sisk felt that they were sentimental (145) and Dodd, "foolishly sentimental" (in Gardner and Ramsey 18); all early fiction series were sentimental, according to Lillian Hollowell (736). Kinlock singled out as "perhaps worst of all for insidious influence, the overly-sentimental girls' school series" (11).

5. One of the most common objections to the series is that, unrealistic and untrue to life, they present false values. In 1964

Margaret Beckman declared that books worthy to remain in the permanent collection of any public library must present "some portion of the fundamental truth of life" (4613), reiterating a statement four years earlier by the Young Adult Services of the Public Library, A.L.A. to the effect that good literature should "interpret life truly." The majority of critics feel that series fail to do so. In statements almost without variation, series books are described as "lacking living equivalents" (Kinlock 10), as supplying "a false view of life" (Hall 868), as encouraging "false value about life" (Mitchell 580). Sisk called them "hypocritical" (145). From 1905 to the present, there is a historical persistence of opinion and objection to series.

6. Closely related is the general feeling that desirable books for children possess "integrity" (Beckman 4613), "sincerity and honesty" (Fenner 559), "a high literary excellence, freshness of imagination" (Bowman 212). The series, on the other hand, are seen as hackneyed, repetitious, and mass-produced. Admittedly, they have been factory produced, using a kind of literary assembly line, written to formula by more than one author for a given series. The quality of inspiration, of creative imagination, or of individual integrity is obviously minimal.

7. "A literary-minded parent is horrified when a child appears with a series book . . . they are certainly not elevating!" (Frank 76–77). The lack of "elevation" or of anything "ennobling" is seen as another important defect in the series. Since girls in adolescence are "emotionally aspiring" and are only "satisfied with books that represent something ideal," they must find in their reading "seeds for spiritual growth" ("New Writers for Girls" 205). Lewis Terman agreed that there is "nothing gained in inspiration" in the reading of series (77).

8. Objections 8 and 9 present a much harsher point of view. The word "trash" occurs frequently. Lucy Kinlock used it twice in her opening remarks about the menace of series books (9). Phyllis Fenner spoke of a fifth grade teacher, who, encouraging her pupils to bring books from home, soon found herself getting series books. "These condemned serials had come from the home. Careless mothers were warned what the consequences would be if their children continued to read such trash"; she specifically mentions Tom Swift as an example of trash (542). To Lillian Mitchell, they are worthless (580),

and to Robert Wallace, good books are "a happy few amid the junk."

9. They may be worse, several critics declare. Dorothy Dodd called them unwholesome (in Gardner and Ramsey 18). In 1918 Clara Hunt declared that a friend's son read nineteen Motor Boys books in nineteen days "and is a long time recovering from the debauch" ("The Child" 490). Lucy Kinlock's feeling is clear in her title, "The Menace of the Series Books"; Lewis Terman urged that some of them might be so "immoral" and "vicious" as to "encourage criminal tendencies" (81); Gardner and Ramsey believed that they "induce mental if not moral deterioration" (15). Clara Hunt agreed: if "read habitually they reduce a child's thinking power to pulp" ("The Child" 489).

10. All the more insidious in view of these various objections is the idea that once a child is infected with the series habit, he or she will never read anything else. Conversely, if the child is given better books, he or she will prefer them. Ruth Viguers's letter, mentioned earlier, commented that "their easy availability has, in fact, done harm in keeping children from discovering books that have lasting values, which are far more interesting and much more likely to turn children into readers for life." This feeling is shared by Gardner and Ramsey in *A Handbook of Children's Literature*: "The worst feature of the series, generally speaking, lies in the fact that when a child has read one book of it, he has read all, but their themes are so fascinating to the immature mind ... that he will read and reread the entire series, filling his mind with useless chaff instead of golden grain" (16). Margaret Beckman argues also that the child will read nothing but the "mind-stultifying series books," and she wearily concludes that "after all, children's librarians have been undermining the Bobbsey Twins for twenty-five years, but they haven't been too successful" (4627).

In summary, the main arguments directed against series are that they are badly written books which contain unreal characters in impossible situations presented sensationally and sentimentally; they are mass-produced without inspiration or integrity; this lack of integrity carries over into the books, which are filled with false values and hence cannot elevate or inspire the child. At best, they are worthless trash; at worst, harmful and unwholesome junk. Once a child has read one of a series, he or

Criticism & Censorship of Series 25

she will read all the rest, in the process ignoring better reading. Chapter 4 will examine the actual construction, technique, and contents of series to see the extent to which they corroborate or confound their critics.

Holding such virtually messianic beliefs, critics, librarians, and teachers made, throughout most of the twentieth century, concerted attempts to censor and eliminate series books. Until the mid-to-late 1960's, public libraries in general "censored" public taste by not buying for their collections Nancy Drew, the Hardy Boys, the Bobbsey Twins, and other such series, including often the Oz books. So far as these publicly supported and maintained institutions were concerned, series books did not exist. Unless a child bought, borrowed, or swapped for *Tom Swift, Jr. and His Race to the Moon*, he or she could not get it; the public library, with the most admirable intentions, one is sure, was exercising de facto censorship over children's reading, for the child did not, even with parental approval, have freedom of choice in library books. Libraries were abetted in this action by the majority of teachers and critics.

Probably librarians have always been forced to do a certain amount of censorship because of the limitation of funds available to them. This fact has meant that certain titles and authors are not acquired. The series, though, are a special case, in that sweeping generalizations caused almost all series to be proscribed. Their proscription was made "unofficially official" in 1929 when Mary E. S. Root prepared "the list" of books not to be circulated by standardized libraries ("Not to Be Circulated" 446). The list included 101 Horatio Alger titles and 140 by Oliver Optic; in addition, all titles by Victor Appleton (Tom Swift, Don Sturdy, Moving Picture Boys), all series by Ralph Bonehill (Dave Porter Series), both Herbert Carter and Howard Payson Boy Scout Series, and both Boy Allies Series by Robert Drake and Charles Wallace Hayes; all the Elsie Dinsmore books were included, along with the Bobbsey Twins, Uncle Wiggily, the Outdoor Girls, and the Campfire Girls; none of the Rover Boys was allowed, nor any of the Frank and Dick Merriwell books. In all, 59 authors were listed, as well as some categorized as "banned by some librarians," a group including Johnston's Little Colonel Series, Caroline Wells's Patty books, and Isabella Alden's Pansy Series of 100 titles.

The books became known as "the list." When the *Wilson Library Bulletin* invited discussion of the list, describing its entries as "the type of juvenile books that most librarians seem to agree is harmful," very few opposing arguments followed. Ernest Ayres defended books on the list, suggesting that they were being denied to the public merely because "librarians do not care for this type of literature" (528). Noting similar treatment of *Tom Sawyer* and *Huckleberry Finn*, Ayres mentioned one librarian who refused to order any book with war or bloodshed in it, thus excluding *Treasure Island* and almost all other "boys' books." Unfortunately, his arguments were not especially strong, based as they were on the "Would any book of absolutely no value have lasted as long as Elsie Dinsmore?" kind of reasoning. His most important point was that citizens pay taxes to support public libraries, but they have to buy series books if they want to read them.

The battle raged for three and a half decades, and indeed skirmishes are still being fought. In 1959, Dorothy Dodd, the state librarian of Florida, presented a list of books that she urged all libraries in her state to withdraw from circulation. Her list included many of the books already mentioned and added, notably, all of the Oz books. The *Wizard of Oz* had not been in the children's room of the Detroit Public Library for thirty years, and while the New York Public Library had *The Wizard* on its shelves, all the sequels were in the main reading room or kept under lock and key in the rare book section. The Milwaukee Public Library, where *The Wizard* was not banned, wore out 135 copies from 1949 to 1957; it owned 50 more and had 25 additional on order. As late as 1964 the public library in Newton, Massachusetts, had no Oz books, giving as the reason that the books were not well written. In 1988 the library still had only two Oz books and no examples whatever of other series.

Martin Gardner, the most able and articulate defender of Oz, offered in 1963 several possible reasons for their exclusion from libraries; most have been applied as well to other series books, though few actually are justified (834–836):

1. They are published in weak bindings, which necessitate repair, rebinding, or replacement. (In fact, most original series, especially those issued by Grosset and Dunlap, were generally well bound and can still be found in good condition in second-

Criticism & Censorship of Series

hand bookstores. Since the late 1970's, however, the majority of new series have been in paperback form and do wear out quickly.)

2. Illustrations are old-fashioned, though they appeal to children. (Few series had more than a frontispiece until the 1950's; since then, they have been more fully illustrated, using up-to-date pictures.)

3. *The Wizard* was badly edited, and some careless writing got into it. (It can and will be demonstrated in Chapter 4 that series writing is quite good, certainly no worse than that in other popular books and often much better.)

4. Librarians feel that if children read one book of a series, they will want all the rest and libraries will have to stock them. (Since libraries did stock some series—Wilder's Little House books and many by Howard Pease—the argument is spurious.)

5. Series books have not the stylistic elegance of the Caldecott and Newbery Medal–winning books. (Yet the medal winners are not read in anything like the numbers of the series, a fact which may mean that, for a child, considerations other than style are important.)

Gardner was eminently fair to librarians, but again one has the frustrated sensation that none of those in control of children's reading was telling the truth, if they even knew what the truth was, and that few had actually examined the books they were condemning. The real reasons seem to be matters of taste, of prejudice, of inertia.

The argument boiled up again in 1965 when, in January, the public library in Provo, Utah, declared that it would discontinue certain popular books issued in series form. Chief librarian Edwin Dowlin reasoned that with limited funds available, "series book replacement would be judged against other books available regarding reading value" ("Series Library Dispute," *Daily Herald*, January 13, 1965). Nancy Drew, the Hardy Boys, and Peter Cottontail were taken from the shelves, and great controversy arose among the public, the faculty of Brigham Young University, the P.T.A., and the library. Mrs. Israel Heaton, a citizen, was especially firm: while she agreed that "some of these are only mediocre reading . . . most of these have a moral in them. They are not filthy and not like horror movies." She defended "our freedom of choice in the public library, citing a library policy that "in children and young adult sections, no book of any series would be purchased, rebound, or replaced until it has been justified on a basis other than popularity." As rebuttal to the claim that children will read nothing else, Mrs. Heaton showed that many children "have complained that going to the library is not fun anymore" ("Explain Opposition on Ban in Library of 'Series' Books," *Daily Herald*, January 1965). Subsequently ten high school students wrote to the *Daily Herald* on February 1, 1965, affirming that the series books had not hurt their minds and had helped develop their reading habits; all received good grades and were on the honor roll. On February 10, 1965, the library stated that series would be available, but that henceforth money would be spent "on substantially better books . . . the decision as to what constitutes a better book is made by a qualified librarian and his staff who are guided by professionally recognized tools. . . . If a child is going to spend a great deal of time with this type of book, he is going to miss other literature of better quality" ("Provo Library Board Gives Stand," *Daily Herald*, February 10, 1965).

Here again is typical critical language: undefined terms, generalization, and rationalization of existing conditions and methods. Such things persist: in 1979 in Oslo, Norway, the public library, which had been buying series books since the middle 1960's, stopped the practice and began discarding worn-out copies. Despite the fact that series were intended to lead children to better reading, they were "sub-standard literature." By 1979, it was argued, "Norwegian books had improved greatly in standards and numbers, and priority should be given to "good Norwegian children's books . . . series were excluded" (Bjorklid 112). Hostile public reaction followed. In the same year, Kurt Kristensen, also from Norway, maintained that the series were detrimental to children (1286).

By the mid-1960's however, Peter Soderbergh recognized a tendency counter to that of the libraries. The two positions he designated as "Classical" (the old "Not to Be Circulated" argument) and "Developmental" ("How to get reluctant readers to read, read, read") (870). Perhaps, he reasoned, it was time to give up discussions of literary merit and see that "series books sustained the reading habit" (869). Four years earlier, in 1975, Susan Fruchtman, children's librarian in Orange, New Jersey, gave a party to honor Harriet Stratemeyer Adams; she planned the event "to initiate a campaign to get the Adams books on library shelves," stating that she circulated Nancy Drew and the Hardy Boys to get children interested in reading, and "hopefully if they enjoy reading, they will keep reading" ("Orange, N.J. honors Nancy Drew" 10).

When Harriet Adams died in 1982, however, an editorial by Ethel Heins in the *Horn Book* spoke in a sarcastic tone, recognizing that "with cool efficiency this woman wrote, and superintended the writing of, hundreds of books during her half-century career—a phenomenon which probably deserves a place in the Guinness Book of Records rather than in a history of children's literature" (254). The editor admitted that to read something is better than to read nothing, but the article was generally negative.

In the same year, Louis Phillips noted the fact that in the early Hardy Boys books, Chief of Police Collig was usually discovered reading comic books, "a sure sign of mental degradation"; the Hardy Boys were intended "to wean a young man away from the land of Dell" (176). Phillips reflected on his fifth and sixth grade reading material, realizing that the Hardy Boys had been educational: "I would rather a child read those books than the works most libraries and teachers would recommend . . . the best paths to the classics are not reading lists . . . but paths that zig-zag in all directions at once. The Hardy Boys provided me with one such path" (177).

For the past quarter-century, many, if not most, public libraries have come to circulate the various series. More than three dozen which were questioned admitted to being comfortable with them, although the children's librarian in Waltham, Massachusetts, pointed out that at library conventions, the Classicists and the Developmentalists still raise the same arguments, now almost a century old.

3 WHAT DO JANE AND JOHNNY READ— BY CHOICE? CHILDREN'S TASTE AND MOTIVES IN READING

WHAT DO CHILDREN, LEFT TO their own devices and with freedom to choose, actually read? Do they by choice read the Caldecott and Newbery Medal books? More important yet, why have they continued to read the series in such vast numbers? If, as Margaret Beckman indicated, librarians have been undermining the Bobbsey Twins for half a century now without much success, why?

"A book is a good book for children only when they enjoy it; a book is a poor book for children when adults rate it as a classic if children are unable to read it or are bored by its contents" (Arbuthnot 2). "Good literature, whether for young or old readers ... carries the reader along into genuine if vicarious experience; it stirs his emotions, arouses his curiosity, stimulates his mind, and gives him a measuring stick for living. The characters in the stories are as real as the people he knows.... Good literature recalls the past, reflects the present, and prognosticates the future" (Adams viii). Evidently "approved" books do not supply such "vicarious experience," do not stir children's emotions, do not arouse their curiosity, do not, in short, satisfy needs and desires that children look to have satisfied in their reading; just as evidently, in view of their tremendous popularity, series books do. One is not now considering the relative quality of either classification: quality never has had, necessarily, much to do with success or popularity. As long ago as 1929, Joe Jennings, surveying the leisure reading of junior high school boys and girls, found that the boys listed only two titles that appeared on the approved list of the *Children's Catalog* and girls listed only three (335).

Since 1920 several observers have studied children's taste, interests, and preferences in reading which they themselves could choose. None of these persons employed the same methods of collecting information, nor did they use the same area of the country for research, the same size sample, the same books, or the same terms: once again this lack of similar definition poses a problem, since "adventure," "imaginative stories with action," "war," "scouting," "chivalry," "historical fiction"—terms which appear often in lists of preferred works—may mean the same thing or may not, depending upon the observer. Consequently, no exact correlation appears among the findings. Yet during this time and despite the difficulties, considerable agreement does exist.

In 1920 itself an informal survey of the reading tastes of 170 boys at a New York summer camp revealed that, except for the magazine *Popular Mechanics*, the boys read only fiction ("What the Boys Are Reading" 35–36). Six years later Arthur Jordan concurred that more fiction was read by boys and girls than anything else and that they liked it better than anything else; in fact, he found that high school girls preferred as ideals characters from fiction rather than from real life (11). The next year, Terman studied an "unselected group" of 2,000 schoolchildren, asking them to keep a record of what they read; the results showed that 27 percent read only series books of adventure and school life (80). A decade later, *The Elementary School Journal*, in an inventory of children's voluntary reading, found the proportion of fiction, especially animal tales and stories of children's experiences, also dominant. With the passage of another decade, Ada Campbell Rose, editor of *Jack and Jill* magazine, concluded on the basis of 18,000 letters a year that "children like, in the first place, continued stories," and that they prefer imaginative stories of action, suspense, and drama ("Editor Makes Plea for Fantasy and Action Stories" 2053). On the basis of the Boys' Clubs of America Junior Book Awards Reading Program (1950–1951), boys were seen to prefer "reading books" (i.e., books of fiction) two to one over "fact books" ("Adventure Stories Preferred" 297).

As a corollary to their liking for fiction, perhaps in spite of it, children generally prefer realistic, modern stories and characters. Marjorie Bloom, who in 1964 taught the sixth grade at Horace Mann School in Newton, Massachusetts, was quite definite on the point. When asked why children were not interested in reading the classic children's books, she replied, "They're classics. The children won't read them. They want something up to date." Her opinion itself was almost classic. As early as 1914 *The Literary Digest* declared, "Boys of today have bidden farewell to fairies and even heroes of adventure and are buckling down to scientific fact." The article asserted also that girls in adolescence are satisfied only with books presenting something which they can apply to their own lives. "One cannot get girls to read stories not laid in the present; history tales are not popular; stories of life in other lands are generally not popular; stories of school and neighborhood life are very popular" ("New Writers for Girls" 205). In 1949 *Publishers Weekly* claimed that realistic, authentic juveniles were currently most popular with children. "Children choose contemporary books for themselves. . . . children now show an almost brutal realism and they will settle for nothing less than a clear presentation of problems and authentic facts" ("Children Want Realism in Books" 1895).

These views run counter to the cherished beliefs of many adults, who would like to keep children reading classics and fairy tales. Yet Marie Rankin in 1944 surveyed forty boys and forty-four girls to discover why they did not like certain Newbery prize books; she found that their reasons numbered 6, 7, and 8 involved a lack of realism (one thirteen-year-old girl said, "I want stories that could really happen to me. I can't stand fairy tales, and if they happened in the past, I want to feel that they could happen to me"); eleven boys and seven girls gave nonrealistic, difficult, or unpleasant language as their fifth reason; six boys and two girls felt that these medal books were "not contemporary" (76). Writing in the 1920's, Arthur Jordan affirmed that in the lower grades, children preferred to read about children like themselves, and in the upper grades, about people like themselves; girls in high school liked novels of the day about manners and daily life (12). Writing in the 1940's, Joan Walker, though she found "a mass of contradictions" in children's interests, did feel that "a story about a boy who single-handedly braves unusual hardships is apt to irritate them," that they "object to the fact that heroes always get the winning touchdown," and that they "won't swallow too fast a rise to the top" in career books (678).

Thus the rejection of unrealistic literature is a long-standing tradition in children's reading.

The fiction series seem to disprove, or at least challenge, all or most of these ideas, since in general they are not realistic. They do, however, have the appearance of reality: their dialogue, descriptions of clothing and artifacts are almost invariably up to date. The Nancy Drew, Hardy Boys, and especially the Bobbsey Twins Series have been consistently rewritten in order to update them and make them more "modern." To such a degree has updating been done in the 1980's that the books bear slight resemblance to their originals. Very new series, for example, the Sweet Valley High and Sweet Valley Twins, are all recognizably contemporary. *The Case of the Disappearing Diamonds*, a 1987 Nancy Drew entry, contains a scene that her first adventure, *The Secret of the Old Clock* (1930), would not even have considered including: "Nancy nearly collided with Frederick Reese, who was coming out of the men's room." On the following page, Nancy actually "darted into the men's room [and] quickly checked each stall and wastepaper basket" (121–122). Dare one anticipate a future revision titled, *The Clue in the Men's Room*?

Within their general preference for realistic fiction, what kinds of stories do children most prefer? Here, too, despite variations from one critical survey to another, a reasonably good correlation exists, certainly sufficient to allow some definite conclusions to be drawn.

Stories of adventure are almost unanimously found first on lists of critics who have surveyed children's reading taste. In fact, in her analysis of reasons for the unpopularity of certain Newbery Medal books, Marie Rankin revealed the chief reason—given by 43 percent of the children studied—to be "insufficient action, adventure, excitement" (76). From a 1920 survey by the *Literary Digest*, to one by Arthur Jordan in 1926, by Terman in 1927, by both Joe Jennings and Franklin Mathiews in 1929, through Joan Walker in 1941 and Marie Rankin in 1944 adventure ranked as the highest reason for reading a particular book.

Hereafter such close agreement cannot be found, but it is still possible to note a high frequency of preference. Sports stories are ranked either second (by Hanna and McAllister and also by A. M. Jordan) or third (by Rankin), as well as appearing on most other lists. School life and activities are found as either third or fourth on a composite list. Mysteries appear on almost all lists, but strangely, in view of their popularity in series, usually in about fifth place. Animal stories also can be found in most studies, averaging sixth place. Realistic stories of daily experience and home life do not show up so often as those already mentioned but they rank very high when they do: in A. M. Jordan (1926) and Scott (1930), where the term applied only to girls, such stories stood first in popularity. Books about Boy Scout activities were read widely from the beginnings of the movement in 1910 to the end of the 1920's; Mathiews estimated (848) that at least ten million such books had been sold by 1929, but after that date few new ones were written, though some were kept in print; the Lantern paperback series for children published a volume of Boy Scout stories in 1948 and reissued it in 1964. Westerns and Indian tales were popular in the early years of the century, but in general interest in them did not survive the 1920's. In tenth place are found stories of war, though their popularity seems to be limited to wartime periods or those immediately following a war; war stories are tied with love stories—for girls—and science fiction, another area rated low by critics, despite its status in series, for example, the Tom Swift and Tom Swift, Jr., Series.

Once more, critics and investigators of the reading taste of young people have not, to any great extent, considered the series. Few mention them; most ignore them. Perhaps this fact accounts for the greater frequency of appearance in the series of types awarded a relatively low position by researchers of "better" books—for instance, mystery stories. At any rate, until 1965 one could assemble a composite list of preferences of the taste of children: stories of adventure, sports, school activities, mysteries, animal tales, realistic stories of daily life and experience, westerns and Indian material, Boy Scout stories, books about war, love, and science fiction. After 1965 mysteries dominate children's reading. So far as the series are concerned, nothing, with the exception of the three Sweet Valley Series for girls, touches the popularity of mysteries. All of the New Bobbsey Twins Series are mysteries. By the time of their stopping in the mid-1960's, the Happy Hollisters had become entirely a mystery series. Nancy Drew and the Hardy Boys always were, and the issuance of one entry a month in the second and third of these latter two series suggests that young readers prefer mystery stories to any other kind: publishers do not continue to produce material that does not sell.

A profile of readers to whose age group the series are directed may demonstrate that such books satisfy not only a child's taste in reading but certain motivational needs as well. The majority of fiction series are read by eight- to twelve-year-olds, these ages corresponding approximately to school periods from the end of grade two (the average series probably cannot be read much before this time) to the end of grade six (when most children have "broken the series habit"). The bulk of series considered here conform to such limitations. It must be noted, though, that several very recent ones, such as Doris Fein, the Nancy Drew Files, and the Sweet Valley High Series, with their strong elements of romantic attachments among the continuing characters, their interest in fashion, and their treatment of teenage concerns, imply a slightly older reader. Publishers indeed state that they are designed for "older readers" or "young adults," yet twelve-year-old girls, and younger, who were surveyed responded to such material as well.

To suggest that a *child* could be found typical of so dynamic a period would be unwise, but the similarity of series books leads to the conclusion that a typical *reader* can be outlined. A review of authorities—child psychologists, sociologists, therapists, students of children's literature, and library science experts—reveals close agreement on what children in these years are like. Following is a list of characteristics discovered in the eight- to twelve-year-old period. Some observers find the same quality— for example, a highly developed imagination—in children of all these ages; one will find a quality at age eight that another finds at age nine, and so on, but with almost no exceptions, all qualities were found in all ages, eight through twelve, by some observer. Though they are presented in order of frequency, often a single digit separates one element from another. Finally, several terms which have substantially the same meaning have been combined in the interests of space and clarity.

1. The most commonly noted characteristic of children in this age group is their boundless energy: they are active, busy, restless, filled with zest and enthusiasm. Such attributes mani-

fest themselves in a search for adventure, for things novel and exciting. For these children, nothing is too difficult; they explore and go out to meet the world. A preference for stories of adventure is quite understandable. The original Nancy Drew Series brought excitement and adventure and were thus different from what Harriet Adams called "goody-goody characters" (Moran and Steinfirst 114): that is, sentimental, domestic, and dull.

2. Children are sensitive, desiring affection and approval; they want to please and to be trusted, and consequently are cooperative and obedient. They fear failure, worry, and take things hard. Heroes and heroines of series never fail. They are consistently praised for their successes and encouraged to go further; rewards, usually in material terms, are common.

3. In this time of life, children are much concerned with the opinions of others, especially those of friends and of adults other than their parents. At about the age of ten, children form gangs and clubs and are much guided by the codes that such groups evolve. Their faculty of imitation is prominent. Interestingly, when television arrived and older Hollywood films were being revived for the new medium, it was felt necessary to change the name of the popular Our Gang series of films to the Little Rascals: "gang" was a threatening term. Yet the Woodland Gang Series of the mid-1980's (a charming, nonthreatening six books) addressed the child's fondness for clubs and for exactly the kind of approval noted; so does the slightly later A.I. [Artificial Intelligence] Gang, though with a strong technological base.

4. At this time also are developing the characteristics of his or her own sex. Friends are usually of the same sex, and each sex expresses contempt for the other. Girls develop an interest in their appearance, in clothing fashions and concepts—to which the Nancy Drew Files are conspicuously pointed—and in babies. Boys are concerned with not being "sissies," and may become, verbally at least, pugnacious; undoubtedly they enjoy the many fights in the Hardy Boys Casefiles for this reason.

5. Children develop a strong interest in social and personal relations. They want to establish a good two-way relationship with others, especially with their mothers, and despite concern for the opinions of persons other than parents, they have a deep

Children's Taste & Motives in Reading

sense of the importance of family life and family excursions. The Bobbsey Twins and Happy Hollisters books address just such areas. Matters of race relations and nationality grasp their attention, and prejudices either weaken or strengthen. While Black people have virtually disappeared from series in the past quarter-century, the number of characters, usually minor, with "foreign" names has increased greatly. Children are sensitive to socially approved attitudes and want to attain socially approved behavior.

6. Hand in hand with the preceding point is the fact that children are building a good ethical sense: matters of justice fascinate them; personal responsibilities become important issues, and they can accept blame when they fail in them. They seek out social information, such as crime and racial issues. They are, moreover, concerned about honor and honesty, protection of the weak, unselfishness, self-sacrifice, and sympathy. Most of the early Nancy Drew adventures were efforts to right various injustices, while the Hardy Boys Casefiles conspicuously aim at combating terrorist activities.

7. In these five years, the imagination of children is very active. They daydream and make up stories; they put on plays. Inveterate moviegoers and television viewers, they are fond of mystery, the supernatural, black magic, and secrets. Boys brag of accomplishments executed with bravado in the world of imagination. The Hardy Boys titles *Night of the Werewolf* (1979) and *Track of the Zombie* (1982) reflect such interests, as does *The Haunted House Mystery* (1985), a Bobbsey Twins entry. In the Not Quite Human Series, number 5, *Terror at Play*, actually sets its events as part of a high school play production. The great popularity of John Bellairs, who is not really a series writer, can be at least partly accounted for by his supernatural content.

8. The quality of independence is general. Children are self-reliant, self-sufficient, seeking independence of adults; they like to sleep in tents, at the homes of friends, and they like to play away from home. Most series, in fact, stand as almost denials of home and family life. Doris Fein occasionally reports her whereabouts to her mother, but is careful to stress that as an eighteen-year-old "woman," she does not feel obliged to do so. The New Bobbsey Twins Series also emphasizes that parents should not be told too much about their children's plans to

prevent worry. At the same time, and ironically, Biemiller argues that the "child's war against insecurity is best fought from the fortress of the familiar . . . children want to know and be easy with the same fictional people" (62).

9. With independence goes an overall equilibrium. These children are well-adjusted; they like their parents, their teachers, and life in general, and they have quite effectively mastered their environment.

10. Highly physical, children are interested in games, competitive sports, and strenuous outdoor activities. Strength is important to boys, as is physical skill, and manual dexterity increases greatly. The Hardy Boys Series has such qualities to a high degree: Moran and Steinfirst see the Boys as "courageous, independent, clever, physically adept at everything, and undaunted" (115). The video game foundation of the Arcade Explorers Series points to the manual dexterity required to play such games.

11. A desire for success or mastery is very important: the child wants to win over opponents, especially those whom he or she considers despicable, and to gain plaudits, admiration, and esteem. Heroes in all series do exactly these things. In the earliest series—the Rover Boys and the Bobbsey Twins, particularly—the same villains appeared and were regularly overcome.

12. Intellectual interests also develop. Eager to learn, children are great fact grubbers; they make endless lists and inventories. They enjoy creating and breaking codes, and they have much information and probably know more about more things than the average adult. In fact, if adults, when examining a series book, find that children easily out-know and out-think them, there is a basis for such ability. In *The Cutlass Clue* (1986), an A.I. Gang title, Wendy readily solves a code that has baffled the adults; it is a simple rail-fence code that young readers could themselves solve. Most series contain brief "lectures" or "essays" to inform the reader about some exotic or at least unusual aspect of life.

That children read for some kind of vicarious satisfaction of these needs must be obvious. Recognition ranges from Fjeril Hess's, "Girls like to see themselves as heroes, just as boys do" (1477), to Marie Rankin's suggestion that one reason Newbery

Medal books are not popular is that "the child cannot live vicariously in them" (90). Psychiatrist and bibliotherapist Thomas Verner Moore believes that the "child may find psychological relief by vicarious participation in the lives of heroes" (5). Franklin Mathiews offers the idea that a boy wants to remain a boy yet act like a man and show men a thing or two (849); his chance comes consistently in series books.

A correlation between reading preferences and psychological and physical drives can easily be demonstrated. With minimal exceptions, all the series are fiction and are, at least in appearance, realistic; until the past decade, fantasy was extremely rare in series. In the 1980's, such series as Not Quite Human involving an "integrated electrologic android" (that is, a robot that looks like a thirteen-year-old boy), whose name is Chip, presumably after a computer microchip, and Arcade Explorers (an interactive series occurring inside one's computer) entered the realm of fantasy, but like the third Tom Swift Series they are actually more works of science fiction than they are pure fantasy.

That publishers are keenly aware of the needs and preferences of their young audience can be illustrated by an advertisement at the back of *The Secret of Skull Mountain*, a 1948 Hardy Boys title. Readers are asked whether they have ever considered why they get so much fun out of the series; the question is answered by nine points:

1. The Hardys are "fellows like yourself" (interest in one's own sex, if the reader is a boy).
2. "They like action and plenty of it" (love of adventure).
3. They are "full of curiosity" (the fact-collecting tendency).
4. They enjoy mysteries (strong imagination).
5. "They think girls are all right—*in their place*!" (interest in one's own sex, if the reader is a boy).
6. "They can drive a car and pilot a speedboat" (well-developed physical ability and imagination).
7. They are at home in the great outdoors (interest in strenuous outdoor physical activity).
8. They "keep their heads in an emergency" (well-adjusted mastery of environment).

9. "They like wisecracks" (no psychologist or sociologist mentions a sense of humor as an important element in children of eight to twelve; publishers and authors feel, correctly, that it is).

The original Hardy Boys Series was read mainly by fourth, fifth, and sixth graders, aged about ten through twelve; Joe and Frank Hardy were fifteen and eighteen; point number 5 above is aimed at a younger boy's actual feelings about girls, while point number 6 appeals to his ideas about what a teenager's life will be. The Boys are now seventeen and eighteen, a strange catch-up in age similar to what happened to the younger set of Bobbsey Twins, but the series since 1979 has clearly been geared to "older readers."

The table of major elements demonstrates more clearly the extent to which various series satisfy both needs and reading preferences. It should be noted that an individual volume of a series may fall into several categories (e.g., *Cherry Ames, Dude Ranch Nurse, Honey Bunch: Her First Little Trip West,* and *Grace Harlowe's Overland Riders on the Great American Desert* all have western settings and Indian characters), while the series to which it belongs is listed only on an overall basis (i.e., career series, family series). Series used are limited to those referred to most frequently in this study. While animal stories bulk fairly large in children's reading taste, only one very recent series—Animal Inn—from the late 1980's is devoted to animals in such a way as to fulfill the initial definition of a series.

Children's Taste & Motives in Reading

Table 1
Series Satisfaction of Needs and Reading Preferences

Psychological or Physical Need	Reading Preference	Series Satisfying
1. Desire for adventure, the new and exciting	1a. Adventure	Cherry Ames Vicki Barr Rick Brant Happy Hollisters Hardy Boys Ken Holt Honey Bunch Lone Ranger Race Against Time Rover Boys Don Sturdy Tom Swift (Sr. and Jr.)
	b. Boy Scouts	Series by Carter, Payson, Shaler, Burgess
	c. Sports	Chip Hilton Grace Harlowe
	d. War	Boy Allies Payson's Boy Scouts Brighton Boys Dave Dawson Red Cross Girls Uncle Sam's Boys
	e. Westerns and Indian tales	Lone Ranger
	f. Mystery	A.I. Gang Cherry Ames Vicki Barr Bobbsey Twins (since 1950's) Judy Bolton Nancy Drew Encyclopedia Brown Doris Fein Hardy Boys Happy Hollisters Rick Brant
	g. Career	Cherry Ames Vicki Barr Sue Barton

Psychological or Physical Need	Reading Preference	Series Satisfying
2. Desire for affection, acceptance, fear of failure, sensitivity	2a. Family life and daily experience	Bobbsey Twins Honey Bunch Happy Hollisters Woodland Gang
	b. Love stories	Sue Barton Judy Bolton Beverly Gray Grace Harlowe Sweet Valley High and Twins
3. Concern for opinions of others, friends and adults other than parents; gangs, clubs, codes	3a. Sports	Chip Hilton
	b. School life	Marjorie Dean Beverly Gray Grace Harlowe Rover Boys (at Putnam Hall) Sweet Valley High
	c. Daily and home life	Bobbsey Twins Bunny Brown Honey Bunch Happy Hollisters
	d. Boy Scouts	Series by Carter, Payson, Burgess, Shaler
4. Interest in own sex and in developing characteristics of own sex	4a. Boy Scouts	Series by Carter, Payson, Burgess, Shaler
	b. Sports	Chip Hilton
	c. Home life and daily experience	Cherry Ames Sue Barton Bobbsey Twins Judy Bolton Bunny Brown Honey Bunch Marjorie Dean All-of-a-Kind Family Grace Harlowe Happy Hollisters Sweet Valley High and Twins

Children's Taste & Motives in Reading

Psychological or Physical Need	Reading Preference	Series Satisfying
5. Importance of social and personal relations; interest in family life	5a. School	Marjorie Dean Beverly Gray Grace Harlowe Chip Hilton Rover Boys Sweet Valley High and Twins
	b. Daily and home life	Bobbsey Twins All-of-a-Kind Family Honey Bunch Marjorie Dean Beverly Gray Grace Harlowe Happy Hollisters Bunny Brown
	c. Boy Scouts	Series by Carter, Payson, Shaler, Burgess
	d. Sports	Chip Hilton
6. Ethics and personal responsibility	6a. School	Marjorie Dean Beverly Gray Grace Harlowe Sweet Valley High
	b. Sports	Chip Hilton
	c. Boy Scouts	Series by Carter, Payson, Shaler, Burgess
	d. Daily life	Cherry Ames Sue Barton Bobbsey Twins Judy Bolton Bunny Brown Honey Bunch Happy Hollisters Red Cross Girls Sweet Valley Twins

Psychological or Physical Need	Reading Preference	Series Satisfying
7. Imagination	7a. Mystery, adventure	A.I. Gang Vicki Barr Bobbsey Twins Judy Bolton Rick Brant Nancy Drew Happy Hollisters Lone Ranger Don Sturdy Race Against Time Doris Fein
8. Self-reliance, self-sufficiency	8a. Sports	Chip Hilton
	b. Boy Scouts	Series by Shaler, Payson, Burgess
	c. Daily life	Sleep Over Friends Woodland Gang
	d. Mystery, adventure	A.I. Gang Cherry Ames Vicki Barr Judy Bolton Rick Brant Nancy Drew Hardy Boys Lone Ranger Don Sturdy Rover Boys Tom Swift (Sr. and Jr.)
9. Equilibrium and adjustment; harmony with environment	9a. Home and daily life	Bobbsey Twins Bunny Brown Honey Bunch
	b. School	Marjorie Dean Beverly Gray Grace Harlowe Sweet Valley High
10. Sports and outdoor activities	10a. Sports	Chip Hilton
	b. Boy Scouts	Series by Carter, Payson, Burgess, Shaler

Psychological or Physical Need	Reading Preference	Series Satisfying
	c. Westerns and Indian tales	Lone Ranger Grace Harlowe's Overland Riders
	d. Adventure	Rover Boys Rick Brant Don Sturdy Tom Swift
11. Desire for success and mystery	11a. Sports	Chip Hilton
	b. School	Sweet Valley High Grace Harlowe Marjorie Dean Beverly Gray
	c. Boy Scouts	Series by Shaler, Payson, Burgess, Carter
	d. Mystery and adventure	Hardy Boys Rover Boys Nancy Drew Tom Swift (Sr. and Jr.) Don Sturdy
12. Fact gathering and curiosity	12a. Science fiction	Tom Swift (Sr. and Jr.) A.I. Gang Arcade Explorers Not Quite Human
	b. Career	Sue Barton Cherry Ames
	c. Mystery	Encyclopedia Brown
	d. Sports	Chip Hilton
	e. Boy Scouts	Series by Payson, Shaler, Burgess, Carter

It is readily apparent from the table that, whatever the attitude of critics, teachers, and librarians, the series books fulfill an extraordinary number of the needs and reading preferences of children. As a corollary, Marie Rankin's excellent study of children's interests in fiction offers several valuable reasons why the Newbery prize winners despite their high critical acclaim and wide publicity, are not popular with children. She found, first, that many are unrealistic in plot and illustration, as opposed to the realism of the series. "Newbery books," she said, "provide very little familiarity" (90). Foreign settings were also characteristic of Newbery books, a fact which evidently strikes children as unrealistic in their terms. Only one-third of books rated as popular by young readers had foreign settings; hardly any series do, except Don Sturdy, occasionally the Rover Boys, and war stories. During the past decade the Hardy Boys have been traveling—to Paris, Africa, and other "exotic" locales—but these settings are not essential, nor do they consume much attention. Possibly the fact that six out of seven Newbery books had historical settings did not satisfy children's desire for fiction by seeming to be too factual (only two out of ten popular books had historical settings; since 1900 historically oriented series have been almost nonexistent). The Newbery books often had no child characters at all, so that children found it hard to identify with them and to live vicariously through their adventures. Many have animal characters of the "wrong type": one boy, speaking of *Gay-Neck*, said, "A pigeon is weak and couldn't save anybody. I don't see where a pigeon could have much adventure" (90).

The reasons children themselves gave number twelve:

1. Insufficient action, adventure, excitement (Series clearly provide these elements.)
2. About foreign people (all heroes and heroines of series are Americans; even their adventures abroad could as easily have happened in the United States; foreign settings and people are not described in any detail.)
3. Wrong emotional tone (Rankin feels that the Newbery books often tried to teach some "majestic concept requiring maturity far beyond children's" [92].)
4. About unpopular characters (The series use children and adults easily identified with.)
5. Children felt that Newbery books were for younger readers (Series invariably use characters three to ten years older than their expected audience.)
6. Difficult or unpleasant style of speech or writing (This item, as the following chapter will detail, is utterly avoided by the series.)

7. Fairy stories (No series uses fairy tale material, the imagination being satisfied in realistic surroundings.)
8. Not contemporary (Almost without exception, the series are.)
9. Biographical (Series are entirely fictional; actual people are almost never mentioned nor do they appear.)
10. No humor (Series always have at least one character whose purpose is to provide humor.)
11. Poor illustrations (This term means stylized and unrealistic illustrations; series, when illustrated, are thoroughly realistic and recognizable.)
12. About fighting and struggle (This is a negligible item mentioned by no boys and only two girls out of eighty-eight sampled; fighting and struggle are a major part of series.)

One additional attraction of the series has appeared recently. Moran and Steinfirst, speaking of the "new realism in children's literature," feel that books involving drugs, abortion, suicide, death, and homosexuality will drive readers away (116). These elements play a minuscule role in any series, except Doris Fein, where they are rather prominent, and the A.I. Gang Series volume, *The Cutlass Clue*, where drugs are discussed with an almost startling awareness by the children.

4 PASSPORT TO ENJOYMENT: STYLE AND TECHNIQUE OF THE SERIES

SERIES BOOKS FULFILL MORE effectively than other children's literature the interests and needs of their readers. While many librarians, critics, and teachers may object to such a statement, it does not necessarily imply praise. Professor Jane Hannigan of Simmons College, Boston, Massachusetts, in answer to my question of why these three groups were so set against a study of children's series, replied in 1964 that perhaps they were afraid such an analysis would reveal that the bases for their objections were not so valid or secure as they supposed. This idea is startling, since it suggests again that these people have read neither closely nor critically the books they so widely condemn. If, however, we take such generally accepted critical standards as the audience for whom the work was intended, the success from a technical point of view with which author and work accomplish their purpose, and the worth of the work from the point of view of its intended readers, we may avoid personal biases and traditional prejudices and judge the series in their own terms. At the very least, we can account for their success.

As noted, few critics have commented in detail on the fiction series. Even fewer have discussed their style and technique, or the general mechanics of these books. Precisely what are the series like in makeup? In terms of psychological and physical needs, reading preferences, and interests the series satisfy children to a greater extent than do "better books"; if the charge that they are poorly written can be refuted and if their style is well adapted to juvenile readers, their popularity can be easily explained.

In 1927 Lewis Terman felt that children prefer books that can be read in a comparatively short time; in 1988 children's librarians in Waltham, Stoughton, and Hudson, Massachusetts, agreed in almost identical terms: kids like them because they are

Style & Technique of the Series

not too long. Marie Rankin contradicted this idea, offering as evidence that the average length of a popular book was 246.5 pages, as opposed to an average of 160.8 pages for the less popular medal winners. Publishers evidently agreed that brevity was more appealing. A few of the early-twentieth-century series books did have a mean of about 250 pages, although Tom Swift and Don Sturdy ran to only 215. Indeed, 215 pages was the standard length for most series through 1956, thereafter, the length came to be fixed at 180 pages. Many series after 1956—the Hardy Boys and Cherry Ames, for instance, became about 35 pages shorter; the Bobbsey Twins had reduced its length three years before, and the Happy Hollisters, which began in 1953, followed suit. The figure of 180 pages comes close to Rankin's 160 for unpopular books.

When we move into the 1980's, series books drop another 30 pages. The Hardy Boys weigh in at about 150, as do the Nancy Drew Files. The Bobbsey Twins drop to an average of 125, while the New Bobbsey Twins Series contain fewer than 90. The third Tom Swift Series rose to 190 pages, but it lasted only from 1981 to 1983; its length may have been a factor in its lack of success. The very popular Sweet Valley Twins Series runs to slightly over 100 pages. The Tom and Ricky Mystery Series, which admittedly is aimed at very young readers and is almost a primer, has only 44 pages.

When children commented that the medal-winning books were for younger readers, their objection was based apparently on size—eight inches by nine—where the series have, since 1900, made an effort to appear as much like adult reading as possible with an average size of five and a half inches by seven and a half. The Nancy Drew Files and the Hardy Boys Casefiles, both of which began in the 1980's, along with the A.I. Gang and Not Quite Human Series, are indistinguishable from adult paperback books, a fact which seems to attract readers who may wish to feel more "adult." In a similar vein, the Newbery and Caldecott books made a definite effort to produce light and colorful bindings. Rankin discounted this trend also as not important, while Polly Ann Scott felt that a colorful cover and binding were definite factors in popularity. Perhaps they are, in a negative sense: light colors may be associated with picture books. Until relatively recently, the series were notable for their lack of color—the Hardy Boys had ugly brown beige covers, the Bobbsey Twins used a dark green for almost the whole of the series, and Sue Barton used a light gray. To be sure, they did have dust jackets of more than one color, but they merely resembled adult books more because of the fact. As late as 1959 the series had not varied much in this area; after that year they did appear with illustrated covers. By the 1980's color had become important to publishers. Very bright yellows, reds, and blues dominate, while cover pictures depict action scenes involving the main characters. *The Secret of Jungle Park* in the New Bobbsey Twins Series shows the children beginning the downward plunge on a roller coaster; the colors are garish and the expressions on the twins' faces makes them appear grotesque. The Hardy Boys Casefile number 10, *Hostages of Hate*, reveals a group of hijackers with automatic weapons taking over an airplane; colors are similarly bright. Children surveyed for this study, however, claimed an interest only in contents; illustrations and colors were negligible factors in their choices.

Rankin felt that the titles of unpopular books did not reveal their subject and contents, nor did their chapter headings (*Gay-Neck*, for example, has several possible interpretations). The series avoid this error entirely. Virtually all their titles identify the hero or heroine and indicate exactly what he or she is: *Cherry Ames, Cruise Nurse*; *Sue Barton, Visiting Nurse*; *Don Sturdy in Lion Land*; *Tom Swift, Jr., and His Deep Sea Hydrodome*. Titles are meant to be intriguing and despite frequent similarity usually are. Well into the 1980's, no change is noted: *The Thief in the Brown Van* clearly indicates its contents as part of the Tom and Ricky Mystery Series, as does *The Missing Will* in the Woodland Gang Series. Occasionally one finds a genuinely imaginative title for a book: *Recipe for Murder* takes Nancy Drew to an international cooking school and *Racing Hearts*, a Sweet Valley High volume, despite the innuendo, is about runners.

Both Carringer and Scott felt that large, clear type was sought, not only by children, but by parents, teachers, and librarians as well; while the Rover Boys, Bobbsey Twins, and early Tom Swift used a slightly smaller type than is now fashionable, it was widely spaced on pages with well-defined margins (both elements that Scott saw as important in juvenile books)

Style & Technique of the Series

and was easily read. Since the 1950's, the series have used a heavier, blacker type. The number of lines on the page, the size of margins, the quality of paper (always heavy and dull so as not to reflect light) have not changed in any major detail since 1900. From a physical point of view, series are easily and quickly read.

Other factors make these books "readable." Style and technique are aimed at creating a fast pace. For instance, paragraphs have always been short; as the twentieth century went on, they became shorter: the original Tom Swifts averaged 6.5 paragraphs per page, while the Tom Swift, Jr. Series had 7.5. The older Bobbsey Twins had 7 paragraphs on a page; in the 1950's the number rose to 9; and in the 1980's a dozen was average. The most remarkable increase is found in the Lone Ranger Series, in which the first volume, published in 1936, had between 4 and 5 paragraphs per page; *The Code of the West* (1954) had between 9 and 10, with some pages running to over 20. The Rover Boys used 9.2 paragraphs, the Hardy Boys and Happy Hollisters 11. The overall average is 9, the number of the 1980's Nancy Drew Files and Hardy Boys Casefiles.

The majority of these paragraphs contain dialogue, many of the speeches quite short. The result is that not only is the number of paragraphs high, but their length adds also to their swiftness: the average series reads with the speed and simplicity of a published play. The Race Against Time Series from the 1980's aims to pack a head-spinning number of events into a brief period of time, sometimes less than twenty-four hours; part of its success in doing so is due to the paragraph structure.

Most critics have seen such elements as important to the success and popularity of series: Harvey (86), Rankin (45, 60), Howard Pease (91) all cited paragraph length, size, and consequent simplicity and speed of reading. Earlier series, such as Don Sturdy, averaged 38.5 words per paragraph; later series— for example Chip Hilton—ran to 28.1; while the Hardy Boys used only 23.2 and the Happy Hollisters, beginning in the mid-1950's, 21.5. Again the overall average for all series studied was 26.2, a not unusual average for an adult *sentence*. It should be noted that several series reveal tremendous variety. Chip Hilton books not infrequently had paragraphs of only 4 words followed by another of 51, in turn followed by one of 14; the Bobbsey Twins alternated quite short with quite long ones; the

Hardy Boys preferred initially medium-length paragraphs interspersed with occasional long and short ones. Such variation in length is recognized as most desirable stylistically in college composition courses.

Sentences also tend to be short: an average sentence in a series entry is 12.9 words. If one takes arbitrarily a half-dozen series, one finds Chip Hilton, 14.5; Nancy Drew, 12.0; Tom Swift, Jr., 12.4; Rick Brant, 13.6; Hardy Boys, 12.2; Happy Hollisters, 11.8. Typically the series keep close to a short-sentence ideal.

Other quite consistent and apparently calculated elements of this kind can be observed. The usual number of lines per page is thirty, but the opening page tends to be much shorter, about eighteen lines. The opening pages are immediately dramatic and exciting to attract children, who, as Rankin notes, sample the first page before buying (60). The first book of the Hardy Boys Casefiles, *Dead on Target* (1987) opens with the death by explosion of Iola Morton, an unforgettable scene. In spite of Howard Pease's feeling that it is difficult to maintain a high pitch of excitement after such a start, most series do begin so. If a child reads the first page—briefer than most of the others and easy to read quickly—he or she will probably go on a bit further into a chapter packed with suspense and will, authors and publishers hope, be hooked for the balance. Josette Frank spoke derogatorily of "the speed of the thriller" (76); unquestionably, the series are built for speed.

What other stylistic and technical devices are used to make series appealing to children? Clearly, one of their basic charms is familiarity—especially familiarity of characters. Children come to know the characters in a series as they do actual friends and acquaintances. Consequently, almost three-fourths of the series (71 percent, to be exact) use "summary beginnings": somewhere within the first two chapters, most often in the first, reference is made to earlier volumes. This reference may be very detailed (the first few Rover Boys, Bobbsey Twins, and Tom Swifts, for example, mentioned all previous titles and the main incidents in each) or very general, such as that earlier books have occurred in the mountains, at the seashore, and on a farm. Usually characters who appear regularly are named and briefly described as to general or specific age, and their relation to plot

Style & Technique of the Series

is made amply clear: hero, villain, comic, parent, and so on. The device is meant to arouse a sense of the familiar, even in readers who pick only one volume of a series: a reader is rarely at a loss for background exposition in a series.

Almost as popular as summary beginnings are "preview endings." This device, found in about 60 percent of series, involves a rather specific indication of what will be going on in the next volume to appear. Very often the title of this subsequent book is given and frequently a notion of the chief source of interest. In the late 1980's actual pages from the next entry are supplied at the end. There may well be a connection between the regular use of the preview ending and the popularity of series which use it.

Some things which do not happen, but which critics, librarians, and the public generally assume happen, should be mentioned. As literary serials, they are often assumed to have the chief quality of movie serials, namely, chapters that end in cliffhangers. As late as 1980 Kurt Kristensen in Norway argued that the "climax of suspense at the end of each chapter is what draws the reader on" (1287). The claim is difficult to support. Once again one sees that observers of series have not read extensively in them and are perpetuating legends. All chapters of motion picture serials after about 1920 ended in cliffhanging. The series books, with a mean number of eighteen chapters, average only six to seven crisis endings—slightly more than one-third. Actually, the series are closer to the earliest movie serials, such as *The Perils of Pauline* or *The Exploits of Elaine*, which had their crises occur and be resolved within each chapter. The Hardy Boys used such a method consistently until the 1980's Hardy Boys Casefiles Series, which have as many as eleven cliffhanger endings. Only a few series justify the claim of frequent crisis endings: the Tom Swift, Jr., Series had twenty chapters after 1958 and fourteen cliffhangers on the average, or 70 percent; the Happy Hollisters had eighteen chapters and fifteen crises—83 percent. The New Bobbsey Twins Series ended only two of its ten chapters with suspense; the Honey Bunch Series used none, and ironically neither did the Lone Rangers, though one might have expected such conclusions. At least an average shows that it is unwise to assume that series in general are cliffhangers.

What they do have might be called "TV endings," scenes concluding with the suggestion that something momentous is about to happen. One chapter in *Hostages of Hate* ends: "We've got a date at the Hole-in-the-Wall. With Lonnie—and maybe the Dutchman" (40). One senses a slow fade-out and a commercial message next.

Almost as popular but even less true an assumption is the idea that series abound in foreshadowing of the most obvious "but as we shall see" variety. On the average, such foreshadowing is used only 2.1 times per book, Tom Swift and the Lone Ranger reaching a high of 4 to 5, the Hardy Boys, Nancy Drew, and Chip Hilton running slightly less than 1; in all of the latter three, which involve either mystery or sports contests, the outcome must be a surprise, and obvious forewarnings would be destructive.

Neither is coincidence used as often as critics believe. The device was seen frequently in the earlier series—the Rover Boys, Tom Swift, and Don Sturdy, for example, average respectively two, three, or four coincidences per book. More recent series average only one, a figure which means that many series do not use the technique at all, while others, such as Nancy Drew and Honey Bunch and Norman do continue a fairly high average of three. Even into the 1980's Nancy Drew indulged in coincidence in virtually every book; many instances hark back to Horatio Alger. In *The Case of the Disappearing Diamonds*, for example, Nancy tells her friends, "I've tied each of you with a magician's knot" (138); fortunately she has been taking magic lessons (though we have not been told so before), and as a result all will be able to escape the villains.

As noted earlier, several critics claim that the series are not well written, although the term has never been adequately defined. If it means that mechanical errors occur, errors in grammar, punctuation, diction, and syntax, the charge is true, as it is of Dickens and Chaucer, but no individual series volume comes close to the number of such errors in Melville's *Pierre* or *The Confidence Man*. Close attention to this area reveals an overall average of 5 errors per book. This figure includes some 50 possible mistakes ranging from universally agreed upon sentence fragments and dangling modifiers, to some usually recognized (such as the use of quotation marks to indicate unspoken thoughts), to clichés and jargon (which some authorities may

Style & Technique of the Series

not wish to include at all). It does not include such things as the use of commas with parenthetical expressions, an area disagreed upon by many. Further qualifications should be made. Five series—Grace Harlowe, the Rover Boys, Payson's and Carter's Boy Scout Series, and Chip Hilton—account for more than half of the total errors found in the various series; these books average 9.5 errors per volume, or twice the overall average. (Ironically, the Grace Harlowe series listed as author Jessie Graham Flower, A.M.) Chip Hilton ran to approximately 6 errors per book, only slightly above the average for all series. Individual books within a series vary as well: in the Judy Bolton Series, *The Yellow Phantom* reached 11 mistakes, while *The Clue of the Broken Wing* had only two; the first title appeared in 1933, the second, in 1958. A general trend can be seen in these two books—in the last three decades mechanical errors have significantly decreased in number, and if the five series mentioned are not included, the average for all series errors drops to 3.5, even including the 1980's Nancy Drew Files with a high of a dozen.

One may conclude then that in general, errors in children's fiction series occur with no greater frequency than they do in any other books, either for children or adults.

If the charge that the series are not well written means something other than mechanical errors, the claim is equally hard to maintain. In the first place, although one might assume that books produced by a group—such as the Stratemeyer Syndicate or the Philip Lief Group—would have unmistakable characteristics, good or bad, in common, such is not the case. A comparison, for example, of *The Cutlass Clue* and *Robot Trouble*, the second and third volumes of the A.I. Gang Series, reveals remarkable differences. Admittedly two different "authors" are credited with continuing the adventures of the same characters; yet the former work, by Jim Lawrence, contains some of the best writing found in any series book, indeed as good as that found anywhere. By way of evidence, toward the end of chapter 12 one reads, "The westering sun was now low in the sky as the long summer day drew to a close, but the air was still brilliantly clear" (102). A page or so later, "The sky was flaming red and gold in the west as daylight faded fast" (104). As the story moves into chapter 13, "The whole sea was turning crimson as the sun sank below the rim of the world" (106), while a page later, "Even as he spoke, the sun dropped out of sight, quenching its flames in the Atlantic, and twilight settled over Ancoteague Island" (107). Matching atmospheric events to actions is a technique that John Steinbeck employed, most notably in his short story "Breakfast," where the sun goes through a similar series of stages. *Robot Trouble*, on the other hand, supplies rich fodder for any antiseries critic: Bruce Coville's favorite connective is *so*, occurring as often as four times on two facing pages. Grammatical errors abound—fragments, lack of agreement between pronoun and antecedent, and others. At 220 pages it is 66 pages longer than *The Cutlass Clue* and almost as long as the original Stratemeyer volumes; the length is insufferable considering how dull and unbelievable it is in relation to its predecessor. A similar comparison can be made of titles in the third (1980's) Tom Swift Series. The first title, *The City in the Stars*, contains writing of very high quality: "They listened to the babble from *New America*, from the incoming shuttles, from the desperately running racers, and from Control. They sat still, unmoving and afraid. All around them, they knew, was the invisible rain of death. Nothing changed; the thirteen containers rippled and bobbed, upset by the movement the two racers had made in attaching themselves" (136–137). Here is excellent parallel style, inversion, variation in length of clauses, and unusual, graphic language. By no means an isolated example, it is previewed earlier: "The strong wind all but toppled him, but he reached the first of the metal struts between the plastic hexes and felt his magnetic shoes take hold. Tom moved along steadily until he could grasp the edge of the inflated patching panel. It was still large enough to cover the hole, although just barely, and it would have to be positioned precisely" (35). Surely such writing can be used as a model for younger readers and writers, in its directness, inventive vocabulary, and rhythms. By comparison, the style of volume 5, *The Astral Fortress*, is heavy, unimaginative, cliché ridden, and ungrammatical: "Everyone settled back into the padded contour couches, holding their breath. . . . Tom glanced at the Skree warrior, still not quite believing that he not only knew, but could converse with, a true alien. A real, nonmovie, not-a-man-in-a-funny-rubber-suit

Style & Technique of the Series

alien. . . . Tom was forced to admire his lightning-fast reflexes" (9, 13, 48). More pedestrian writing could scarcely be found. The Nancy Drew Series is notable for quite high-level writing: style is consistently varied in type, length, and beginnings of sentences; the vocabulary, so far from playing down to readers, actually encourages a level of language higher than that conventionally employed by them; almost without exception, plots are true mysteries, in some cases rivaling successfully good adult mystery novels. On the other hand, the Arcade Explorers Series are stylistic insults to a second grader; in fact, the Tom and Ricky Mystery Series, avowedly aimed at that grade, are far more honest, trying to give their very young readers something better than the verse of Dr. Seuss.

The first Tom Swift books were overblown in rhetoric, filled with jargon and clichés, and grammatically embarrassing; as the series moved into the 1920's, however, its writing became more sophisticated, at times almost elegant.

What one must say, then, is that in general the series stand up well against such adult classics as Melville's *Pierre*—almost unreadable—and worse, *The Confidence Man*—utterly unreadable. The awkwardness and stylistic horrors of the middle and late Henry James are not found in the series. If one applies the only valid critical criterion—Does a work succeed in doing what it attempts for the audience at which it is aimed?—then the series overall are actually good models for young readers to emulate in their own writing: clear, coherent, generally correct, and convincing. Whatever the claims of certain critics, the test of a child's book is not that it appeals to an intelligent adult, but to an intelligent child. The entire series genre cannot be dismissed when in even a particular series individual volumes display marked differences. As earlier noted, judgments of series fiction often do not bear close scrutiny.

Let us look further into technical aspects that make series attractive to children. Marie Rankin felt that it was difficult to find a passage descriptive of scene or setting in a series book (60). Her conclusion is correct. Description is generalized and undetailed. Typical are the descriptions of Honolulu in the Rick Brant book, *100 Fathoms Under*: "modern city of brown and white and green" (7); of New York in the Judy Bolton *The Yellow Phantom*: "a new world of gray buildings and flickering light" (13); of a harbor in *Don Sturdy and the Port of Lost Ships*: "busy place, crowded with every variety of craft, seething with a picturesque and colorful type of humanity" (67). Many times, as in *Don Sturdy on the Desert of Mystery*, scenes are "beautiful beyond description" (86). The same words exactly are used in *Nancy Drew and the Mystery of the Moss-Covered Mansion* (4), and as though to prove the point, none is attempted. Often, as in *The Bobbsey Twins in Washington*, one reads that a building "is very wonderful and beautiful" (133); there might be a bit more to say about the Library of Congress. The new home in *The Happy Hollisters* is "a large, three-story house. Big lawns stretched on each side. The lake touched the property in the rear" (19). Bert Bobbsey "stood gazing at the rocky panorama that spread red and purple before him" (*The Campfire Mystery* 36).

Carter's Boy Scouts visit the Rockies; Grace Harlowe, the Great American Desert; Don Sturdy, Africa, Alaska, and Egypt; none is described in any terms except those of the Sunday supplement. When a full page of description is found, as in *The Boy Scouts and the Army Airship*, where an old house used by the Army is fully detailed, the book bogs down and almost stops because the normal pace is so fast. The point is precisely here: as noted earlier, children want and are given in the series a swiftly moving story. Description slows it down. When plot is the main issue, long descriptive passages are unnecessary. Although few children's books are richer in description than Robert McCloskey's *One Summer in Maine*, children do not buy it or, apparently, pick it up to read. In short, children do not like description. One imagines that they pass quickly over passages longer than a sentence or two.

Sometimes series writers set scenes memorably. In *The Boy Scouts and the Army Airship*, we find, "Above him the stars twinkled. Beneath was a long, white hill, chequered vividly here and there with inky splashes of shadow" (181). "Blue and sparkling in the sun," the reader is told in *Honey Bunch: Her First Little Trip to the Seashore*, "miles and miles of beautiful, dancing water lay spread before her. The waves were still running upon the sand and back again, but each one as it ran back left a ring, a wet ring, and on the edge sparkled hundreds of bubbles with rainbows flashing through them" (73). In the 1987 Hardy Boys

Style & Technique of the Series 59

entry, *Hostages of Hate*, "The Uzi [machine gun] snarled again, stitching a line of broken runway in front of the police" (9). But children have excellent imaginations, and perhaps a suggestion of scene or person is sufficient. Furthermore, if a short, fat, dark-haired boy reader is asked to identify with a tall, muscular, blond hero, the job is not easy; it is made easier if Tom Swift remains as "a lad of no ordinary appearance or attainments."

Another element frequent in series is the inclusion of "lectures," brief passages which explain unfamiliar terms or processes. In some series they occur very often, ranging from four in Tom Swift and Don Sturdy to six in Tom Swift, Jr., Rick Brant, and Chip Hilton. In most instances they are much longer than descriptions: some, as in Thornton Burgess's *The Boy Scouts in a Trapper's Camp*, run to an entire chapter of twenty pages, and four-page lectures are not uncommon in the Don Sturdy books. The science and technology series of the 1980's, such as the A.I. Gang, Not Quite Human, and the third Tom Swift Series, abound in informative data. Paradoxically, such facts are not, like passages of description, unwanted. Considering the desire in children of eight to twelve to acquire information and facts, it is not strange that they like these passages. Every boy surveyed mentioned them, particularly in reference to sports series, where they are usually blueprints for football plays or strategies for basketball and baseball. The boys described them as helpful and interesting.

Humor is also aimed at the eight- to twelve-year-old reader. It takes three forms. First, humor is gained through misunderstanding or mispronunciation. Small children, ignorant and unintelligent adults or foreigners, or hard-of-hearing people are chiefly responsible for this variety. Bunny Brown's sister, Sue, pronounces *certificate* as "stiff cut"; Freddie Bobbsey mixes up "peccadillos" an "picalilli" (*Pilgrim Rock* 165); Honey Bunch thinks that a lifeguard is sitting in a high chair for babies when she goes to the seashore (92), and her friend Norman tries to speak French in *Honey Bunch and Norman Play Detective at Niagara Falls* with "mercy bokoo hacho" results (118–119). Occasionally this form of humor reaches unexpected subtlety (possibly unintended), as when the loquacious Jenny Jenks in *Don Sturdy in the Land of Volcanoes* talks about finding "the tomb of old Paresis" (27).

Humor comes also from slapstick. During *The Bobbsey Twins in the Country* the family cat gets loose on the train and disturbs a sleeping woman by swishing its tail in her face (16); Judy Bolton's cat, Blueberry, does the same in *The Yellow Phantom* (3). On the way to the seashore the Bobbsey's duck, Downy, repeats the cat episode (11); and later Freddie Bobbsey falls into a flour barrel, and his sister's efforts to clean him off with water turn him instead into paste. Norman spills his orange juice into his cereal and eats the result anyway (*Niagara Falls* 110). The Hardy Boys' friend, Chet Morton, bites his thumb while eating; Nancy Drew's friend George pours liniment over the young detective's head; the Sturdys' maid, Jenny, repeatedly swallows her gum. The Woodland Gang Series from the 1980's was replete with slapstick passages, suggesting that children still respond to them.

Sometimes, a character is given a particular mannerism which produces humor. Here the most famous, and probably the only character other than a hero or heroine to attain stature in the memory of readers, is Wakefield Damon of the original Tom Swift Series. Damon is recalled by practically everyone who read the books, not always by name, but as the man who blessed everything in sight: "Bless my sewing machine," "Bless my wallet," "Bless my shoelaces," Damon would exclaim, an average of thirty-six times per volume (he reached a peak of fifty-two blessings in *Tom Swift and His Wireless Message*). He played no important part in the action usually, but even an adult waited expectantly for the next variation. The Tom Swift, Jr., Series tried to repeat the trick in the character of Chow Winkler, who used "Brand my fuselage" and other such phrases, but it was more contrived and no reader of the series mentioned it.

Some new developments in recent series are robots programmed to speak with often unexpected results. Paracelsus, the A.I. Gang's talking bronze head, had been given "some of the most sophisticated programming in the world. But lately... Roger had taken to adding clichés and punch lines from old joke books to the automaton's programs, along with certain clues for when to spout them" (*Robot Trouble* 73). In *The City in the Stars*, Tom Swift eats a huge meal laden with garlic; when he comes to make a call to Earth, the operator assigns him a booth, and as he is turning to go says, " 'Take these too. Take the whole

Style & Technique of the Series

package' . . . smiling broadly as she held out a half-used roll of breath mints. Tom took them, blushing furiously" (73). In *Revenge of the Desert Phantom*, an excellent in-joke is pulled by Joe Hardy. He is "lying on a park bench with his head tilted back to stop the flow of blood from his nose," after a fight in Paris; "Joe laughed as he mopped his lip with a tissue," and with reference to the many similar brawls that occur in the series, remarks, "It reminds me of home" (33).

The remaining elements of technique can be summed up rather quickly. Plots, of course, are the main interest. In general, they are not unified, tightly organized affairs pointing to one end. Most series are loosely connected, episodic, and picaresque tales, often with several lines of development. *Grace Harlowe's Plebe Year at High School* is typical, though any of Grace's other years at school might be used as well, or the school lives of Marjorie Dean or Beverly Gray. Grace's friend, Anne Pierson, tries to win the freshman prize of $100 and is accused of stealing the examination on which it is based; Miriam Nesbitt repeatedly tries to discomfit Grace and her friends; the girls are attacked by wolves; there are Thanksgiving and Christmas parties. At best the Bobbsey Twins books were a set of scenes and problems: Where is the lost dog? Who broke the window and will Bert be blamed? What kind of show shall we put on? The Tom Swift, Jr. Series used, chiefly for suspense, scenes not involved with the main line of development: Tom has to avoid a speeding truck or be crushed, but the truck has nothing to do with the main plot. The device was still being used in the third Tom Swift Series from the 1980's: in *The City in the Stars*, a hole is found in the protective covering of the space station, threatening destruction, but it is easily and quickly repaired and we get back to the plot. Escapes and rescues follow escapes and rescues with the regularity and often the ingenuity of a novel by James Fenimore Cooper. Cherry Ames is captured by and escapes from penicillin thieves and counterfeiters when she is a clinic nurse. Shaler's Boy Scouts rescue a man from a balloon in *The Boy Scouts and the Prize Pennant*, as do the Bobbsey Twins in *The Camp Fire Mystery*, while Payson's Scouts rescue a girl from a bull and several people from a sinking ship (*Army Airship* 125, 248). The Hardy Boys and Don Sturdy average three rescues and three escapes per book, and Tom Swift continually escapes from such varied threats as a disabled airplane, storms, earthquakes, mudbanks, sharks, whales, and starfish. Almost none of these episodes needs to happen in view of the story involved; all add suspense and interest.

Suspense is further increased by changes in point of view. The Lone Ranger Series often ends a chapter with some crisis about to happen to the masked hero, shifts the scene to someone else for a chapter, then returns to the Ranger. The Rover Boys constantly shifted from character to character, keeping suspense at a peak. The recent A.I. Gang employs the technique consistently. Shifts occur in the Nancy Drew books to allow a reader to see a crime committed or to meet the criminal before Nancy does.

Until relatively recently, plots were quite uncomplicated. In *The Camp Fire Mystery* (1982) thieves are stealing children's bicycles. One questions how large a market there can be for such efforts and how much money it can produce. Indeed, the subject seems absurd, used only because of possible reader identification; when one discovers that the thieves "sent their spies in a phony police car" (120), the absurdity deepens. The plots of the latest Nancy Drew cases, however, have become very complicated, able to stand comparison with adult detective stories to which they are often superior.

Motivation in series is rudimentary. As will be discussed later, Tom Swift is a hero because he is a hero in a series, not because of particular actions he performs; Danny Rugg is a villain and consequently does mean actions. With very few exceptions, characters are seen in terms of one quality: genuine three-dimensional characters rarely appear and instead, sharply distinct black-and-white characters are found. Thus the child's desire for security is served, since one always knows how to take each character.

Should any doubt exist, a reader need only follow the central character's lead. In *Don Sturdy on the Desert of Mystery* we read, "Abdullah was a clean-cut young fellow, and the party had taken a liking to him at once" (77); in *Nancy Drew and the Hidden Staircase* we learn that "Nancy had taken an instant dislike to Gomber" (5) and in *The Haunted Bridge*, "Nancy had taken a dislike to him" (7). Later in *The Hidden Staircase* readers can relax when "Nancy concluded that Wharton was not withhold-

Style & Technique of the Series

ing any information" (173). When Joe Hardy says in *The Phantom Freighter*, "I like him" (33), readers do too and can rest secure that they are right. Even with updating, neither series has changed in this regard.

Only rarely does real motivation creep in. An "overbearing doctor" is introduced in *Sue Barton, Student Nurse* with the explanation, "He's got a terror of a wife. This [hospital] is the only place where he can get any respect. . . . What a glorious place a hospital is for henpecked doctors" (102). Dr. Grotz in *The City in the Stars* is a true psychopath, one for whom normal rules and restraints have no meaning: his sole concern is power and he relentlessly removes enemies and opponents. Assuming again that plot is the main interest of readers, then insufficient character motivation is not so serious a flaw. As with description, children want to know where they are: is a character good or bad? Once the fact is established, they can get down to enjoying the action.

Finally, something should be said of diction, and here one's feelings are divided. The best series from the point of view of plot, action, and originality often use a heavy, stilted language. Nancy Drew is a notable example; as mysteries the series is by far the best of any, yet in *The Mystery of the Moss-Covered Mansion* Nancy can say, "Truly this is a dreadful place. And dreadful deeds may be going on behind those moss-covered walls" (9). On the other hand, Shaler's Boy Scouts Series, at once the most realistic and believable of any of the Boy Scout books and the dullest (for perhaps the same reason), used a language devoid of bombast and jargon: "If we only had plenty of time . . . we might make a lean-to out of branches that would shed the rain. I've helped do it before" (*The Prize Pennant* 8). Most of the trouble with language occurs in dialogue. Straight exposition is usually direct and simple.

Some of the difficulty, though by no means all, is due to the period of time in which certain series were written. "A beautiful night," says Dora in *The Rover Boys on Land and Sea*, "but who can enjoy it when we do not know what tomorrow will bring forth?" (109). Shortly thereafter, Dick Rover says, "Gracious! he is going to attack Mr. Barrow." The time is 1903. Seven years later, Grace Harlowe, at the age of seventeen, asserts that "The Sophomore Class will not tamely submit to such impositions"

(*Sophomore Year at High School* 18); she had not mastered her jargon by 1921, when in Grace Harlowe's *Overland Riders on the Great American Desert* she was still saying, "None knows better than you the perils that lurk there for the unwary traveler" (52). Some excuse may exist for describing the Lone Ranger's horse, Silver, as "the great, glistening body" (*The Lone Ranger* 15), since the series tried to create a romantic and legendary tone, but none may be claimed for allowing the killer, Murdock, to refer to "these pore, benighted Injuns" (108). Sixteen years later in 1952 Cherry Ames was guilty of an improbable piece of rhetoric: "I can learn a lot about a patient when I hear his actual voice—the inflections, the pauses, the little monosyllables which can mean so much" (*Clinic Nurse* 5). As recently as 1982 Bert Bobbsey in *The Camp Fire Mystery* observes that "his most outstanding feature was his long hair" (65). Can such language be usual for a twelve-year-old? Later, when Nan is asked for her opinion, she replies, "Most definitely" (82), and Amanda Freedman, who is about Nan's age, comments, "Precisely" (95).

On the other hand, Helen Dore Boylston, author of the Sue Barton books, acknowledged in *Senior Nurse* the help of Jane Ayer Cobb, "whose criticism and knowledge of modern young conversation have been invaluable, both in this book and the volume preceding it." The result was some of the brightest and most realistic dialogue in any series. As a rural nurse, for instance, Sue has to perform mouth-to-mouth breathing on a newborn baby to dislodge the mucus from its throat. Her friend Marianna cries, "An'—an' you got it out—like that?" Sue replies, "Well, I certainly didn't get it out by singing to him" (221). In *Sue Barton, Senior Nurse*, Connie reveals that "the nicest man I ever met fell down the subway stairs on me" (112). The Hardy Boys also use good, natural speech, utterly free of bombast, yet a good model for young readers, if they emulate the language of the heroes. Similarly, the 1987 *Nancy Drew and the Case of the Disappearing Diamonds* has natural dialogue: "Karen said she'd ask Larry to get in touch with me. If I don't hear from him soon, I'll have to track him down" (54). While the Chip Hilton series generally had excellent, realistic dialogue, occasionally it went too far, for example, in its assumption that athletes, both players and coaches alike, use very bad grammar and slurred pronunciation: in *Touchdown Pass* a friend of Chip's says, "Speakin' of pilin' it on, now come clean,—who done it?" (12) Later we find, "Nothin' doing! Nothin' doing! I got a plan for these chocolates and it don't include no football players." In the recent Nancy Drew Files efforts to be current produce annoyance and boredom: in *Deadly Intent* (1986) characters begin far too many sentences with, "Hey, how are you?" "Hey, what's happening?"

A 1983 Ph.D. dissertation by Mavis Olive Cariou pays the series an unintentional compliment: "The popular series novels had the highest means for vocabulary difficulty and diversity" (in *Dissertation Abstracts International* 1613). It appears that the series are offering to children a higher-level vocabulary than other children's books provide. On the negative side, by the 1980's profanity had begun to appear in both the Doris Fein and the A.I. Gang Series. Harry Grubb in *Dr. Doom: Superstar* (1978) speaks of Cucamonga, saying, "wherever the hell that is" (28); later he claims that "I'm one of the best damned police reporters" (31). When Doris's image in the mirror agrees that she is too fat, Doris observes, "No one loves a wiseass" (*Deadly Aphrodite* 3). Early in *Robot Trouble*, Trip says, "we have already succeeded in thoroughly screwing up his plans" (82), and when caught by a sentry robot, Ray yells, "Oh, God, get me out of here quick" (105).

By way of conclusion, we might cite Marie Rankin's observations about the style of popular books as opposed to that of the relatively unpopular medal winners. Popular books, she said, use a "conventional narrative style," while the Newbery winners employ "a unique, unconventional one." Rankin believed that the emphasis in the latter books was on form, not content. The popular books use little description and are "packed with incident and written in a dynamic style suited to fast-moving action. Setting and character sketches are supplied through incidents in the story directly. The popular books give short, direct statements with much action. Characters are directly introduced. The language of the Newbery books was described by children as 'queer,' 'too lofty,' 'silly,' 'not the way people talk' " (92). Her conclusions, while in no way aimed at or involved with the series directly, are admirably borne out by them. Thus, we may say that there is technical as well as psychological justification for series popularity.

PART II:
ATTITUDES, BELIEFS, VALUES

GENERAL INTRODUCTION

ALTHOUGH NONE OF THE SERIES books for children is admittedly didactic, from these books young readers gather general principles governing conduct, ideals, attitudes, beliefs, and values; in short, they find object lessons which adults apparently want them to have. These lessons have been written into the books, which parents have either bought or at least allowed their children to read; critics, librarians, and teachers have, to be sure, railed against them, but almost invariably from a "literary" point of view. Few have commented on what the books actually say and have been saying with only minor variations since the Rover Boys appeared in 1899. Is it not reasonable for children to assume that these series books contain views which agree with the attitudes, beliefs, and values that society wishes them to share? At an age when they wish to please, to cooperate, when they value the opinions of adults, when they are concerned with social and personal relations, when they are building an ethical sense and their prejudices are forming, series readers are ripe for suggestions presented in the kind of reading they enjoy most—fiction—and in the form of fiction—series—they seem to read most. Series teach not by assertion but more emphatically by example. Didactic or not, these books cannot help but affect the attitudes and values of their readers. When these values are reinforced by one of the most effective rhetorical techniques—repetition—and are embodied in characters whom they like and admire, it is worth bearing in mind the fear of many critics that if children begin to read the series, they will read nothing else.

Whether the values are desirable or not is important. In overall construction, format, and style, series are calculated to be popular, and they are aimed at interests the child already has. Everything is working to make them a powerful educative force. If they are to be criticized, it should not be for their literary qualities, but for the image of life and its elements which they offer to their young readers.

Rather than approach this most significant area haphazardly or alphabetically, we can divide the area of attitudes, beliefs, and values into three broad categories: human relations (to be treated in Chapters 5 and 6), social institutions (to be treated in Chapter 7), and elements of character and personality (to be treated in Chapter 8). Each of these main divisions has an almost infinite number of subdivisions. Since the turn of the twentieth century, there has been a close correlation and agreement among the various series, all the more remarkable considering the variety of subjects, types, and scenes covered by the books. Even granting that several series are products of syndicates, not all are products of the same syndicate or of one publisher, and certainly a century is time enough to modify the opinions even of a syndicate. (Changes in fact have occurred definitely and deliberately, as in attitudes toward policemen and Blacks.) Actually, who writes or publishes a series does not matter; what does matter is the numbers in which the books are read. If only a single person were producing all the books for all the children, what those books contained would still be significant.

Without further preface, let us turn to what the series have to say to children about their relations with others, the elements of their world, and their own characters and personalities.

5 FAMILY LIFE AND RELATIONSHIPS

PARENTAL IMAGE

THE SERIES PRESENT OVERALL an ideal of youth, nowhere more clearly seen than in their images of parents. In countless books, fathers and mothers are shown in similar terms. Cherry Ames's mother is "sweet-faced," "still young," and "still youthful" (*Senior Nurse* 22, 96); moreover, she is "slender, active, and gifted with a sense of humor" (96). Mrs. Bobbsey is a "charming, pretty woman" (*Horseshoe Riddle* 14); the Hardy Boys' mother is a "petite, pretty woman" (*The Tower Treasure* 19). Compare the mother of Honey Bunch: "Mrs. Morton laughed. She was a very pretty mother and she laughed often" (*First Little Trip to the Seashore* 4); Honey Bunch's friend Stub also has a "pretty mother" (*First Little Trip West* 31). The mother of Tom Swift, Sr., was a nonentity, but that of Tom Swift, Jr.—the Mary Nestor of the original series—is another matter: she is "pretty" in *Rocket Ship* (37), "attractive" in *Caves of Nuclear Fire* (9), where she is also "slim," and "slender" in both *Visitor from Planet X* and *Race to the Moon*. In *The Camp Fire Mystery* (1982), the Bobbsey Twins are in New Mexico with Kathy Leonard, "a college friend of their mother's [who] was a tall, attractive young woman" (10); Mrs. Bobbsey must be considered young also if they were at school together. The mother in *All-of-a-Kind Family* (1951) is even more attractive: "Most of the other Jewish women in the neighborhood had such bumpy shapes . . . like mattresses tied about in the middle. But not Mama. She was tall and slim and held herself proudly." An additional comment makes the point: "The children were very proud of Mama" (65).

Fathers fare well also. Cherry Ames's father is "good-humored" but also "business-like" (*Senior Nurse* 22). Mr. Bobbsey is a "tall, good-looking man" (*Horseshoe Riddle* 14) and "an athletic-looking man with a broad smile" (*Pilgrim Rock* 9). Both he and his wife are "young in spirit" (*In the Country* 7). Honey Bunch's father "laughed a great deal" during *Her First Little Trip West* (41) and later in the same book "just loved to tell jokes" (114). In *The Caves of Nuclear Fire*, the father of Tom Swift, Jr., himself the hero of countless books of his own, is a "tall, distinguished-looking man with twinkling blue eyes" (9). The tendency to good and frequent humor is found also in the father of the *All-of-a-Kind Family Downtown*. Papa is a source of whimsical amusement to his daughters, as for example when he tells Gertie, the youngest girl, to inform "the little man inside the [mail]box where the letter is going, otherwise it'll never get there" (166). The rest follow eagerly to see whether she will take the advice seriously, which she does, but Papa never cracks a smile. When Henny stays out too late in *More All-of-a-Kind Family*, Papa, in the dark, mistakes her friend Fanny for his daughter and spanks her; when the error is realized, "both Papa and Mama were laughing so hard they couldn't stop" (48).

The description of Rick Brant's father is rather more interesting: He is a "youthful-looking man in casual slacks and sport jacket. Mr. Brant had his son's lean hardness and unassuming friendliness. More than once he had been mistaken for Rick's older brother" (*100 Fathoms Under* 2). Various television commercials use the same theme—the difficulty of telling mother and daughter apart because mother is so youthful; one manufacturer illustrated the idea with two dachshunds.

Nancy Drew's father takes a much more active role in that series than most parents do in such fiction; he is variously beaten, robbed, and kidnaped, and often assists in the solution of crimes. Like other fathers already noted, Carson Drew is "tall," "handsome," and in "robust health" with "a sturdy constitution" (*The Hidden Staircase* 23, 181); in fact, he pounds his chest in the same book and declares that he can be tough (23). In *The Mystery of the Moss-Covered Mansion* he grips the steering wheel with his "strong hands" (63); in *The Mystery of the Tolling Bell*, Nancy is told that her father is the best lawyer in the state (3). To some extent time caught up with him. By 1986 his hair had become pepper and salt (*Deadly Intent* 34) and a year later in *The Case of the Disappearing Diamonds*, upon arriving home, he "sank into his favorite leather easy chair" (1). Even signs of a generation gap between him and his daughter appeared in *Deadly Intent*, when Nancy notes that her father is at the hotel "getting ready for the opera. He's not too big on what he calls 'that music you listen to'" (191). But Father fought back, and in the same books he jogs regularly, is clearly in top physical condition, and engages in what seems to be an incipient romance.

Like Carson Drew, Fenton Hardy, Joe and Frank's father, is a strong character in the Hardy Boys Series. At first a retired detective on the New York police force, he became a private detective, and by the time of the 1980's Hardy Boys Casefiles, he was an international figure, head of security for a presidential candidate in *Dead on Target* and a high official in the Intelligence Security Commission in *Hostages of Hate*. He too is slugged, captured, starved; he fights as well as his sons in emergencies. The only parent whose age is given in a series, Fenton Hardy is "a tall, distinguished-looking man of forty-five. His sons loved his sense of humor and admired his brilliant mind and thorough methods" (*The Hooded Hawk Mystery* 21). "We're Fenton Hardy's sons," the Boys say proudly in *Program for Destruction*. "Solving cases comes naturally" (152). Only five pages earlier, however, *they* have saved *him*.

A summary reveals certain parental ideals in series: both mother and father are youthful in appearance and attractive; both have good senses of humor; mothers are pretty and slim; fathers are tall, handsome, and vigorously athletic.

Exceptions to the foregoing are impressive. In several series, and especially in what are likely the two most famous of all series the Rover Boys and Tom Swift, parents are shown to be feeble, old, and grossly ineffectual. The reason is probably to give children the major role in the books; nonetheless, the picture is extraordinary.

In volume 6 of the first Rover Boys Series, *The Rover Boys in the Mountains*, the father of Dick, Tom, and Sam tells his sons, "I'm getting old and I want no more trouble" (90); later we read, " 'Do as you think best, Dick,' sighed Mr. Rover. 'From now on I shall leave these business matters in your hands. I realize I am too feeble to attend to them properly' " (262). At the time, the Boys are still in prep school and range in age from fourteen to eighteen; logically their father should be in his forties, hardly a time of life to call oneself old and feeble, let alone futile at business. Yet the image is consistent in the series. Don Sturdy's father is also in poor health, and Don is accompanied on his adventures by a more robust uncle, a fact true also of the 1980's Race Against Time Series. Tom Swift's father is referred to as aged, the aged inventor, and his aged parent throughout the original series. Tom himself is always called young—in the early books—he is a teenager—and though he eventually married before the series ended, he remained apparently in his twenties. How old could his father be? Yet "Mr. Swift was getting along, and his long years of brain work had made him nervous" (*Airship* 20); Mr. Swift was "a man unversed in the ways of the world" (*Airship* 131), while one supposes that his son, a youngster in his teens, is much better equipped to deal with worldly matters. Sue Barton's "white-haired" father appears only in *Sue Barton, Rural Nurse*; in that book, Sue cries, " 'Oh, no! . . . Daddy darling, you mustn't get old!' But he was" (35). Sue's age in that book is twenty-three.

Such a view may be valid in *Charlotte Temple*, where it also appears, considering the lower life expectancy in 1794; it is substantially less so in the 1920's. Tom Swift and the Rover Boys ceased with the death of Edward Stratemeyer in the early 1930's and such a father image is pretty much, though not exclusively, limited to series which he controlled. In view of their great popularity, though, one wonders how much influence they had in convincing younger readers that their parents were "the older generation" and even "the old folks." To compare the series with the other form of popular entertainment most readily available to children in these years—the movies—is also revealing. The most popular movie star and the ideal of eight- to twelve-year-olds was Douglas Fairbanks, Sr.; Fairbanks came to films when he was thirty-four, and he produced one of his most athletic swashbucklers, *The Black Pirate*, when he was forty-three—just about the age of most fathers in the series mentioned and probably that of most fathers of the children who read them. There was nothing feeble about Doug.

IMAGES OF FAMILY LIFE

The Wizard of Oz concluded in 1900 that there is no place like home. To prove the idea on the basis of the series published in

Family Life & Relationships 75

the twentieth century would be difficult. All series say that family life is good, desirable, and necessary; paradoxically in only a handful is family life shown to exist at all. Certainly it does not in the twelve books about Don Sturdy (1925–1931), largely a geographical-travel series. Don is never at home in any book after the first chapter or two, and in those he gets permission—easily—from his parents to go traveling. Nothing remotely resembling a family is shown. The life of Tom Swift, Jr., is spent in the laboratory, in outer space, at the bottom of the ocean; he may inquire occasionally about the health of his parents, but there is no more sense of family life than is shown in the Don Sturdy books. Grace Harlowe's high school career is involved exclusively with scholastic and extracurricular matters. Referring to a visitor in *Grace Harlowe's Junior Year at High School*, Grace says, "She called on mother yesterday afternoon, and, for a wonder, I was at home" (125). Grace spends Christmas of her plebe year with a friend, Mrs. Gray, and that of her senior year with a friendly judge. In any given volume, she is seen at home for a dozen pages at most. The series is filled with orphans, broken homes, and deserting parents, but never are home and family life offered as an ideal alternative. Once Grace finished college, married, and had a daughter, all semblance of family relationship disappeared. In the Overland Riders, the fourth and longest series about Grace Harlowe, Grace leaves her infant child with relatives, bids her husband farewell, and spends every summer in the Kentucky Mountains or on the Great American Desert, in the High Sierras, and elsewhere, with two girl chums and the husband of one of them.

The Rover Boys, as their name implies, were indeed rovers. Educated at boarding school, they were involved in the bulk of the books with adventures on land, sea, and mountain—but never in their own home. As noted earlier, their father was so infirm and elderly that he could never have provided a normal home for three boys anyway. Sue Barton's life is that of hospital or slum; Cherry Ames lives at home once in a while, but her stories have nothing to do with family life; as an airline stewardess, Vicki Barr clearly spends most of her time in the air. Virtually all the many books about Boy Scouts take their principal characters away from home, a necessary occurrence if they are to go scouting. Like Tom Swift, Jr., Rick Brant, a less-successful counterpart, spends his days in Egypt or under the sea. The Race Against Time Series in the 1980's consistently leaves the thirteen-year-old hero, Stephen, in the hands of his uncle Richard; both agree that there is no reason to inform the boy's parents about what they are doing, since only worry would result. By the 1980's also, even the Bobbsey Twins were spending the bulk of their time away from their family; *The Camp Fire Mystery* (1982) finds the parents missing altogether and the children staying with "Kathy Leonard, a college friend of Mrs. Bobbsey" (10), though in the first volume to appear about the Twins, *Merry Days Indoors and Out*, Mrs. Bobbsey was too occupied with family life to acquire either a college education or a college friend. All the military series (Uncle Sam's Boys, the Red Cross Girls, the Brighton Boys, Dave Dawson, and so on), of course take their chief characters to war in places distant from their home environment.

The abnormality of family life is deepened by the fact that many series heroes and heroines have lost a parent. Neither Tom Swift, Nancy Drew, nor the Rover Boys have a mother. Chip Hilton's father is dead long before the series begins, and once Chip gets to college, his mother all but disappears as well. In addition, Don Sturdy's best friend, Teddy, has no mother, and Judy Bolton's protégée, Irene, is also motherless and supports a crippled father. According to *The Case of the Disappearing Diamonds*, Nancy Drew's mother died when the eighteen-year-old detective was three. All of the four major characters in the Woodland Gang Series are orphans.

At least two major series and several minor ones do present a much more satisfactory view of home and family life. In the longest-lived series, the Bobbsey Twins (beginning in 1904 and in 1988 still producing a book a month), the Happy Hollisters (starting in 1953 and running well into the 1960's), and the All-of-a-Kind Family Series (appearing first in 1951 and continuing sporadically for several years thereafter) family life is warm, close, and satisfying. All four Bobbsey children are together constantly: the fact that there are two sets of twins gives each a logical playmate; they are all good friends and throughout the series they make their own fun by giving plays, arranging circuses, culling treasures from the family attic, and going on many trips together to the country, the seashore, Washington,

Family Life & Relationships

Plymouth, and elsewhere. By the 1980's they were playing in their own rock-and-roll group. The Happy Hollisters were very much the same family, though the books emphasized mystery to a greater extent (actually the Bobbsey Twins became primarily detectives as well in the 1950's). The All-of-a-Kind Family duplicated their family relationships and their activities. Bunny Brown had only his sister, Sue, but the "author," Laura Lee Hope, also wrote the Bobbsey Twins and the Six Little Bunkers books, and apparently her name was the sign of tales about close families: plots of the three series were identical. Bunny also gives shows, goes South, and visits Grandpa's farm in the close company of Sue and their parents. So does Honey Bunch. Although she is an only child, the Honey Bunch books have a close sense of family and home life.

Despite what has been said, it should not be assumed that even in these series any degree of closeness exists between parents and children. Indeed, the worlds of adults and children are distinctly separate. The exceptions prove the rule. Parents and children travel together, enjoy holidays in common, go on occasional vacations and picnics together; adults are sometimes invited to attend the plays their children perform. But these are unusual cases. During the daily round of activities the two worlds have little to do with one another. " 'After dinner,' their father said, 'we'll all have fun making a jack-o'-lantern' " (*The Bobbsey Twins at School* 97). Clearly the occasion is a special one—Halloween. The All-of-a-Kind Family Series, stories about a Jewish family in New York, coincides in time (1912 and following) with the years of the early Bobbsey Twins publication. Much is made of religious holidays, and the five girls and eventually their infant brother share Yom Kippur, Rosh Hashanah, and other such holy days with their parents and family—all are special occasions.

Forty years later in *The Bobbsey Twins and the Horseshoe Riddle*, Mother "was in the living room playing the piano. And Daddy was there too, singing a new song" (54). The children are elsewhere. Mr. and Mrs. Bobbsey, we are told, "were young in spirit, and always took part in their children's joys and sorrows" (*In the Country* 7)—not, however, in their games. "Togetherness" had not been invented when the Bobbsey Twins were born, and the children seem quite contented, even though Dad is not out playing with them. An exception does occur in *The Bobbsey Twins at Pilgrim Rock*: "Mrs. Bobbsey often played games with her children and sometimes surprised them by winning" (125). *Pilgrim Rock*, though, is a much later book, 1956, and one must insist that a statement is quite different from a dramatization. Mrs. Bobbsey is never shown playing with the Twins.

Although the publisher's blurb for *The Happy Hollisters* (1953) tells a reader that Mr. Hollister is never too busy to play ball with his children, we do not see him do it. We do see that Daddy Morton is a good sport—in amusement parks and on the beaches. Nancy Drew and Joe and Frank Hardy solve mysteries with their fathers, but a usual family relationship is hardly implied by the fact. It has already been shown that the age, illness, and infirmity of the parents of Tom Swift, Don Sturdy, and the Rover Boys preclude their active participation in the lives of their offspring. The attitude is well summed up in Thornton Burgess's *The Boy Scouts in a Trapper's Camp*: Mr. Upton has been asked by his son and his son's friends to join them for a tour of New York night life. He replies, "I have an engagement for this evening, though I would much rather join you youngsters than keep it. I feel that I am to lose something really worth while—a rare pleasure"(27).

By the 1980's, as is observable in life as well as fiction, parents, particularly the mother, are chauffeurs for the children, taxiing them everywhere, however inconvenient. In *The Secret of Jungle Park*, Mrs. Bobbsey asks, "When will your rehearsal be over?" Bert answers, "Could you pick us up at four-thirty?" His mother replies, simply, "Okay" (45). By the time she picks them up, they have almost been killed on a sabotaged roller coaster. "Have a good time, kids?" she asks, and the Twins respond, "It was, um, interesting" (59). No communication whatever exists between parent and children. Later, pressed by their detective activities, the Twins tell their parents that their equipment has been left at the park: "Your mother and I will bring it," says Mr. Bobbsey (71). Parental agreement is taken for granted in both cases. One may go further and say that all adults exist for such purposes: in *The Camp Fire Mystery*, Bert asks their mother's friend, Kathy, with whom they are staying in New Mexico, "Would you mind taking

Family Life & Relationships

us to the Camp Fire office?" Kathy answers, "It's number one on my list of things to do today" (37).

In 1939 Dorothy Dohm felt that she had found a different trend in children's books. She admitted that fathers played no role in certain "standard books for children" (*Tom Sawyer, Heidi, Rebecca of Sunnybrook Farm*), agreed that many childhood heroes were orphans, allowed the fairly frequent appearance of the "ineffectual father" (in *Little Women* and *Hans Brinker*), and the villainous one (in *The Prince and the Pauper* and *Huckleberry Finn*). But she concluded that by 1939 fathers were playing a more interdependent role in juvenile literature: in some Newbery award books, fathers share the pleasures of their children as well as their problems. This change Dohm saw as an indication of "the current attitude that father is now flesh and blood" (397–401). As is so frequently true, the series do not bear her out.

Perhaps there is some connection between the occupations of parents and the attitudes they display toward their children. Many series parents are professional people, a fact increasingly true of recent series. In the Sleepover Friends books, Kate Beekman's father is a doctor, and both Patti Jenkins's parents are professors of history at the university. Parents in the A.I. Gang are mainly scientists, computer experts, and artists. The fathers of all three generations of Tom Swifts were either scientists or inventors; Carson Drew is an attorney, as was Grace Harlowe's father; Fenton Hardy may be considered a professional involved in law enforcement. Some are small entrepreneurs running their own businesses, as is true of the Bobbsey Twins, the Happy Hollisters, and the mother in the Race Against Time Series; even Papa in the All-of-a-Kind Family, while he is a junk dealer, is nonetheless self-employed. What problems of identification such occupations may pose for readers with less pretentious parents may be set aside here, but "professional" parents may be too involved with their own work to spend time with or in consideration of their children.

Whatever the reason, parents in series are revealed generally as ineffectual, permissive, and frequently nonexistent—what may be called "the invisible parent." The ineffectual father has already been shown in the Tom Swift, Rover Boys and Don Sturdy series. In addition, Carson Drew tells his daughter, "I was just thinking how you always manage to get your own way" (*The Mystery at Lilac Inn* 17), and he "smiled indulgently" as he says it. In *The Mystery of the Moss-Covered Mansion* he worries a bit about the fact: "I know I'm making a mistake to let you have your own way" (179). He lets her have it, however. The mother of Rob Blake in *The Boy Scouts and the Army Airship* is a plaintive and timorous woman. When Rob reminds her of events in the previous volume, she says, "Oh, Rob, I cannot bear to hear such things. . . . You might have been killed by those Indians" (49). Such is the sum total of her dialogue in the book. Nevertheless she allows her son to become involved with dangerous enemy agents.

" 'Don't worry, Momsy,' [Tom Swift, Jr., says] using his childhood name for her." He is leaving for outer space. Mrs. Swift, a weeping handwringer, does no more than smile forlornly as her eighteen-year-old son climbs into his rocket ship. A generation earlier, Don Sturdy's mother had also deplored her son's worldwide travels and adventures, but in the end she always agreed—so often, in fact, that a scene near the beginning of each book in which she wept and pleaded in vain became conventional and a bore. "I'm sure they [his mother and sister, Ruth] will come around," said Don in *On the Ocean Bottom*. "They always do" (31). His father rationalized his own abdication of authority by saying repeatedly that he didn't believe in wrapping boys in cotton wool. The same assurance is seen in *The Boy Scouts at the Panama-Pacific Exposition*: "I don't believe Rob's parents would object if he wanted to go hunt for the South Pole" (34); he has no greater trouble in *Under Sealed Orders* when he wants to join a search for an insane man: "The boy had no trouble at all" (23). One sees how absurdly simple it is for children to manipulate their parents. Almost three-quarters of a century later, nothing has changed. In *Kate's Campout* (1988), volume 6 of the Sleepover Friends Series, the girls invite Lauren to spend a weekend in the country; unhesitatingly, Lauren responds, "I'm sure Mom and Dad'll say okay" (4). Of course they do.

Throughout the life of the modern series, parents have invariably forgiven their children's peccadillos, disobedience, and bad manners. As early as 1910 readers met such a mother in *Grace Harlowe's Plebe Year*. Mrs. Nesbitt "was a very shy, quiet

Family Life & Relationships

woman, almost entirely wrapped up in her only son. Miriam had always been too much for her, and she had long since given up attempting to rule or direct her brilliant, willful daughter" (54). After a wild automobile ride, which ends with Miriam's wrecking the car, her mother protests weakly, "I do wish you'd let one of the boys drive." "I prefer to do the driving, mother," replies the "spoiled girl" (163). Grace encounters another such parent later in her junior year: "My dear child," Jessica Bright's father tells her, "you know you may do as you please" (91). Indeed, the girl is Bright's disease. In *Patti's Luck* (1988) although asked to keep their noise down to accommodate Kate's father, who has had a hard day at the hospital, the girls in their exuberance crash through hedges and make a great racket; all Mrs. Beekman does is sigh. Later the girls use purple styling gel on their hair, not knowing that the water has been turned off and they cannot wash it out. When Stephanie's mother discovers their state, " 'Oh, dear,' she groaned. 'What a mess!' " (32). No reprimand is administered, however, not even a verbal one. Indeed, parents seem almost fearful of offending their fifth graders, or those younger, and make no complaints.

Most alarming, it seems that the more unpleasant a child is, the easier it is for him or her to overcome parental disapproval. Through the various entries in the All-of-a-Kind Family, Henny consistently disobeys and ignores rules. Nothing happens, beyond a shrug that seems to imply, "Oh, well, what can we do with Henny?" In *More All-of-a-Kind Family* she stays out so late that she misses dinner, an action she had performed also in the first book. Papa locks her out, but then spanks her friend by mistake and the incident ends in general hilarity. As usual, Henny escapes any criticism. A similar character is Jessica, one of the Sweet Valley Twins, who regularly performs actions that warrant Devil's Island. Yet because everyone loves her and is resignedly amused by her deeds, punishment is light and infrequent. In volume 4, *Sneaking Out*, her twin, Elizabeth, tells Jessica, "I think you're about the lowest, sneakiest sister anybody could ever have" (93); Mrs. Bramble, whose dog she was to care for but whom she allowed to run away, forgives her with, "I'm sure . . . you won't forget the lesson you learned today" (97). Eleven volumes later, in *Second Best*, the prophecy is still unfulfilled. Jessica is a consistent liar, and even her older brother, Steven, is "disappointed that Jessica had gotten off so easily" (8).

Even the updated Bobbsey Twins suffer from permissive parents. Once almost models of rectitude, the recent Bobbseys pretty much decide how they will live and act. *The Camp Fire Mystery* offers the children the chance to spend an extra day on a planned overnight trip; the council director asks whether they will be able to stay on: " 'Oh, yes,' the younger twins exclaimed gleefully" (44). They never even consider asking permission of Mom and Dad. When Flossie asks whether she has to eat any more meat loaf, Mrs. Bobbsey replies, "Just eat what you can, Sweetie" (*The Secret of Jungle Park* 18).

Series are dominated by children ranging in age from four to eighteen. They rule their parents, who are insipid, irresolute, and utterly baffled by what Carleton B. Morse in *One Man's Family* used to call their "bewildering offspring." One wonders whether art imitates life in the series, or whether life, through the influence of the series and television, is imitating art. Generally speaking, children are left on their own, to make their own mistakes and solve their own problems. Often they are told by parents that they have been brought up to make the correct decision, but readers have only the parents' word for evidence. So innocuous, so invisible are they that any real directive force on their part is incredible. Invariably, children are shown to be wiser, more courageous than adults; although parents are said to know best, clearly children do know best. Children are urged to obey their parents as final authorities, but by any standard, children are the prime movers in society: parents merely bumble along in their wake. In the latest series to appear in the 1980's, children consult each other, not their parents or any other adults, about criminals, politics, and drugs.

Much of what has been noted is summed up in the Doris Fein Series. Blessed with professional parents (her father is an ophthalmologist, her mother, a nurse; Uncle Saul is a dentist), Doris drives a $50,000 sports car and has a personal income of $3.7 million inherited from friend Harry Grubb. Clearly she is independent of her parents, neither of whom would consider attempting to advise her, let alone make demands. A remark in *The Mad Samurai* is quintessential: realizing that she is late, Doris decides to call home, but she states that she does not have

Family Life & Relationships

to do so, since she is a grown woman (at eighteen) and of voting age. However, "I don't like my Mom to worry" (76). The usually hard-to-please *Horn Book* described Doris as "an intelligent, self-confident teen-ager with remarkable intuition" (publisher's blurb for *Deadly Aphrodite*).

Perhaps not too ironically in the face of almost superfluous parents, series children often reveal an insufferably patronizing attitude toward the older generation. Grace Harlowe did so regularly, as in her junior year at high school she says, "You are just like Mrs. Gray, Judge . . . always imagining yourself old, when you know you're just a great big boy" (254). Jessica Wakefield in *The Haunted House* (number 3 of the Sweet Valley Twins) responds to her father's question of why the girls believe that Mrs. Mercandy is a witch with " 'Daddy,' Jessica explained, as though her father were six" (7). While Dr. Werner Wendell has come to Ancoteague Island with several other scientists to perfect a machine that can actually think, to his daughter, Wendy, his highest accomplishment is his ability to cook (she is called "Wonderchild" because of her own ability to use computers; she is twelve). When her mother forgets a crucial ingredient for the night's meal, Dr. Wendell is upset. "Poor dad, he's deeply hurt, thought Wendy. Which meant that he was likely to sulk throughout dinner. And her mother in turn—furious at him for making her feel guilty—would get revenge by smacking her lips over the moo goo and remarking how good Chinese food tasted for a change. Wendy sighed. Adults were so childish at times!" (*The Cutlass Clue* 35–36).

To be sure, Tom Swift, Jr., paid lip service to his father, the indefatigable hero of thirty-seven books of his own, in *Race to the Moon*: "As always, when in trouble, he asked himself, 'What would Dad do in this situation?' " (170). But Tom Jr., at the age of eighteen, has been eclipsing his father for 169 pages of that book and for the eleven books preceding it. The statement of confidence seems to lack motivation. Likewise Carson Drew may be the best lawyer in the state, but in what is now well over a hundred volumes, he has never beaten his daughter to the solution of a mystery. When Nancy tells him in *The Mystery of the Moss-Covered Mansion*, "you are the best judge of what is best" (72), no reader believes her.

Mr. Hollister has invented many gadgets, and he runs a combination hardware shop and toy store, yet when the store is robbed in *The Happy Hollisters*, it is the children who find the solution. Again and again, Fenton Hardy is extricated from peril by his sons, although undoubtedly he is one of the two or three strongest adult characters in any series. Despite their larger-than-life scientific parents, in the A.I. Gang Series the children create a complex detective program for the computer ("Sherlock"), build robots (a dog named Rin Tin Stainless Steel and a talking bronze head called Paracelsus), construct successfully a flying wing and an outerspace rocket, and throughout the series pursue enemy agents.

Finally, with the exception of the All-of-a-Kind Family, children in series have no household responsibilities. Even in the various family series they never take out trash or garbage, rake yards, mow lawns, or make beds; indeed, they seem to have no academic responsibilities, even in scholastic series—all heroes do well in school automatically. Once in a while they feel the need to get to football practice on time, for the good of the team. Though Chip Hilton is supported by his widowed mother, and though, in order not to be unfair or harsh, we might assume that he does help around the house, as so often happens in series, we never see him in such actions. Only in the All-of-a-Kind Family Series do children have regularly assigned tasks. The family is very poor, and with five girls and a baby, mother is fully occupied. True, she makes the tasks as much fun as possible and she does at times have to goad or fool the children into performing them; for example, she claims to have hidden twelve buttons in a particular room and offers a penny to the child who each week can find all of them while cleaning. In general, however, all children do in the series is play, play, play. The most recent series, those of the past decade, are the worst offenders. Children watch television, talk about boys and make themselves up (if they are girls), go to the Mall, eat Chinese noodles in restaurants, and dream up schemes to get to rock concerts which their parents feel they are too young to attend.

The inescapable conclusion is that there is no true "family" series, no series which displays the daily activities of children and their parents. Instead, when family life is presented, it is seen in its unusual aspects—on trips, vacations, holidays, and at

Family Life & Relationships

parties. Families are seen together chiefly at such occasions, and while parents are often described as close to their children, such closeness is only rarely demonstrated. With few exceptions (notably Nancy Drew and the Hardy Boys) parents are "invisible," and when visible, they are ineffectual and indulgent. The world is of, by, and for children, who, almost without exception, disprove the idea that "Father knows best."

MAN–WOMAN, HUSBAND–WIFE, FATHER–MOTHER RELATIONSHIPS

A *Booklist* review of *Doris Fein: Phantom of the Casino* states that "Doris Fein . . . is rapidly becoming a Nancy Drew type for modern tastes . . . a balanced feminist-feminine perspective" (publisher's blurb for *Dead Heat at Long Beach*). The balance is hard to find in the books. In *Phantom*, for example, Doris is offended when Jack Ford calls her "Miss Fein . . . to him the word 'Ms.' doesn't exist" (36). A year later in *Deadly Aphrodite*, Mario the masseur calls her "Miss Fein," and Doris bridles, "That's Ms." (42). A doctor in *Murder Is No Joke* further raises her ire for referring to her as "Miss," and Doris castigates him soundly: "It's Ms., not Miss Fein" (10). When she bawls out Georgie Stark later in the same book for the same offense, he retorts, "Ms., Schmiz . . . What's the difference if you're healthy?" (25). It is probably only coincidence that Georgie is murdered further on.

Except for the Doris Fein Series, however, feminism and gender issues have not taken root in the children's fiction series. With one early exception, the Grace Harlowe Series, which ran from 1910 to 1924, nowhere can one find a picture of American life dominated by women. The emergence of women as dominant—the chief consumers, creators of taste, resolvers of family problems, or until the 1980's as chauffeurs—does not appear in these books. The husband-father rules the home. In the adventure and mystery series, it is the father who decides to allow children to leave home, to travel, to get involved in crimes. In *The Secret of Wildcat Swamp*, the Hardy Boys' "quiet, pretty mother said that she would leave the decision to their father" (7). Invariably Don Sturdy has his first-two-chapters' difficulty in getting parental permission to travel to "lion land," but he can rely on his father's feeling that boys should not be wrapped in cotton wool, and eventually "Mother usually does what Dad thinks best" (2). Nancy Drew's father is thoroughly masculine, and although Nancy outdoes him in detective accomplishments, from the first volume to the latest, she is his housekeeper and never questions his decisions. Though she gets into trouble and danger, in none of the books does she really dispute his authority or go against his expressed wishes. Chip Hilton's father is dead, but there is no doubt about his position in the household when he was alive: Mrs. Hilton, in fact, has done everything she could to bring Chip up to resemble him; Chip is allowed to make the major decisions as "the man of the house." Throughout the All-of-a-Kind Family Series, which is to be sure historical (laid as it is in the early teens of the present century), Papa is patriarch; at all the many Jewish festivals, his position is supreme, and though Mama is charming and resourceful, she and the other women sit at the back of the synagogue separated from the men.

Naturally one sees more of the mother in the Honey Bunch and Bobbsey Twins books, because the children are very young (Honey Bunch is only five), and with father at work, mother would be more involved with the children. When decisions concerning the whole family need to be made, they are usually worked out by both parents, a fact true of the Happy Hollisters also. The mother of Tom Swift, Jr., is decidedly a weak figure, interested in her son's and husband's work but owning to little understanding of it. She acceded to her husband's wishes for twenty-five volumes.

It would be fair to say that children who read the various series receive a quite different image of the man-woman, husband-wife, father-mother relationship from that put forth by television, movies, and other kinds of literature—an image which does not square with the mores of contemporary U.S. society represented by other popular media, sociologists, or social critics. The dichotomy between life and books here is very sharp. By the 1980's Mrs. Bobbsey worked part-time as a reporter for the *Lakeport News* but there is no implication that the job is a career: her main occupation is still wife, mother, and chauffeur for the children.

The one exception, and a startling one, is found in the Grace Harlowe Overland Riders Series. Once having married Tom Gray, her sweetheart through high school and college, Grace proceeds to leave him regularly each summer in order to travel with friends. The series retains her maiden name and she is even called Harlowe by friends in the books themselves. Tom gives in readily to Grace and allows her to spend the summer months with three other women and Hippy Wingate, a comic character, in various parts of the United States. Early in *The Great American Desert* we read, " 'I am going back to the hotel to lie down for an hour,' announced Grace. 'Tom, you go and do a little shopping for me while I am resting' " (34–35). Tom goes without comment. Very slightly later he tells Grace, "No wonder you are successful in managing a husband . . . Even the dumb animals bow to your will" (37). In a different kind of book, one might suspect an analogy. The next year, Grace leaves him again, this time for the Kentucky Mountains. Hippy teases her, saying, "What's this? Henpecking your husband again, Grace Harlowe?" (20). Note that he does not call her Grace Gray, her married name. Taking over before Tom has even left, Grace—not the men—does all the searching for lost articles and lost people, she ropes a bear, and after a wild gun fight in the forest, she says, "I will look after the camp for the rest of the night" (71), despite the presence of a male companion, Hippy. For a series of seven volumes, there is no change in the relationship.

While the husband-wife relationship in this series is not typical of series in general, in another respect it is. Because the fiction series are written for children, husbands and wives live together in nonsexual terms; probably it could not be otherwise. The situation is most apparent in books where parents are widowed or widowered—Tom Swift, Nancy Drew, the Rover Boys, Chip Hilton. Voluntary separation of parents also occurs, however. Grace Harlowe is one such example. Each summer means total separation for Grace and her husband; not only is the sexual relationship destroyed thereby, but so is the whole family, since their daughter, Yvonne, is placed in a boarding school or with relatives while mother goes off adventuring. One can conceive of no reason for this marriage beyond the producing of the child. Much the same thing happens in the Honey Bunch books. In *Her First Little Trip to the Seashore*, for example, Daddy Morton delivers her mother and Honey Bunch to the seashore, planning himself to return home immediately, where he will remain for the entire summer, not even excepting weekends. Thus, there is no question of sex. Both Fenton Hardy and Tom Swift, Sr. (in the Tom Swift, Jr., Series) are described as thoughtful, considerate men in family matters. "When he was working on a problem," we are told of the elder Swift in *Tom Swift, Jr., and his Flying Lab*, "one thing he never failed to do was to keep in touch with his family if he could" (138). The trouble lies in the last three words: he very often cannot, since, like his son, he is usually under the sea or in the stratosphere or at least closeted in his laboratory. Fenton Hardy too is "an intensely considerate man and his first thought was always for his wife and boys" (*The House on the Cliff* 81), but thoughts are cheap and he is more often away on a case than at home. The image of the parents of Sue Barton and Don Sturdy as aged and infirm makes a sexual relationship seem unlikely. Mr. and Mrs. Bobbsey and Mr. and Mrs. Hollister are together a good deal of the time—on picnics, merry-go-rounds, or trips; they sing around the piano, but no suggestion of other intimacy can be found. A perceptive cynic might find food for thought in the series title—the *Happy* Hollisters. Parents never so much as kiss each other. When one considers the vigorous, youthful image of parents presented in the series overall, their good looks and vitality, such complete lack of physical feeling is all the more remarkable.

As a corollary to the virtually platonic relations of husbands and wives, one finds that parents have no lives whatever beyond the family. Of course the focus of the books is on children, their problems and adventures, but in the series, once parents leave the house, they cease to exist: they have no personal, private, business, religious, moral, or psychological problems. They are disembodied, anemic spirits, in spite of being handsome, athletic, and good-humored. Mr. Hollister runs The Trading Post, a hardware, sporting goods, and toy shop, certainly a romantic-sounding combination, and although his children do help at the store, particularly in the first volume, he disappears in the morning and is seen thereafter only at meals or on family

Family Life & Relationships

outings. In *The Bobbsey Twins at the Seashore* we learn that Mrs. Bobbsey's sister "had been a society belle when she was married" (54); may we not reasonably assume that Mrs. Bobbsey must have led a similar life? Yet no suggestion of any past existence creeps into the books. Although Fenton Hardy, Carson Drew, and the elder Tom Swift all have occupations that figure prominently in the series, even they are seen as foils for their children and they engage in no activity not somehow or also involving Joe and Frank, Nancy, or Tom Jr. All of the Woodland Gang are orphans, but Mrs. Tandy, their housekeeper, stands in the role of adoptive parent; she is equally ready to join the children in their activities, such as building their clubhouse. Even when Mrs. Tandy inherits an English house and the children recognize that she probably wants to examine her new home, a potential mystery lurking in the wings causes her to say, "I'm dying to go to that castle as much as you are. We can unpack later. Let's go" (*The Old Gold Coins* 47).

Mothers and fathers never discuss business, never visit other adults, belong to no lodges, clubs, or other social organizations—indeed, they never attend a P.T.A. meeting, though Mama in *The All-of-a-Kind Family* does visit the library—once—with her daughters. If fathers have careers, they are pursued solely for the maintenance of their families, not for personal satisfaction. So far as one can tell, parents get no pleasure from life that does not involve their families. To readers, then, is offered an ideal of total family devotion and absorption. The baby-sitter, almost an American institution, almost a myth figure, appeared in no series until the 1980's, when the Babysitters Club series appeared. Parents take complete responsibility for their children. Moreover mothers and fathers never lose their tempers, have headaches, or worry; the worst that can be said is that Kate Beekman's father "had a rough day at the hospital, and he's exhausted" (*Patti's Luck* 8). Not only are their lives free from any kind of sexuality; they are also free of any passion or feeling whatsoever, unless a sense of humor can be considered feeling.

Because of the lack of parental existence beyond the family, the lack of anger, fear, doubt, or passion, parents provide the ultimate in security for their children. As noted, they rarely reprimand and almost never punish. They seem, in fact, to subscribe fully to the notion that the feelings of children are never to be hurt. In the series, children live in an assured moral and psychological world.

In *Honey Bunch and Norman Play Detective at Niagara Falls*, Norman forgets his carved boat, which he wanted to take on his trip. Despite their being at the station, with none too much time, Daddy Morton turns right around, drives home, and brings the boat in the nick of time. Norman thus experiences only momentary discomfort. Early in *The Yellow Phantom* the reader learns of Judy Bolton's father that "Dr. Bolton's manner was reassuring as always" (11); sprinkled through the rest of the book are numerous other examples of the security he provides. The publisher's blurb for the first volume of the Happy Hollisters Series assured the prospective buyer that Mrs. Hollister "is always ready to meet a sudden need, for a surprise picnic or to lend a helping hand." Fenton Hardy "was never too busy to talk to his sons" (*The House on the Cliff* 52). At the seashore, Honey Bunch tells her friend, "There's such a lot to do. . . . Daddy likes to do it" (158).

Exceptions to the image are rare. In the Judy Bolton book, *The Clue of the Broken Feather*, Mr. Lake tells his daughter, Polly, "Your papa was wrong. Parents make mistakes" (161). Once in a while, parental permissiveness is pernicious: the mother of Trip Branders, a villain in *Uncle Sam's Boys in the Ranks*, "abetted his idleness by supplying him with too much money" (17).

Substantially, clear marital and parental ideals are given in the series: a strong father who heads the family and an acquiescent mother; a relation between a husband and wife devoid of any passion except concern for the family and no life beyond the family; parents whose entire interest is the welfare, comfort, security, and happiness of their children. Childhood is pictured as a golden time, without pressures or emotions and only short-lived sorrows or tragedy, enlivened by vacations, trips, and wholly unreal and unlikely mysteries.

Richard Mandel's valuable 1964 study of the Dick and Jane books, long used by many elementary schools as primers in grades one and two, corroborates the foregoing conclusions. Since the books were used directly in the education process for beginning readers in their most impressionable years—six to

Family Life & Relationships

eight—Mandel feels that they reveal exactly what society wants to instill in the child: "society's most fundamental system of values and motivations, which will make up his basic attitudes and behavior for the rest of his life" (190). Most of these qualities are found also in the fiction series.

1. The mother of Dick and Jane does housework, but has time to go to the zoo and on other trips, and she joins father in games with the children; both spend a good deal of time with the children.

2. All adults are ready to help children, who have good times and are approved of and fostered by adults. There are no bad children.

3. All situations that call for reprimands work out well for Dick and Jane. If they take mother's food and open a sidewalk store, mother laughs, takes back the food, and they all have a good dinner. If a boy takes cookies and gives them to friends, he receives no lecture or advice: Mom has just baked cookies and he may have them. No standards are taught, thus. Children are rewarded for taking what does not belong to them.

4. Parents are not seen as people to whom children are obedient; the love of parents is automatic and need not be earned. Dick and Jane have few rules. They spend much time talking to other children and have slight interaction with adults or adult authority. Their time is spent in playing, in school, or in activities described as funny or silly. An amazing amount of time is spent at parties and in other peer group activities. Gregariousness and social activities are seen as desirable. Children's roles and identities are molded, not by parents, but by peers. Their world is distinct from that of adults. (198)

Adults, as represented by publishers and authors, seem to want certain ideas instilled in children. Both the Dick and Jane books and the fiction series are mutually supportive in this regard. They are reinforced as well by the series' view of women and girls.

In the many series with girls as main characters, they are fearless, capable, intelligent, and adventurous, in fact, to a much greater degree than the males who struggle along after them. The situation is obviously logical in such series as Cherry Ames, Sue Barton, Vicki Barr, Nancy Drew, and Doris Fein, whose appeal is chiefly to girl readers. In contrast, the image of girls and women in series where they are not focal points is quite different. "Girls can't be soldiers," says Freddie Bobbsey, aged four, in *Merry Days Indoors and Out.* "They have to get married, or be dressmakers, or sten'graphers, or something like that" (21). In *Don Sturdy Among the Gorillas*, Emily declares, "It's mean that you boys should have all the adventure" (39). But they always do, because as Don says in *On the Ocean Bottom*, "girls aren't any good on an expedition like this" (78): they have to be protected. After some days on a desert island in *Tom Swift and His Wireless Message*, Tom and the men realize that the group will have to go on half rations; the men, however, are willing to go on quarter rations to be sure that the women have enough and also that they will not be frightened (190). Disguising Tom Wat as a girl in *Footprints Under the Window*, the Hardy Boys give him advice about how to avoid detection: "You mustn't forget to giggle every few minutes, for no reason at all, and powder your nose whenever you see a mirror" (112).

Except for books with girls as heroines, it's a man's world in the series; just as families are ruled by men with slight assistance from women, so is the view of life a predominantly masculine one. At the seashore, the Bobbseys admire Dorothy for acting like a boy: she swims, rows, paddles, and climbs trees, provoking the comment that "girls don't have to be babies and be lady-like" (85). That Ruth is a good sport is the highest compliment that Don Sturdy can pay. The Hardy Boys and the Swifts, father and son, had girl friends who played minor parts; not until the 1980's did Joe Hardy become a real womanizer. Strangely, the Chip Hilton books, twenty-two of which were published between 1948 and 1964, present an utterly girl-less world, strange because Chip goes through high school and his junior year in college during the series with no interest whatever in girls. Girls rarely even appear, and none has a major role to play. Chip's only interest is sports, yet not even a female cheerleader is seen. This series made its appeal to boys of ten and eleven and to their interest in baseball, football, and basketball. As they were shown the world in these books, it belonged to males.

THE GOOD LIFE

On the basis of what has been said so far, one can form a clear idea of what, according to the series, is the good life. Almost

Family Life & Relationships

without exception, the ideal is the unusual. The best life is one free from responsibilities—no school, no job, no family, no church, no nation. Peter Pan and Tennessee Williams's Baby Doll reign supreme in the series world. To be good, life must be abnormal, exciting, changing. One must never repeat actions or experiences. The normal life of everyday existence is specifically condemned, and dissatisfaction with the usual is encouraged.

Perhaps a reader would expect the life of Tom Swift, Jr., to be extraordinary: he builds and pilots a rocket ship, goes to the bottom of the ocean in a deep sea hydrodome, engages in a race to the moon, and battles asteroid pirates. One should remember that Tom is eighteen years old—the age of a high school senior. Certainly Tom lives in a "large, comfortable house," but it is surrounded by a magnetic alarm field and one needs to wear a special badge to get through it (*The Caves of Nuclear Fire* 9). Even more extreme was the life of Don Sturdy, who was only fourteen when his series began in 1925 and only seventeen when it ended six years later; Don went to Egypt, the North Pole, Alaska, Africa, and like Tom Swift, Jr., and Rick Brant, the bottom of the sea.

If one examines the series that seem most likely to present a normal way of life, he finds the Bobbsey Twins *On a Houseboat*, *On the Deep Blue Sea*, *Treasure Hunting*, *In Eskimo Land*, *In Mexico*, *In Tulip Land*, and *In London Tower*. Honey Bunch Morton is only five years old, yet we find her taking a trip on the ocean in 1927, a trip west in 1928, a trip to the Great Lakes in 1930; she solved a mystery in 1935, went on a treasure hunt two years later, and when the series name changed to Honey Bunch and Norman, she and her friend had adventures in the Castle of Magic and solved a whole series of mysteries. Evidently, the Happy Hollisters also felt that happiness lies in the rare: almost half of the books had "mystery" in the titles; volume 4 concerned an Indian treasure, volume 9 a secret fort, and volume 18 adventures in Denmark.

But titles are one thing: they sell books. Editorial comments and observations by characters are another. What kinds of opinions about the good life are found in the series?

The one career series—indeed, almost the only series of any kind—to be praised highly is that involving Sue Barton, nurse. In each book, Sue has something new to learn and to face. As a student nurse and then as a senior, she naturally progresses from stage to stage: classes, wards, the operating room, and so on. Along the way, however, the usual routine of hospital life is never seen. Instead, a particularly difficult patient has to be won over, a potential suicide must be averted, a couple that does not want their baby must be reconciled to the child. When she leaves the hospital to become a visiting nurse, we find that Sue "had never been inside a tenement in her life" (33). As a rural nurse, she helps locate the source of a typhoid epidemic. Only a rare temperature is ever taken; no bed pans are ever emptied.

The other main career series, Cherry Ames, makes scarcely any attempt to be authentic. "My whole nursing career has been just one scrape after another," Sue says halfway through the series (*Clinic Nurse* 67). Even as a senior nurse, in the second volume, Sue is involved with the attempted theft of the formula for penicillin; the prevention of this theft, not nursing, is the core of the book. Grace Harlowe may have been voicing no more than the average feeling of a high school sophomore when she sighs, "Oh, dear, I wish that examinations and school were over. . . . I can't go to the woods alone, and I can't get anyone to go with me" (*Sophomore Year in High School* 224). She certainly is not average when, after getting married and having a child, she still goes off adventuring, saying, "Safety's not the ambition of our young lives [she is now beyond her middle twenties]; at least getting into difficulties and perilous situations has become a habit with Grace Harlowe" (*Great American Desert* 124). Judy Bolton expressed the idea thus: "Death could be kind to old people who were through with romance and adventure. But Irene had so much to live for" (*The Yellow Phantom* 176). The implication is quite clear that the young live for romance and adventure. The idea is explicit in Herbert Carter's Boy Scout Series. *In the Rockies* presents a group of boys "who yearned for excitement in any shape or style, so long as it thrilled their pulses—which was the natural boy spirit, always feeding on action" (8). In Howard Payson's Boy Scout Series is seen the terrible alternative: "Rob Blake secretly sighed when he contemplated having to put in a whole summer around the home town" (*At the Panama-Pacific Exposition* 11); the statement comes just after reference has been made to the Scouts' previous adventures in Mexico, Belgium, and Panama.

Family Life & Relationships   95

A similar feeling is expressed by another Scout in *Under Sealed Orders:* "When you, Rob, and Andy were taking in the splendid sights of the great fair out on the coast, and enjoying the remarkable scenery of the Canadian Pacific woods on the way back home, there I was with my folks at that dinky little village in Maine, visiting my mother's people" (7).

Such attitudes characterized all the Boy Scouts series except that by Robert Shaler, at once the most realistic, the most satisfying, and the most indicative of normal Boy Scout activities and ideals. *The Prize Pennant,* for example, deals with the efforts of rival scouting troops to perform enough good deeds and to learn enough about woodcraft to win a prize pennant. "They've learned that a fellow can get heaps and heaps of fun out of life without playing mean tricks or being cruel to birds and animals" (25). In the fourth Nancy Drew book, *The Mystery at Lilac Inn,* Nancy, after considerable work, is able to engage a servant-housekeeper. Her reaction is quite different from that seen in *The Prize Pennant*: she is "delighted to be relieved of responsibility" (25). It is sufficient to note that readers of ten, eleven, and twelve are being asked to identify with her.

The urge to avoid the ordinary and average is nowhere more clearly expressed than in the Don Sturdy Series virtually dedicated to the rare and exotic in experience. "It's a mighty risky project," Professor Bruce tells Captain Hardy, Don's uncle. "That's what makes the idea so alluring. . . . I wouldn't give a copper for anything that didn't have some risk connected with it" (*Desert of Mystery* 1). Whenever Don goes a-traveling, his companion is the Captain; his mother and father, representing the normal life, stay at home. *On the Ocean Bottom* informs the reader that "it's a great thing to live. To go places and see strange things. That's the life" (101).

Let us observe the two types of life side by side. Bruce Langley in *The Port of Lost Ships* complains, "I'm tied down to the humdrum life. My father is head of a bank in Norfolk" (31). His sentiments are exactly those of Slim Robinson in the Hardy Boys entry, *The Tower Treasure*: "I'll have to give up all those college plans and settle down to the business world. . . . I'll have a chance to learn supermarket work from the ground up" (80).

The recent Sweet Valley Twins and Sweet Valley High Series are devoted to an avoidance of the average. All of *Sneaking Out,* for example, involves getting to a rock concert and meeting the star singer. The A.I. Gang Series uproots the several children, taking them to Ancoteague Island with their parents and involving them with mystery, espionage, and scientific development; school is a thing of the past. While it was a most "acceptable" series in the sense of not allowing children to perform actions that persons of their ages could not, the Woodland Gang presented four orphans, with more than adequate money, no parent-child conflicts, no real rules, no responsibilities beyond homework, and a permanent and loving housekeeper. The Tom and Ricky Mystery Series for very young readers is just what its title proclaims; all the books involve mysteries. The two boys have no home life or school life; they are as remote from reality as the Dr. Seuss books. Notably the reading level is exactly that of Dick and Jane and its appeal is to the same audience. Don Sturdy spoke for all the series when he said in *On the Ocean Bottom*, "There's everything in doing what you like to do"; and perhaps the point is made most vividly as Don sets sail for Lion Land: "Now they were heading toward the land where it was always summer, the land of glamour and mystery, and perhaps of tragedy" (65).

6 EXTRA-FAMILY RELATIONSHIPS

EXTERNAL JUDGMENT OF PERSONS

THE CHILDREN'S SERIES ARE generally black and white in their attitudes, morality, and motivations; to their readers they present definite, uncomplicated ideas, reinforced by repetition from book to book, series to series, publisher to publisher. In fairness, little direct moralizing or explicit attitudinizing is done. Readers are not told how to judge or react. Gradually, however, certain set beliefs, established with slight variation, become taken for granted. All the fiction series have heroes and villains, and rarely the twain do meet: a bad character may reform by contact with a good one, as Dan Baxter did in *The Rover Boys in New York,* but a good character can never become bad. The devices used to allow readers to tell bad persons from good are so unequivocal that a transfer from fiction to life may be easily made.

First, physical appearance provides an infallible revelation of character. A good character, for example, is instantly recognizable by his or her looks. When Sue Barton first meets Phil, the beau of her wealthy friend, Connie, one glance shows her a firm chin, grave mouth, steady eyes: "This was no fortune hunter. This was a very nice boy" (*Senior Nurse* 119–120). The Payson Boy Scout Series is more general in details but just as specific in attitudes: "He's a fine-looking gentleman, I must say," Rob Blake observes. "I think you'll have no trouble making fair terms with him, if I'm any judge of faces" (*Panama-Pacific Exposition* 275). Nancy Drew has only momentary doubts in *The Haunted Bridge*: "It did not seem possible that this dignified, quiet young woman could be the member of a disreputable gang . . . she didn't look the type" (36). The Hardy Boys feel they have a friend aboard the phantom freighter, because "unlike the others on the ship, he had a fine, intelligent face. The Hardys wondered how the man happened to be part of a smuggler's crew" (208). Although Honey Bunch has some initial trouble in *Her First Days in Camp*, she too knows a friend: "This boy had a kind and merry face, and such truthful brown eyes that Honey Bunch liked him at once" (35). In *The Caves of Nuclear Fire*, both Tom Swift Senior and Junior know that Alvy Tompkins's "strong face and direct gaze reflected his integrity" (37). Uncle Sam's Boys are sure that Sergeant Brimmer can be trusted since he is "a man about thirty, tall, rather slender, erect, thoroughly well built, with light, almost golden hair and mustache, and a keen but kindly blue eye" (*In the Ranks* 66). One is compelled to worry about the other eye and to wonder how many children may be misled by the often-charming appearance of child molesters.

Descriptions of heroes and heroines invariably reveal their roles. One should remember, though, that series descriptions are often quite general, to allow as many readers as possible to identify with them. Perhaps the fact of broad, simple strokes makes the point even stronger. Cherry Ames is slim, lovely, with black hair and eyes; her cheeks and lips are cherry red; she is "fresh and glowing as a rose" (*Senior Nurse* 23). Nancy Drew is poised, pretty, and originally blond, though her hair eventually went reddish. Pete Hollister is twelve, blond, with a crew cut and sparkling blue eyes; Pam Hollister is ten, blond, with brown eyes; Ricky Hollister is seven, lanky, redhaired (usually mussed), and freckled; Holly Hollister is six, dark-haired, with pigtails and dancing brown eyes: such variations in hair and eye color in one family rather stretch Mendelian theory, as happens with the Hardy Boys—Frank is tall, dark-haired, with clean-cut features, while Joe is blond, blue-eyed, and curly-haired. Grace Harlowe has chestnut hair; she is tall, slender, with regular features and cheeks glowing with health. Chip Hilton has cropped blond hair; he is tall and "streamlined." Honey Bunch is blond, "all that was lovely, and good, and sweet." While the Lone Ranger cannot be described facially because of the mask he wears, he is seen as a giant who moves with the "easy, effortless grace of a perfectly conditioned athlete." Don Sturdy is clean-featured, robust, tall, muscular, strong, well-built, brown-haired. Tom Swift is tall, muscular, well set-up physically; Tom Swift, Jr., is tall and slender. In the 1980's Sweet Valley High Series, the twins, Elizabeth and Jessica, have "shoulder-length, sunstreaked blond hair, the same sparkling blue-green eyes, the same perfect skin"; the girls are five feet six and are "generously blessed with spectacular all-American good looks" (*Double Love* 2). Here readers are told almost directly what they should look like if they are to be truly American. What about those, one asks, who do not share such qualities?

Possibly there is a relationship between their appearance and the fact that almost without exception heroes and heroines of series have distinctly Anglo-Saxon names: Ames, Bolton, Brant, Davis, Drew, Hardy, Harlowe, Hilton, Swift, Wakefield, Wendell. When in the All-of-a-Kind Family Series, whose characters are Jewish, a non-Anglo-Saxon designation is called for, no surname at all is supplied. Doris Fein, also Jewish, is a notable, though recent, exception; in series before 1978 such a "foreign" name would have implied a villain.

Occasionally social position may be a means of judging character, as it is in *Cherry Ames, Clinic Nurse*: "He's one of Hilton's most respected citizens, so he couldn't have had anything to do with my kidnaping," Cherry asserts confidently (94). Social position is not so secure a yardstick as appearance, however, and occurs rarely in series.

If it is easy to identify good people, it is even easier to identify bad ones. Villains can also be detected by physical appearance, facial expressions, and clothing. The villain in *The Horseshoe Riddle* appears to the Bobbsey Twins as "an ugly man [with] a crooked red scar on his forehead" (41). The Boy Scouts' adversary in *The Prize Pennant* is a man with "a gorilla-like face that just then looked to Arthur as though he could chew a file, it was so lined with a scowl" (99). Both Nancy Drew and the Hardy Boys, who make a career of foiling criminals, must make quick assessments of people. In the many Nancy Drew books there is a whole gallery of evil people, all detectable by their looks and manners. Nathan Gomber, for instance, in *The Hidden Staircase* is short, thin, rather stooped, with a shifty gaze; he is also Jewish. Trying to hire a maid in *The Mystery at Lilac Inn*, Nancy meets a woman "obviously sent by the agency"—"obviously" because of her "wiry build and dark complexion," "her impudent look," "her sly look," and "her bold manner" (18). Later in the same book, one of the male villains wears a flashy suit, walks with a bold swagger, and has a hooked nose. In *The House on the Cliff,* the Hardys encounter a woman, "hard faced and tight lipped, with gaunt features; she was not prepossessing, and her untidy garb did not impress the boys favorably" (98); her husband they also dislike: "short and thin, in need of a shave... his complexion was swarthy, and he had narrow eyes under coarse black brows" (98). Later they are able to identify Shackley ("his lips were thin and cruel") as a bad man: "he is evidently a lawless and desperate man" (124).

In *The Mystery of the Tolling Bell* Nancy Drew meets a hotel clerk, "an unpleasant-looking fellow with shining, heavily-oiled hair"; he is reading a comic book and staring insolently at Nancy (57–58). Indeed, hair, or the lack of it, is consistently a sign of villainy in the series. In *Tom Swift, Jr., and His Flying Lab* the villain has "sleek, black hair" (11) and is later called "the pomade kid" (18) and "an oily-haired sneak" (23). The Bobbsey Twins in *The Camp Fire Mystery* meet "two stringy-haired thieves" (114); at first sight of them, noting their "stringy blond hair [that] hung about their faces," Nan observes, "They look mean" (21). Pia, the villainess of *Hostages of Hate*, is similarly denounced: "her dark hair was stringy." In *Deadly Intent,* Roger Gold has "spiky black hair and a single silver earring" (7), while the head villainess, Vivian, has dark hair that "gleamed with henna-red highlights" (40); when we are told that she wore a blue sweater "cut low in front," she is condemned out of hand. Cherry Ames's kidnapers are "a small, birdlike girl, with coarse sandy hair," and Jake, "a bald, thin, bearded man with shifty eyes" (*Clinic Nurse* 48). Akutu, the villain of *Revenge of the Desert Phantom,* is also bald; if it had not been for Frank and Joe, wails Aunt Gertrude, "that horrible bald general would be president" (153).

Nancy Drew judges as evil a "dwarfish stranger" who makes a "display of bad table manners... 'he reminds me of a brown-skinned elf... only he has such mean, cruel eyes' " (*The Mystery of the Tolling Bell* 163–164); when two pages later she sees that he has "a misshapen back," the conclusion is that hunchbacks are evil people. The chief woman villain of *The Clue of the Black Keys* has "a loud, brassy voice" (12). "You wouldn't like her, Nancy. She wears loud clothes and makes herself conspicuous" (151).

Heroes and villains are not the only persons to be judged by external qualities. At first thought, the image of fat people may

Extra-Family Relationships

seem an unimportant area, yet it implies some basic facts about series, and it is a constant in them; the conception of the fat person changes in no respect whatever. If few readers of the series, however much they might identify with a hero in fantasy, could never measure up to his picture, the stout person could do so least of all.

Fat people are invariably cast as fools; with the exception only of Doris Fein, they provide comic relief. They are jolly, pleasant, easygoing, and good-natured; they are also ridiculous and laughable. Friends and helpers of heroes, they never attain first rank in any series but that devoted to Doris Fein. In general, they are clumsy, awkward, and ineffectual. Consistently the subject of insult and ridicule, even from their friends, the heroes, they bear all with good humor. Indeed, they seem little disposed to avoid such insults, for they all eat hugely and often. Occasionally, they have names, such as Bumpus Hawtree in the Carter Boy Scout books or William Philander Tubbs in the Rover Boys Series, which seem calculated to add to their comic condition. From 1900 to 1978 nothing is done to change their image. Typical is "fat Hilda Grayson" in the Sue Barton books, who in *Student Nurse* is called "fat girl" (21), "the very fat girl" (35), and again, "the fat girl" (41). The technique here is common to all series—never to allow readers to forget a particular concept or picture. As noted, character development is limited to a few broad strokes, and type casting is one means of providing a sense of who a character is. Unfortunately, however, stereotypes are also maintained by this means. In *Sue Barton, Senior Nurse*, we find that "fat, pretty Hilda, of course, was a darling. She was no intellectual giant, but she was sweet" (47). The "of course" underscores several assumptions about Hilda: she is pretty, sweet, not bright, and a darling—though fat. Both the younger Bobbsey Twins, Freddie and Flossie, are fat. Flossie's father calls her his "fat fairy" throughout the series, and Freddie is his "fat fireman." During their trip to Washington, Freddie sees a large boy at the theatre; ironically he says, "Oh, look at the funny fat boy over there. . . . He's awful fat, isn't he?" (195). Freddie is in no position to point a finger, yet he is apparently not aware that he too is funny. Perhaps young readers may not be aware of the fact either—until they read it in the series. Bumpus Hawtree, "who answered to the suggestive name of 'Tubby,' " is told by a fellow Scout that he could live a week on his own fat (*In the Rockies* 32): perhaps it was simply not a day for Good Deeds. Another Boy Scout series, that by Payson, contains the most offensive portrait of a fat person, also called "Tubby." He is "corpulent Tubby" in *The Army Airship* (16) and "fat boy" in the same book (25). Later, when a group of Scouts arrive at camp, they hear a voice asking, "Say, where do you keep the grub?" "That must be Tubby," the leader, Rob Blake says, without a moment's hesitation. After they have seen the army airship fly, Tubby guesses that he will stick to the ground and not try to fly. The main hero tells him, "You're too fat to do anything else" (123). At the Panama-Pacific Exposition, the Scouts introduce Tubby as "our fat chum, Tubby" (8), though, since he can obviously be seen, the adjective seems egregious. Later he is referred to as a tub of jelly (187), but luckily "nature had given him a cheerful disposition" (189)—"gloom and Tubby never agree" (190). When Tubby turns in for the night, the author suggests that Tubby "was almost certain to snore, as stout people are apt to do" (*Under Sealed Orders* 292). Worst of all, when disguises are being considered, Tubby is told, "You could never pass for anything but yourself, or the fat boy in the freak show" (174), and to make certain that no stout reader missed the point, he is further informed, "Athletes alone make good air-pilots, and a fellow who had the shape of a tub would only be useful as an anchor, or something like that" (*Panama-Pacific Exposition* 179). In the Grace Harlowe Series, Hippy (for Hippopotamus) Wingate is a "round, roly-poly boy, famous for his appetite" (*Plebe Year* 176). Throughout the series he is called "fatty" and "fat one," but he grins good-naturedly and eats his four meals a day (*Great American Desert* 86). On Honey Bunch's *First Trip to the Seashore* she meets Anne Wade, "a fat little girl [who] laughed most of the time" (84), despite the fact that she is jeered at and called "Anne Wide" (86). To reaffirm a point made earlier, it is not for reasons of stylistic inelegance that many series deserve criticism.

In no sense is this general attitude toward fat people limited to the early-twentieth-century series. The first Hardy Boys book, *The Tower Treasure*, published in 1926, introduced Chet Morton, "a plump boy who loved to eat" (7); rewritten in 1959, the book made no change whatever in Chet. Nor had any occurred by 1985: in *Revenge of the Desert Phantom*, he is still "Iola's overweight brother," and when he encounters hungry Africans, Chet "was so ashamed of his over-ample physique" (68). The 1986 Nancy Drew Files entry, *Deadly Intent,* shows that Bess wakes immediately at the suggestion of food; her friend George groans, "look who finally rises at the mention of her favorite sport" (151). A most impressive instance of author-publisher attitudes toward fat people is found when the original Honey Bunch series became the Honey Bunch and Norman Series; originally, no mention was made of Norman's size, but when he became a more important character, he also became "the roly poly boy": he seems in fact to have been recreated fat for the new books—the 1950's and 1960's evidently found fat people as amusing as did earlier years.

Though she quickly became a series heroine, Doris Fein was a secondary character in the book that introduced her: *Dr. Doom, Superstar* (1978). She was also obese and the usual butt of insult and jokes. Larry Small, the actual hero, is editor of the high school newspaper and narrator. He describes Doris: "about five feet four and I'd say she weighs easy a hundred and fifty-five pounds. . . . Almost all of Doris Fein is large and soft" (14); "there ain't no doubt, buddy. Doris makes two of me" (21). When she runs up to him, Larry thinks, "Last time I saw that much meat in motion, it was a delivery" (22). But Larry is no student, and Doris is "pulling an A-minus average this year" (27). She also became in the next volume a heroine who was able and attractive, though fat; she acquired a boyfriend, Carl Suzuki, a detective in the New York Police Department, and she was pursued by various other men as well. Though she has been compared to Nancy Drew, Doris is far better developed as a character and solves far more complicated and realistic mysteries, actually more in a class with adult fiction. By *Deadly Aphrodite*, in any case, her weight eventually overwhelms her: "Doris Fein, you are gross!" she exclaims to her mirror, and later, describing herself as "Mt. Fein" (38), she checks herself into Aphrodite's, a weight-loss spa, the site of the crime involved; Chapter 1 is titled, "The Incredible Growing Fein." Remnants of past attitudes persist, however, and reviews of the various entries, as in *Booklist*, the *Horn Book*, and *The Bulletin of the Center for Children's Books*, all speak of Doris's sense of humor, evidently, like that of her earlier counterparts, needed to accept herself.

Clearly, if children are overweight, they can identify only with such characters as these when they read the series, because in these books, that is whom they resemble. Their image is readymade, and they are shown unequivocally how their friends and society regard them. By way of summary, then, we can draw certain conclusions. Heroes and good people of any kind are tall, slender but muscular and well built; usually they have sparkling blue eyes and a straightforward, frank expression and manner. They are "fine looking." Often one finds a preference for blonds, though some are dark, and a few, red-headed. Overall, they are athletic, well-coordinated, quiet, and dignified. Variation from such "norms" implies villainy: evil people are short, small, and thin; they have squinty, shifty, close-set, narrow eyes, and an expression and manner variously described as bold, insolent, swaggering, or devious. Ugly or at least unpleasant looking, they have heavily oiled hair, or hair that is coarse, stringy, sandy, or nonexistent. Men may have mustaches, generally in series a sign of villainy, as it was in B westerns. Evil people often have deformities, and frequently have loud voices and clothes to match.

Can there be any argument about the didactic force of series?

JUDGMENTS OF RACE AND NATIONALITY

The didactic force of children's series becomes pernicious when it is applied to matters of race and nationality. Since 1899 the image of Black people in these books has not changed significantly. They lost their dialect in the 1950's, and certain words of description and identification that had unpleasant connotations ceased being used at about the same time, but their position in society, their general character and personality have varied in no important way.

Until the 1950's, when agitation for civil rights became a major issue in the United States, Black people in the fiction series always spoke in dialect. In the earliest series with which this study is concerned, the Rover Boys' family had a Black servant named Alexander Pop. Aleck never lost his dialect or

Extra-Family Relationships 105

even modified it ("Yo' is a sight fo' soah eyes, deed yo' is," he says during *In the Mountains* 98), despite having lived in the North for decades. When the Rovers went South in *The Rover Boys in Southern Waters*, they found that all Blacks spoke in dialect. In *The Rover Boys Shipwrecked* (1924), Aleck was still saying, "Can't say as I's much younger, but I ce'tainly doan feel no older" (30).

The Bobbsey Twins, begun in 1904, introduced Dinah, a cook, maid, and mammy, and Sam, her husband, a handyman and driver; both spoke in dialect. Dinah tells Freddie about "pickin' cotton in de Souf" (*At the Seashore* 30), and when the family visited Washington in 1919, her dialect was as strong as that of Uncle Remus: "What's all dish yeah I heah Nan say? ... What you gone an' done to yo' l'il broth' an' sistah?" (22) The Tom Swift Series introduced a comic Black man, Eradicate Andrew Jackson Abraham Lincoln Sampson, always called Eradicate, because he eradicated dirt. As long as he was in the series, Eradicate spoke dialect: "Suffin's gwin t'happen," he says early in *Tom Swift and His Motor Cycle* (1910); later he adds, "I trabled all ober, and I couldn't find no jobs" (58, 165). By 1928, in *Tom Swift and His Talking Pictures*, Eradicate says, "An' ef I kotches de feller what done planted it I—" (21).

Blacks abound in *Bunny Brown and His Sister Sue in the Sunny South*; a porter on the train tells the family, "De do' am closed" (61), and a Black woman at their destination warns a boy playing in the street by saying, "Dat frisky li'l nigger suah will be splatter-dashed" (93). In *Grace Harlowe's Overland Riders Among the Kentucky Mountaineers* (1921), Washington Washington appeared, using the most incredible dialect imaginable: "He war peekin' at yuh-all, an' when he seed ah sawed him, he snooked an' ah didn't sawed him no moah" (132). His speech is twice imitated by Emma Dean, who also shies a stone at him; in both cases he is made fun of because of his manner of speaking. Blacks in the original Hardy Boys series all speak in dialect, as do all of Sue Barton's patients in *Visiting Nurse*, and all Blacks, when they appear, in the Nancy Drew Series as late as *The Mystery of the Tolling Bell* in 1946.

So pervasive was the assumption that Blacks spoke in dialect exclusively that Eva Knox Evans found even Black children conditioned to expect it in books. Her *Araminta's Goat* was read to her kindergarten class as she was writing it; not until the book actually appeared in print could the class see by the illustrations that Araminta was Black. They protested that she did not speak as Negroes were supposed to. When Evans pointed out that the class, all of whom were Black children, did not speak in dialect, they answered that in books, colored people do (650). Although some writers, Adelaide Rowell, for instance, feel that "dialect is the folk flavor in the speech of all people of all nations" (*Negro Dialect in Children's Books* 1556), since the early 1940's controversy has existed over dialect in children's literature. It is now gone from series books, and since its use there was almost invariably degrading—it was a source of humor and an indication of inferiority—one applauds its disappearance.

During the 1950's efforts were made to eliminate dialect from the series by rewriting the original volumes. Where the Bobbseys' handyman, Sam, would say in 1919, "I'll put back de hay fo' yo' all " (*In Washington* 32), by 1953 he was speaking quite differently: "Well, I don't know.... Folks say that if a horseshoe is thrown so that it lands with the two ends pointing toward you, that means good luck" (*Horseshoe Riddle* 1). Phonetic spelling disappeared; both Sam and Dinah put *g*'s on words ending in *ing*, "yo' " became "you," and *d*'s became *th*'s. When Wanderer Books (Simon and Schuster) brought out in 1979 Commemorative Editions of the first three Bobbsey Twins books, an introduction, the same for each volume, stated the publisher's position: "In 1950 and again in 1961 the first three Bobbsey Twins stories were completely rewritten.... Dinah and Sam continued to work for Mr. and Mrs. Bobbsey but all traces of their dialect were gone; and while their relationship with the Bobbseys was as pleasant as ever, it had become quite clear that they were a considerable cut above their earlier servant roles" (i). Referring to the forty-six titles then in print and the new ones to be released, the introduction continued, "they will continue to reflect society's changing view of itself" (ii).

Some of this rewriting is curious. In the original first book, *The Bobbsey Twins: Merry Days Indoors and Out*, Dinah enters after hearing a flower pot break. "Well, I declare to gracious!" she exclaims. "If yo' chillun ain't gone an' mussed up de floah ag'in!" (20). In the 1950 update we find the same scene, but Dinah now says, "Well, I declare to gracious! If you children

Extra-Family Relationships

ain't gone an' mussed up the floor again!" (5–6). The earlier dialect may be softened by these "changes," but they are surely minimal and a sense of Dinah's ignorance is still conveyed by the "ain't." Three years later in *At Pilgrim Rock*, Dinah has become "the plump colored woman who helped Mrs. Bobbsey"; speaking to the Twins she says, "You all had better be mighty careful" (2). The traditional figure of the fat Black woman remains, as does a hint of dialect, but the grammar is correct, and Dinah seems less of a servant by becoming the woman who helps Mrs. Bobbsey: she seems, indeed, to be conveying a favor.

If their speech underwent improvement during the 1950's and after, Black peoples' position, role in society, character, and personality did not. In the first Bobbsey Twins volume, Flossie has a Negro doll named Jujube; she used to explain to friends, "He doesn't really belong to the family, you know" (79). Indeed, so secure were authors and publishers that children would recognize Black people by their jobs that often the race was not identified. In *The Twisted Claw*, for instance, a Black man is called merely "the porter," but the work he does, his dialect, and the fact that he calls Joe and Frank Hardy "massa" meant that no one was expected to miss the point.

Black people remained servants and slaves, always in inferior positions. They are porters in Payson's Boy Scout series, the Hardy Boys, and Nancy Drew; they are maids and cooks in the Bobbsey Twins; they are handymen and butlers in the Rover Boys; and they are mammies in Bunny Brown and the Bobbsey Twins; in the Grace Harlowe Series they are ineffectual servants, ranch hands in the Honey Bunch books, laborers and cleaners in Tom Swift; Blacks are elevator operators and grease monkeys in the Rover Boys and washroom attendants in Nancy Drew and Don Sturdy. As late as 1942 in *The Bobbsey Twins in the Land of Cotton*, the most astonishing stereotypes are found. That "land of cotton" should be used as a generic term during World War II itself seems unlikely. Even more so is the image of the plantation, which comes directly from Thomas Nelson Page unchanged. "'And over there,' said Mrs. Bobbsey, 'are the cabins of the plantation workers.' 'Aren't they cute?' said Flossie" (123). Mrs. Percy, their hostess, refers to her husband as "the Colonel" and explains that they have sharecroppers on their land as workers. Later the Twins are told that a sharecropper "gets share and share alike wiv the master . . . a sharecropper, mah honey, is a planter dat raises cotton on de land he rents from de master, wiv tools de master done lend him" (132). After this rather romantic view of economics, the Twins visit the cotton fields: "The Negroes, both men and women, were gaily-dressed in bright-colored shirts, or sunbonnets and aprons. Most of them were singing. 'They must like the work,' said Nan. 'They seem to be happy.' 'Cotton picking is healthful exercise,' smiled the plantation owner" (139). Later the Blacks sing and dance to entertain the children. As the book ends, the Twins say, "I feel sorry for anyone who hasn't been to the land of cotton—it's so much fun there" (216). Two years before, *Intruder in the Dust* had not been so sanguine. In any case, Dinah was still "the faithful servant" and Tom Swift was "massa Tom" throughout his series.

As Blacks were awarded inferior social and occupational status, so were they supplied with traits of character and personality calculated to develop their inferiority even further. By way of example, when Sue Barton takes a job as a visiting nurse, she is sent to Harlem. "You'll love working with colored people," she is told. "They're so willing to cooperate, and so eager to learn" (133). Sue concludes that "she was not there to exploit colored people, or to be grandly feudal, but to help them stand on their own feet" (134). Yet she persists in treating her patients like children or babies, and they respond by saying, "Yes, ma'am. Thank you, ma'am" (140).

Appearing consistently as subservient to Whites, Black people were also presented as lazy, ignorant, good-natured, cowardly; they were invariably patronized. In *Sue Barton, Visiting Nurse*, they have "enchanting black babies" (134); Dinah smiled and grinned through every volume in which she appeared, while her Aunt Emma's face "was crisscrossed with wrinkles that made it seem as if she were smiling all the time" (*Land of Cotton* 49). Bunny Brown and Sue also meet "a fat, jolly-looking colored woman," Mammy Jackson, and their father says, "I'll see if I can have one of these easy-going colored boys to drive me uptown" (*In the Sunny South* 110).

A different view of Blacks is seen in *Nancy Drew and the Mystery at Lilac Inn*, when a Negro applicant for a housemaid's position arrives "dirty, slovenly in appearance and [with] an

Extra-Family Relationships

unpleasant way of shuffling her feet when she walked"; she also answers "in an unsatisfactory manner" (16). Washington Washington in *Among the Kentucky Mountaineers* is the most offensive portrait of a Black in any series. He is dirty and refuses to wash (22); futile and stupid in emergencies, he is an abject coward throughout the book. Aleck Pop, the Rover Boys' servant, is without exception fooled by plays on words and by the most basic references, his ignorance being revealed thereby. Eradicate Sampson is so abysmally stupid as to be only a caricatured comic fool.

None of these pictures of Blacks is improved by the terms, which, until the 1950's, were liberally applied to them. Shocking to a contemporary reader, they were taken for granted by writers, publishers, and, apparently, readers. "Nigger" is quite common. It may be used as part of a phrase, such as "nigger in the woodpile" (*The Boy Scouts at the Panama-Pacific Exposition* 103), or applied directly to a Black person, as in *Don Sturdy in Lion Land* (183) and in the Tom Swift Series, where Eradicate calls himself "nigger" frequently (*Motor Cycle* 60, e.g.); the term may be found as "They told us to work like niggers" (*The Rover Boys on Land and Sea* 244), or as in *The Rover Boys in Southern Waters*, where Gasper Pold has "cheated many a white man and nigger of his savings" (13); in *Bunny Brown and His Sister Sue in the Sunny South* a Black woman refers to a young boy as "dat frisky li'l nigger" (93).

Sometimes the word is used in dialect, as "niggah," the pronunciation used by Washington Washington. A Black man is referred to twice in *Tom Swift and His Motor Cycle* as "darky" (58, 165), and twice as "coon" (140, 170). In *Tom Swift and His Airship*, a Negro man is a "black rascal" (36). Black children are called "pickaninnies" in the Grace Harlowe Series.

Other means of debasing the Black person's status are accomplished by the use of certain stereotypes, a device that further equates all Blacks. The majority of Black women, for example, are fat: Dinah, her Aunt Emma, Mammy Jackson, already mentioned. Dinah and Sam have "kinky heads" (*At the Seashore* 9), and they love watermelon (6). Eradicate Sampson carries a razor as a weapon of defense in *Tom Swift and His Airship* (39). Washington Washington plays the harmonica.

Notable exceptions to what has been said occur, though their number is absurdly small. One is an effort to remove some of the onerous clichés seen earlier; for example, in *Sue Barton, Visiting Nurse,* "All the apartments [of Blacks] were clean" (134). "They had a tradition of cleanliness and were proud of it. An apartment was seldom cluttered . . . no speck of dust lingered anywhere" (139). Another is an attempt to individualize Blacks by allowing them to be courageous: after the Hardy Boys are attacked by three criminals in *Hunting for Hidden Gold,* suddenly two Black men appear (the same criminals had earlier run over their chickens). One is "an enormous Negro" (77), and he and his friend proceed to beat up the hoodlums. Throughout the scene they act fearlessly and with considerable ability. Before the last decade, few instances of Blacks as villains are to be found, a role that would have allowed some balance. In a late book, *Tom Swift and His Talking Pictures* (1928), Tom is captured by two Black men and taken to see some movie moguls who wish to steal Tom's television machine. The men speak well, without dialect—in fact, their language is superior to that of the heroes. Tom is struck by the fact that the "language of these Negroes was above average." Note the assumption, "They did not talk like poor old Eradicate. Rather their talk was that of the man who has seen service in wealthy families" (177). Thus, Blacks can learn from Whites; they are still seen as servants, however. Only one attempt was made to portray the housing situation of Blacks realistically. In *Sue Barton, Visiting Nurse,* "the moment a Negro family moved into a tenement, the rent would go up" (138).

In general, until the last decade, Blacks are never allowed in the series to develop as real characters, as real persons; instead they are revealed as century-old clichés. Never really bad, they can never really be good. Like fat people, they are consistently one-dimensional.

In the wake of civil rights efforts from the 1950's on, the bulk of derogatory implications vanished from the series. One senses conscious efforts to change the way Blacks were being shown to young readers. Gradually over the past two decades and especially in the last seven or eight years, the picture has modified, in a few instances notably. Several "new" series began in these latter years. The Nancy Drew Files, the New Bobbsey Twins,

Extra-Family Relationships

the Hardy Boys Casefiles were basically extensions of earlier series, quite different from their originals; others, such as the Woodland Gang, Doris Fein, the Race Against Time, the Sweet Valley High and Sweet Valley Twins Series, were entirely new. Overall, it may be said that Black people, again *when they appear*, are portrayed more realistically. Whether the attempt to do so reflects a genuine concern is questionable: the stigma of tokenism cannot be entirely dispelled. In any case over the past quarter-century four basic trends can be recognized.

First, the original editions of many series books have been edited and in some cases rewritten to remove traditional images and, as mentioned, repellent language. As Barbara Moran and Susan Steinfirst observed in 1985, during the 1960's and 1970's the Nancy Drew books were revised "to eliminate stereotypes of blacks and other ethnic groups" (115). The most striking instance of rewriting is the Hardy Boys title, *The Hidden Harbor Mystery*, published first in 1935 and reissued in 1961. Here are found not simply the removal of dialect and conventional portraits, but an entirely new plot and predominantly new characters. Such a sweeping change was called for by the fact that in the original, the chief villain, Luke Jones, was a thoroughly despicable Black man responsible for all the criminal actions. To retain him and still satisfy the need for a better image was out of the question.

In 1935 Luke puts his feet on the opposite train seat, though told by the conductor that the rules forbid his doing so. "Luke Jones don't stand for no nonsense from white folks.... Ah puts mah feet where Ah please" (84). Later he tries to kill Ewald Rand with a boulder and tears up the Hardys' camp. Luke also heads a secret organization of Blacks, one of whom is described as "bullet-headed . . . and rather stupid looking" (180). The frontispiece shows the scene—it was clearly important to the writer and publisher—with Luke dressed like Sporting Life in *Porgy and Bess*, flashy and threatening. The group kidnaps Ewald and strikes Mrs. Rand, giving her an ugly head wound. But Luke is "a coward at heart" (196), and his "natural cowardice asserted itself" later (197). Frank Hardy tells him that he is "the worst scoundrel we have ever come across" (199). It is a racially unflattering portrait, and when the book was redone in 1961, every trace of Luke was removed: the villain was now

White. The Blackstone Estate does have a Black servant who has no dialogue at all and is not even described beyond the statement that he wears a white coat. There is a "sly looking negro boy" (60), who plays a minute and unimportant role. Before 1950 Jenny Shringle's work as a seamstress would have stamped her as Black, but there is no implication of color in 1961. Grover is called "the old servant." He says, "my father served the Blackstones, and *his* father did, too. Used to be a grand family, way back" (113). His color is not mentioned.

A second direction can be noted in the first entry of the New Bobbsey Twins Series, *The Secret of Jungle Park,* which uses in a minor role, Beverly Baku, "a tall, slender, black woman [with] hoop earrings" (27). Unlike the "kindly," "easy-going," "slow-moving," "humorous" Black characters of earlier series, Beverly is arrogant, uncooperative, and hostile. Thus she is allowed to be realistic: Black persons are as likely to have such qualities as previous generations wished to believe they did not. Her surname suggests Africa (at one point she is said to have left for a holiday in Kenya) and she trains animals, especially lions: hence a racial stereotype would seem still to be present. Yet in a picture of her, Beverly hardly looks Black at all: there is a suggestion of an Afro haircut and her lips are somewhat thicker than those of other characters shown. As events turn out, she is a help to the Twins in solving the case. Thus we have a Black woman in a small part shown to have only slight racial features and a unique personality. Perhaps these facts are meant to be reassuring to readers.

A stronger and better series of Black characters in important roles are to be found in the 1985 Hardy Boys adventure, *Revenge of the Desert Phantom*. Central is Niki Jerusa, whose father is president of a small African nation. Niki is repeatedly called pretty; in fact, so pretty is she that she wins a beauty contest in Bayport, beating out Joe Hardy's girlfriend, Iola Morton. As she accepts the prize, "the teenaged African girl was even more stunning than they'd imagined" (51). In Paris the Hardy Boys meet Michelle, a Black runaway from wealthy parents, who "are rich and spend their time traveling with the jet set all over the world, so they have no time for raising me. The boarding school is just an excuse so they won't feel guilty about abandoning me. Oh, I hate them so much" (44). Michelle's boyfriend, Phillippe,

Extra-Family Relationships

is not identified as Black and nothing indicates that he is. Blacks are not differentiated by their speech. When he is told that the Hardys want to get something straight, Mantu, though he is an emissary from Niki's father, replies, "Okay, what things?" (54). In Africa, Niki greets Bidoli, her father's supporter, with "Hi!" (102). Later, Bidoli tells Frank and Joe, "I rigged that myself" (124), and speaking of the rebellious Totas, he says, "They reneged on it" (127). While Niki is idealistic and naive, Charlie, another Black, is opportunistic, a greedy and cynical man.

In this book, Blacks have a social and financial status much higher than they have had in any previous series volume. Far from being pigeonholed, they have various personal characteristics and are allowed to be individualized. Yet considering the wide range of settings in the Hardy Boys Series and the superficial treatment given to subjects, one speculates as to whether the publishers simply felt that a "Black issues" book was needed, or one about African problems. Tokenism is still a possibility.

No such charge however can be leveled at the Woodland Gang Series one of the most delightful and satisfying series, which began and regrettably expired in 1984 after only six volumes. Four children comprise the Gang: Dave Stern, who is sixteen; Bill, fourteen; Kathy, thirteen; and Sammy, ten. All are orphans and all but Dave were adopted by the Westburgs (or as it is sometimes spelled, Westbergs). All are White, except Bill, who is Black, short, fat, strong, and "very kind" (*The Hidden Jewels* 8). Hence we have a unique series hero—a Black Jewish orphan, who does most of the central legwork, Dave being confined to a wheelchair.

Bill is aware of and quite frank about his color. In *The Missing Will* he thinks of his color as the first possibility when an antique-shop owner orders the children out: "Maybe she wants me out because I have brown skin" (11). After Cris starts a fight with him in *The Stolen Animals*, Bill speculates, "It isn't on account of my brown skin, or he'd have started something weeks ago when he first came here" (11). Throughout the series he refers to his skin as brown, not black, possibly because author Irene Schultz is White. In *The Hidden Jewels,* when the villain, Mr. Cook, says to Bill, "You dirty little black boy," Sammy charges at him, fighting mad, screaming, "Don't you call my brother names, you rotten sneak" (86). The line is a remarkable advance over Flossie Bobbsey's description of her Black doll, "He doesn't really belong to the family." Clearly Bill does.

The Missing Will expresses directly an attitude that is general in this series: "Our one country is made of people from so many different places. It even says on our coins, 'E Pluribus Unum... Out of many, one.'" All the characters present in the scene begin naming their national backgrounds—Scotland, Norway, Arabia, England, Russia, Ireland, Israel, Poland, Mexico, and Italy. Bill says, "Mine [came] from Africa, hundreds of years ago ... and from Viet Nam" (102–103). Instead of the indirect teaching of earlier series, the Woodland Gang teaches very directly a most desirable—and American—concept. In *The Hidden Jewels* Bill expresses concern about being accepted: "What if the kids don't like me? I bet I have the only brown skin in this town." Kathy argues, "You'd make good friends here even if you were bright green, instead of brown" (9). Young readers see that his character and personality are what count, not any superficial quality.

Lest these examples suggest too roseate a picture, it must be noted that they are based upon a small number of series and in fact upon only a few entries in these series. Those mentioned represent virtually all the appearances by Blacks in recent fiction series. Bill Westburg is the only instance in a series of a Black central character; even more deplorable, he is one of a handful of Black characters who are likable, intelligent, and brave. The final trend in such books is therefore to eliminate Blacks altogether. J. F. MacDonald felt in 1979 that the reediting already noted removed prejudiced and derogatory terminology and gave young readers healthier and more realistic ideas (545). How, one asks, can healthy ideas be revealed about persons who never appear? For example, the very popular Sweet Valley High and Sweet Valley Twins Series might be subtitled the California *Wasp* Series, so empty are they of any but one social group and level. Series which began after the 1960's—those which were genuinely new, as well as those which, while actually new (e.g., the Nancy Drew Files), continued to use earlier characters—contain virtually no Black characters at all. While the number of titles in such series is often astronomical, a scant 4 percent are books with Black characters.

Extra-Family Relationships

To examine the settings of several of these series can be instructive. *The Bobbsey Twins and the Red, White and Blue Mystery* (1971) occurs in Colonial Williamsburg. *The Bobbsey Twins: Dr. Funnybone's Secret* (1972) is laid in Florida. *The Bobbsey Twins and the Tagalong Giraffe* (1973) is set in Africa. Nancy Drew's *Mardi Gras Mystery* (1988) happens in New Orleans, while the Hardy Boys' *Swamp Monster* (1985) takes place in southeast Texas. Though in each of these locations one might expect to find Black characters, none actually is found. The issue is thereby sidestepped. Slurs against Blacks are edited out of books, which are rewritten to play down offensive attitudes. One series with a strong Black hero begins and ends in a single year with only half a dozen titles. Overall, Blacks have disappeared from the major children's fiction series. Readers are thus denied their acquaintance.

More significant, even ironic, are the Commemorative Editions of the first three Bobbsey Twins titles. Published in 1979, all three are identical to their originals, with the dialect and the racial stereotypes intact; even Flossie's description of Jujube remains. The three books seem designed as pieces of nostalgia for their original readers, who presumably have been adversely affected by their contents. The common introduction informs the reader, "You will find yourself transported to a bygone era in American Literature which reflects the social mores and world view of the early 1900's. Dinah and Sam, the Bobbseys' cook and houseman, were a happy-go-lucky couple whose colorful Southern drawl brightened the series." (Should we not, then, regret the loss of all that amusing dialect?) In our own time, we are assured, the Black stereotypes of Dinah and Sam "have disappeared into nostalgic oblivion." But here the books are, available to children as well as adults in public libraries, still able to spread their contagion. That an eight-year-old reader can discriminate between today and three-quarters of a century ago is doubtful.

The Doris Fein Series presents the first Jewish heroine in a children's series. Except for Bill Westburg in a defunct series, no Black hero or heroine has emerged. Despite the frequent appearances of Black characters in various television series, no children's book series has a continuing Black character, let alone a main one. No intellectual Blacks are to be found, nor any cultured ones. No series about Black athletes exists, though sports would seem to be an area where skill, not color, is the issue, and certainly many actual, and excellent, Black sports figures can readily be named. To exclude negative elements is well and good; to *include* positive ones would be far better.

Children, as Ruth Viguers points out in her contribution to *A Critical History of Children's Literature*, are not aware of racial, national, or religious intolerance; economic and social fears that create intolerance in the world of adults are not natural in the world of children. Clearly, however, children may take attitudes and prejudices that they see displayed (Meigs et al. 550), and as Spencer Brown put it, children's books may become a "fertile breeding ground for prejudice" (5). Eleanor Nolan is even wiser in pointing out that the prejudices and attitudes a child forms through reading may be more serious than actual contacts with minority groups. The child, for example, may never know a Black person except through the pages of a book. "The place to combat race prejudice is with the child's first books and first social relationships" (349).

Foreigners or persons with foreign-sounding names fare no better than Blacks. To say that all foreigners in children's series are villains would be an overstatement; nonetheless, many, many villains are foreigners. Furthermore, those foreigners not cast as villains are shown as inferior people—servants, weaklings, clowns. In no series does a non-American play a major role except as a villain. No foreigner is ever a hero, though occasionally he may assist a hero who is visiting outside his own country. As J. F. MacDonald says so strongly, "foreigners are second-best to healthy, intelligent, courageous, rational White Americans" (534–535). Those persons who actually live abroad are seen as ignorant, unwashed, thieving, sinister. The series, he continues, present a "dramatic picture of race consciousness, xenophobia, and imperialism" (534). Many startling, often infuriating, assumptions are made about non-Americans in the series.

First, one can always tell a foreigner. As Louis Phillips, speaking of his early reading of the Hardy Boys, says, "A crook looked like a crook in those days ... in the world of the Hardy Boys, the villain is most likely to be a foreigner" (176). In *The Bobbsey Twins at the Seashore*, a heavily tanned lifeguard "looked like some foreigner, for he was almost black" (115).

Extra-Family Relationships 117

Trying to solve the mystery of the tolling bell, Nancy Drew meets a woman "obviously of foreign birth" (7), yet the woman turns out not to be foreign; hence, while the word "obviously" suggests that foreigners are easily identified, implicitly it is shown that they are not. While in Canada investigating the mystery at Devil's Paw, the Hardy Boys meet two men in the woods; "I'll bet they're foreigners," Joe says (165)—but in upper Canada, foreigners to what and to whom? Don Sturdy meets Joshki, unknown to him, but "obviously [again] of foreign birth, probably a Russian by nationality, for his flat nose and high cheekbones were clearly of Tartar origin" (*Land of Volcanoes* 95). Uncle Sam's Boys also state that "Carl was unmistakably German" (*With Pershing's Troops* 91).

Such statements imply that individual nationalities have immediately recognizable characteristics. The Irish, for example, are redheaded, as witness Pat Malone in Burgess's Boy Scout Series and Nora O'Malley in the Grace Harlowe Series; both talk with brogues—the more strange since Nora developed hers as the series continued: in high school, she had none, but once she married, her brogue became quite strong. Nora has a "charming, sunny nature, and always saw the best if there was any to see" (*Plebe Year* 7); she is hot-tempered but softhearted (8). Pat Malone shares these qualities. Also in the Grace Harlowe books the maid, Bridget, again Irish, is superstitious, stupid, easily frightened. All these characters are used for humorous effect; in fact, Nora marries fat Hippy Wingate, who is never taken seriously either. In *The Boy Scouts at the Panama-Pacific Exposition* we read, "He has a red face, wears big glasses, and is scrawny enough for a Scotchman anyway" (13). Later in that book the reader is told, "The professor is like most Englishmen, for he loves his pipe" (15). The Japanese are fond of the word "honorable," using it often in series. Alain Bakaru, an Arabian in *Don Sturdy on the Desert of Mystery*, talks like a character from Washington Irving's Alhambra, suggesting that all Arabians speak like storybook figures. Ramo Stransky, the Gypsy villain of *The Mystery of the Moss-Covered Mansion,* is instantly identified by Nancy Drew because of his earrings and bandana (69). Granted that Turk Mallane in the Rick Brant book *100 Fathoms Under* is a bad man, his statement about Otera, the native cook, is still quite strong: "Filthy native swine."

Wouldn't change clothes unless told to" (59). In passing the foreign exhibits at the Panama-Pacific Exposition, the Boy Scouts remark that "in some of these squalid villages of foreigners they have some ugly yellow cur dogs hanging around" (339). "Spain is a land of beggars," says Eleanor in *Grace Harlowe's Junior Year at High School* (42), though Eleanor herself turns out to be Italian in Grace's senior year—Italians in that book being described as "a race that swear vendettas" (42).

Don Sturdy was told that "life is pretty cheap in this country [Arabia] " and later that "the natives all look alike to our eyes" (*Desert of Mystery* 14, 17). When visiting *Among the Gorillas*, Don was similarly reminded that the "natives presented a grotesque rather than a ferocious appearance . . . low foreheads, flat faces, a protruding jaw . . . uniform broad grins" (73). John Shepard felt that when Americans are used as villains, no specifically American qualities are associated with them, but that when foreigners are villains, they very often have some stereotyped images of nationality applied to them (672). The series prove him correct.

Only occasionally are racial and national characteristics seen as positive. Notable instances are the Chip Hilton Series and the Woodland Gang Series, both of which were scrupulously fair to all races. "Steeltown," one reads in *Strike Three*, "was . . . a steel mill town and all the men who handled and turned out the pig iron and steel for which the town was famous were from sturdy stock. The population was predominantly Polish, Lithuanian, Swedish, and Norwegian. And the boys who played on the high school team were well named. The iron men" (155).

But foreigners are inferior to Americans. Sometimes this idea is stated directly; sometimes, implied. Often it is put condescendingly; often, maliciously. In *Sue Barton, Visiting Nurse*, the slum area of New York is a polyglot district: "They were Irish, Jewish, colored, and plain American" (211). "Plain American" says very obviously that there is a difference between Blacks, Jews, Irish, and "Americans." When Sue was a student nurse, the supreme irony was uttered by Mrs. McCarthy, an Irish woman who speaks with a heavy brogue and who describes Mrs. Pasquale, an Italian, thus: "Them foreigners is always a queer lot" (55).

Extra-Family Relationships

The most extreme expressions of this kind of feeling are found in the Don Sturdy books, basically a geographic series. In Egypt, Don is told by his uncle that the "natives of a country never do anything. It is the outsiders, after all, who do things" (*Desert of Mystery* 3). Alain Bakaru, despite having an "outlandish name," is "much superior to the usual run of natives," although he is "steeped in superstition like all of them" (27), and Don himself comments, "If time were money, these fellows would all be millionaires" (52). Twice during *Among the Gorillas* Captain Sturdy wins over African natives with "a handful of brightly colored beads" (71, 110).

Some prejudiced descriptions of foreigners are clearly the product of special occasions. For example, *Uncle Sam's Boys with Pershing's Troops,* published in 1919, contains several slurs against people with German names, and *Tom Swift and His Undersea Search* (1920) calls all Germans "huns." Before World War I Germans were approved characters in series. The Rover Boys had a German friend, Hans Mueller, in 1907 (*In Southern Waters*) and as late as 1913, a fellow student, Max Spangler, who was a German-American (*In New York*). As soon as war broke out, sympathetic Germans disappeared from the series, and never again were they shown as anything but suspicious figures.

Undoubtedly, Asians come off the worst of any foreign people in series. In 1911 the United States signed with Japan the Treaty of Commerce and Navigation, which included the Gentlemen's Agreement of 1908 by which Japan agreed not to issue passports to coolies emigrating directly to the States and to abide by President Roosevelt's order of 1907 to exclude all Japanese laborers coming from Mexico, Canada, or Hawaii. In the same year (1911) two children's series, at least, showed that they were not convinced of Japanese integrity. The most outspoken was *Uncle Sam's Boys on Field Duty,* where Japanese are seen by one old man as a distinct threat to America: he calls them "pesky brown critters" and likens them to "rattlers and grizzlies" (78); later, the man, asked whether he has ever seen a Japanese person, replies, "Nope, young man, but what's that got to do with hating 'em?" (120). Anti-Japanese feeling is presented directly in *The Boy Scouts and the Army Airship*: one of the two main villains, the sinister Hashishi, is introduced by a one-sentence paragraph—"The man was Japanese!" (63). In context, the line is designed to raise goose pimples. Later he is likened to "a small and venomous snake" (70), and a page later one reads that Japanese "are not friends of Uncle Sam's, however much they pretend to be." Since one of the heroes of the books makes the statement, it was obviously intended to influence readers.

Not until the Doris Fein series in the late 1970's and 1980's does a strong and likable Japanese character appear. Doris's boyfriend, Carl Suzuki, is a detective on the New York police force when they meet; by 1982 in *Deadly Aphrodite* he is an Assistant District Attorney, and in *Murder Is No Joke* (1982) he is planning to go into politics. In *Phantom of the Casino* reference is made to "racially-mixed necking" (15) when he greets Doris; Carl proposes marriage to Doris, and tells her that she would be a "perfect wife for a rising young legislator" (*Murder* 158). Carl is "a Japanese-American and an extremely proud and honor-bound man" (*Aphrodite* 11), and the Fein family has a long discussion about the injustice of Japanese internment during World War II in the course of *Phantom of the Casino*. Things sound fine. We almost feel that foreigners are getting a new chance, until we read in the same book that "Carl is about as Oriental as MacDonald's" (25); that he grew up in New York "eating Jewish food. In fact my Aunt Lucille's silent partner in the restaurant was Mr. Berkowitz. They kept company for years and years"; that he is "tall for a Japanese" and that his "face reminds you of a typical Ivy-Leaguer's" (15). In short, he is as far from being Japanese as one can get. Perhaps this fact makes him acceptable to the Feins and to readers.

The attitude toward Chinese characters is somewhat better balanced—there are honorable Chinese in series—but the image of the "yellow peril" is also prominent. The Hardy Boys faced a number of perilous Chinese. In *The House on the Cliff* Chinese are the main sources of criminal acts, as smugglers of narcotics. In *Footprints Under the Window*, Louis Fong, also a smuggler, is particularly evil and stereotyped: he was "the most villainous-looking Oriental the boys had ever seen. [He had] a long lean face and high cheekbones. His head was pointed and almost bald . . . a cruel mouth was partly concealed by a drooping wisp of mustache. His eyes were cold and glittering as those of a snake" (6). Sax Rohmer was still producing novels about

Extra-Family Relationships

the worst of Chinese fiends, Fu Manchu, when the Hardy Boys first appeared; Louis Fong's description is remarkably like that of Dr. Fu's. Interestingly, Louis speaks with a strong dialect, while Sam Lee, a good Chinese, does not. Similarly, Yel Bow, in *The Code of the West*, a late entry in the Lone Ranger Series, also speaks a pidgin English, evidently because he too is a hatchet man, conscienceless and hypocritical. As late as 1986 in Nancy Drew's *Deadly Intent,* reference is made to the People's Republic of China as "the one major country to operate without copyright laws" (37), and the villain of the book is James Li, who gives "a demonic laugh" (137) as he leaves Nancy and her friends to burn alive.

Although Chinese are not bad characters in the Grace Harlowe books, Ping Wing in *The Great American Desert* is a virtual fool, cowardly and superstitious. Chinese are called "heathen" in this book. An attempt to be generous is made in *The Bobbsey Twins in Washington*, when the children meet a Chinese family at a play: the father "spoke in English, but with a queer little twist to his words, just as we would speak queerly if we tried to talk Chinese" (199).

Although the Sweet Valley High Series is not notable for using more than one kind of character or social level, the best portrait of a Chinese person—indeed of a Chinese family—in any children's series is found in *Out of Reach* (1988). A high school sophomore, Jade Wu has been training as a ballet dancer for several years. When she wins the starring role in the school music and dance show, she faces immediate discord with her father. Jade "wanted to be American in every way. She wanted American clothes, American food, American friends. If she could *look* American, she would be overjoyed. But Jade was the epitome of Oriental beauty." A major shift in series attitude is conveyed in this line, comparable as it is to the description of Niki Jerusa in *Revenge of the Desert Phantom*. Despite his Ph.D. in physics from Cal Tech, Dr. Wu "distrusted Americans" and "wanted to make sure [Jade] maintained her ties with Chinese culture" (8).

In this book, then, we find a unique series attitude: instead of a White American rejection of Chinese, or foreign, values, we have just the reverse. Moreover, here one finds a picture of a cultivated, educated Oriental family. Jade is beautiful, talented, and completely accepted by her fellow students; she even begins a romance with David Prentiss, a White classmate: " 'Jade's American,' Lila observed wryly. 'Just because her father was born in China doesn't mean she isn't American' " (4). The influence of stereotypes, though, is seen in Jade's dread of anyone's discovering that her grandparents, who pay for her dancing lessons, actually run a laundry; she and David almost part because of his inability to understand why she places such emphasis on hiding this "traditional" Chinese occupation in America. In the strongest statement about foreigners to appear in a series, Mrs. Wu explains matters to Jade:

> My parents were both born in China. To come to this country took extraordinary effort for them, but they made it. . . . You also know what self-sacrificing, self-less, loving people they are. They spent the best years of their lives giving and giving to my sisters and me. . . . That laundry supported us all for years. . . . I think you should show more respect for your own heritage. To be ashamed of your own family—It's that attitude you should be ashamed of, not your grandparents. (109)

The speech has definite links to the passage noted earlier from the Woodland Gang Series about the "foreign" origins of most Americans. Interestingly, a similar conflict exists in the Nancy Drew title, *The Witch Tree Symbol* (1955/1975), in which an Amish father has to become reconciled to his daughter's desire to live a more contemporary American life than her German religious family beliefs allow.

Italians come off quite well in series, even during the 1920's and 1930's when the number of Italians reputedly involved in gangsterism was seen as quite high. The Hardy Boys have a close Italian friend, Tony Prito, who, as a companion of the heroes, receives tacit approval. In *The Tower Treasure* another Italian, Rocco, is the victim of criminals: "Rocco was a hard-working man who came from Italy only a few years ago. He was a simple, genial person" (110).

Two more points about foreigners should be mentioned. Almost without exception, when they appear, they speak with an accent. Sometimes the accent is rendered explicitly in phonetics. Chinese speak pidgin English in the Hardy Boys books.

Extra-Family Relationships

In those about Grace Harlowe dialect is extremely bad: "one blad man," "tlomatoes," even "jlump" are used in *The Great American Desert*, and Anne says, "Every 'r' is an 'l' with a Chinaman ... that's what makes their pidgin English so quaint" (150). The "r's" are hard to find in the preceding words, however. Sometimes, as in the Tom Swift, Jr., books, where villains are almost always foreign, they speak with "a slight accent," though it is not reproduced, nor is the country of origin specified: this series is one of the few that invents foreign countries. As with Black people, one finds dialect used to humiliate and to emphasize ignorance and stupidity, even when applied to characters with a positive role, such as the Amish people in *The Witch Tree Symbol*.

Slang designations of foreign countries were to be found rather commonly in early series; it comes as a shock to modern readers to find Hippy Wingate referring to a Mexican lariat as made by a "greaser" (*Great American Desert* 40), or the Rover Boys pointing out "those two dago sailors" (*In New York* 211), or the villainous Brox of *Don Sturdy in Lion Land* calling African natives, "These niggers" (183). Few such terms are found after 1930 and none at all after 1940.

A kind of tokenism has emerged in regard to foreigners in recent series. Though one still finds no series with a foreign hero, almost a United Nations list of European names has come to be applied to minor characters, as Linda Ferrare, Barton Novak, and Ann Nordquist in *Deadly Intent* or Narosonia Spatz in *The Camp Fire Mystery*. The names of heroes and heroines are almost invariably Anglo-Saxon. Although these characters are positive, foreign names are still a tip-off to villainy, as in *Hostages of Hate*, where one finds Gustave Laru, the Dutchman, and Gil Da Campo. The "best" of such names is undoubtedly Gustave Villen.

J. F. MacDonald was perhaps too sanguine when he observed in 1974 that "today such literature [that is, with such stereotypical handling of foreigners] is no longer being produced. The few series that have survived are being reedited so as to remove prejudiced and denigrating terminology" (545). Yet one is pleased to find in the first of the Doris Fein books, *Dr. Doom: Superstar,* a thorough condemnation of Arnold Whitman, who is called a "superpatriot," and his father Clark Whitman, "a would-be Hitler" (154), who writes hate literature, "racist crap" (49). As with the portrayal of Black people, some progress has been made. One wishes it were greater.

As is true of many aspects of children's series, the ironies here are overwhelming. In celebrating the hundredth anniversary of the Statue of Liberty, the United States seemed to reaffirm the words of Emma Lazarus lodged in the base: " 'Mother of exiles.' From her beacon-hand / Glows world-wide welcome." The concept lies at the heart of American values, of the principles of the nation of all nations founded and populated by foreigners. The series, with their didactic potential, have consistently "taught" something else.

Blacks and foreigners appear regularly in series, and conclusions about their position and image can be drawn from extensive evidence. Since westerns are not prominent among the series, the Indian does not bulk large as a character in them and conclusions must be based on relatively few appearances. Except for the Lone Ranger Series, where Tonto was the second hero, no Native American was a major character until the short-lived third Tom Swift Series in the 1980's.

The traditional view of the American Indian as stoical and impassive is used for almost every Indian who does show up in a series book. On their trip to the Rockies, Carter's Boy Scouts meet an Indian "bearing his burden with that stoical indifference peculiar to his race" (69). In *The Lone Ranger*, "Tonto's Indian blood kept him from expressing his feelings" (181). The Haida Indian, Fleetfoot, whom the Hardy Boys meet at Devil's Paw, also displays this quiet acceptance of success and failure; he is described as "impassive" (54). Moreover, readers are assured that Indians have an inherent nobility. Tonto is "a whiter man than most of 'em who boast about their color" (193), and the Boy Scouts feel they can rely on their guide, for "surely an Indian keeps his word" (*In the Rockies* 111).

Yet one faces a fine contradiction, for the Indian is also a potential savage, and *The Boy Scouts in the Rockies* contains the warning, "I'd go slow about trusting him, Thad; these here Injuns, I've heard, are a treacherous lot, take 'em as a whole" (71). Frank Hardy is tossed in a blanket by Indians, who want to test a white man; if he fails and betrays fear, he must go through a circle of burning arrows. Although the likelihood of such an

Extra-Family Relationships

event in 1959 is doubtful, the explanation is that the Indians "had reverted to the savage customs of the Alaska wilderness" (*The Mystery at Devil's Paw* 112). The word "reverted" is peculiar, since the Indians involved had never left the Alaska wilderness. "Ze injun sell anyt'ing and do anyt'ing foe wheeskey!" says Spic Gomez in *The Lone Ranger* (111). Like Queequeg, however, they retain their barbaric virtues: they know direction implicitly and can read any footprint. "When Indian not want to be seen, no one see 'um," says Fleetfoot (133).

Withal, they remain basically children. Tom Swift, Jr., as late as 1959, fully expects them to respond to "several cheap bracelets" (*Flying Lab* 23), and Fleetfoot declares in the same year that "Indians love dance. Never get tired" (117); the only payment he wants for helping the Hardys is a ride in their helicopter.

Like Blacks and foreigners, Indians speak in dialect or pidgin English. "Me think maybe those men break law too," says Fleetfoot (79). Despite many years of association with the Lone Ranger (whose speech, not remarkable in the first book, improved to a very high level as the series developed), Tonto always kept to a primitive form of dialogue: "Me cook 'um medicine for sick boss in railroad camp. Sick man got son, young boss. Maybe so Gunner Maxim get rid of young boss too, plenty quick" (*The Lone Ranger* 35). On her first little trip west, Honey Bunch Morton is told—in 1928—that Indians must be communicated with by sign language (167)!

Indians, like Blacks and foreigners, remain the White's inferior. Notwithstanding his important role in the series, Tonto is virtually a servant. The Masked Man rides a magnificent white horse, Silver, while Tonto makes shift with a "ratty-looking but tough little pony" who is nameless. In *The Lone Ranger and Tonto*, the Indian waits on the Lone Ranger, cooking, performing the most distasteful and dangerous errands.

Finally, one notes two rather opposed views. In 1913 Herbert Carter presents the reservation as a place where Indians "enjoyed many of the comforts of civilization [the reservation is, evidently, beyond the pale of civilization] and some of the luxuries, too, even to pianos that played themselves, and boxes that sang songs, and played the violin, and gave all sorts of orchestral music" (*The Boy Scouts in the Rockies* 76). Yet fifteen years later in the Honey Bunch Series, Indians are shown, "sad to relate, sitting on the curbstone before the post office with their feet in the gutter, eating bananas" (*Her First Little Trip West* 167).

Not until the 1980's did a series produce a different portrait. The third Tom Swift series, which began in 1981, had only one central hero, Tom himself; in constant evidence throughout the books, however, was Benjamin Franklin Walking Eagle, a member of the Cherokee tribe and as near a second-rank hero as any Indian, foreigner, or Black ever attained before. Called "the young native American" (*The City in the Stars* 46), Ben is a computer wizard: "Ben could explore even the most private circuits in any computer with one hand tied behind his back" (*The Astral Fortress* 20). Hence the image of the Indian who is inferior to the White man is broken; Tom and his friends are consistently rescued from danger by Ben's ability.

Even more surprising, the series had not just one Indian, but two, Ben's cousin, Kate Reiko One Star, a "tall beautiful Indian girl with the almond-shaped eyes inherited from her Japanese mother" (*Fortress* 8). Like Ben, Kate has abilities not found in earlier series Indians: "Kate was an expert on survival under hostile conditions and had considerably more experience dealing with this kind of situation than any of them" (*Fortress* 18). Tonto was a fearless expert also at such matters, but never was he treated to such a description.

The series went out of its way to stress the ability and contribution of Indians in general and in unusual and non-stereotypical areas. In *The City in the Stars,* Tom refers to the Cherokees as the "high-iron people" (47), and Ben, who "knew his own Indian heritage" as well as he knew computers (*Fortress* 9), replies, "Yeah, my ancestors have been climbing around high up for generations. I've had a family who worked on the Empire State Building, the Twin Towers of the World Trade Center, and the Sunset Arcolog" (*City* 47). Even if one feels obliged to say the same thing for many other ethnic and racial groups and to feel a certain tokenism, still the interesting implication is that the Indian had a significant role in building modern America. The total effect is marred by Tom's comment, "Funny how one group had this special talent" (47). The line is comparable to the supposed Black sense of musical

Part II: Attitudes, Beliefs, Values 127

rhythm and the Chinese talent for running laundries. One welcomes such a series gesture nonetheless and laments the short life of this series—only two years—making its possibilities vanish like the Woodland Gang and its very favorable portrait of a Black hero.

7 MISCELLANEOUS ASPECTS OF LIFE AND SOCIETY

ECONOMIC CONCERNS

THROUGHOUT THE TWENTIETH century there is a definite class consciousness in the series books. "The business section of Valley Falls was situated close to the river on the west side, but the sloping hill was devoted exclusively to residences. The majority of the west side inhabitants might have been classified as white collar workers, while the south side residents were made up of the hard-working labor class [i.e., those who wear white collars do not work hard]. The south side boys came from rugged stock; they played hard and intensely" (*Strike Three* 44). Not only does this 1949 passage from the Chip Hilton Series illustrate the distinction between classes; it indicates also the two broad attitudes found in the various series.

One is a desire to maintain the distinction. "Such impudence," thinks Nancy Drew, who is sixteen at the time, while interviewing a prospective maid, "one would think she was an heiress instead of a kitchen girl" (*Lilac Inn* 77). When a theft occurs aboard the ship carrying Don Sturdy to the Land of Volcanoes, Don's friend, Teddy, observes, "It's out of the question that any of the passengers can be guilty." Don, a year younger than Nancy Drew, replies, "That goes without saying.... They're all people of the highest class, and there can't be a breath of suspicion against them. And the same is true of the officers.... It must be some member of the crew" (98). The Hardy Boys refer to Sam Bates, a truck driver, as "evidently not a man of gigantic intellect" (*The House on the Cliff* 85). Both the Tom Swift, Jr., and Happy Hollisters series maintained the class distinction. Tom addressed all employees at his father's plant by their last names, even the elderly, and the Hollister children call their father's employee, Roy Tucker, by his last name, though they range in age from four to twelve and though the year is 1953. Although Miriam Nesbitt in the Grace Harlowe Series is a villain, the terms she employs indicate clear attitudes toward classes: "I have a suspicion her mother takes in washing or something . . . we can't invite a girl like that to our class parties. She would disgrace us" (*Plebe Year* 8); in the girls' sophomore year, she expresses identical attitudes: "She is the daughter of a third rate actor . . . why should girls of good Oakdale families be forced to associate with such people?" (90). Grace, in an attempt at democracy, calls Miriam "an unmitigated snob" (*Plebe Year* 11), but her mother counters with the statement, "Remember that feeding people on the back steps and asking them into the parlor are two different matters altogether" (20).

The latter idea suggests the other main attitude toward classes: a desire to break down distinctions.

> "Queer," remarked Nan . . . "the two girls I thought most of in Meadowbrook were poor . . . somehow poor girls seem to be real and they talk to you so close. . . ."
> "That's what we call sincerity, daughter," said Mrs. Bobbsey. "You see, children who have trials learn to appreciate more keenly than we, who have everything we need." (*The Bobbsey Twins at the Seashore* 5)

Indeed, the poor are lauded at length in this book, although the Bobbseys are clearly not poor. For instance, they admire the day coach more than the Pullman, for in " 'the Pullman cars there are so few people and they're always—' 'Proud,' put in Flossie. 'Yes, it seems so,' declared her brother, 'but see all the people in this car, just eating and sleeping and enjoying themselves' " (*At the Seashore* 9–10). Despite the words, there is an unmistakable tone of condescension in what the Bobbseys say.

There is none in the All-of-a-Kind Family books, which began in 1951, early in the affluent post–World War II years. Here the characters are truly poor: "Almost no East Side child owned a book when Mama's children were little girls [the first volume occurs in 1912]. That was an unheard-of luxury" (12). Father is a junk dealer, and even the illustrations reveal the poverty of their lives. What lingers in the memory, though, are the warmth and closeness of the family, seen, for example, at the end of chapter 5, "The Sabbath": "In the lovely hush of the Sabbath eve, they once more gathered around the table, the children with their books, Mama with her magazine, and Papa with his Jewish newspaper. All heads were bent low over their reading while the candles flickered and sputtered. It was quiet except for the whispered sounds of Charlotte's voice as she read aloud from her primer to wide-eyed Gertie. So they would continue reading until the candles burnt low. Then they would undress and go to bed" (80–81). As the series developed, the family became more comfortable, but strengths developed in their lean years are patently their greatest asset.

Like Grace Harlowe, Judy Bolton is also quite democratic. In *The Clue of the Broken Wing*, "Irene, who had been looked down on as one of the mill girls, could sing as well as play the piano and violin" (105), and Judy says, "The house where we lived was the dividing line [between the upper class and the other side of the tracks]. It isn't as sharp as it used to be, Irene. You and I pushed it way up the street" (139). But clearly the line is still there.

The four books by Thornton Burgess about Boy Scouts worked hard to get "opposite extremes of the social strata . . . on the ground of true brotherhood—the brotherhood of democracy" (*In a Trapper's Camp* 17). While recognizing that social distinctions exist, Burgess brought together a "representative lot. Two were the sons of well-to-do merchants, one was the son of a broker, another was from the modest home of a patrolman on the police force, and a fifth was the son of a subway guard"; of the remaining two, one is named Bernstein, a boy "whose features unmistakably stamped him as a Hebrew of the upper class, and Sparrer Muldoon, newsboy and street gamin" (48). Burgess claims that there is no social distinction among Scouts: "money and that sort of thing doesn't count" (53). So far as Sparrer is concerned, "the fellows were good scouts, all right, and treated him just as if he were one of them" (53). Yet the subjunctive indicates sharply that he is not—in their eyes, or in Burgess's. Attempts at breaking down social barriers always carry a slight reservation; a real sense of social democracy does not exist in most series.

The most likely reason is that the majority of heroes and heroines are well off financially and socially. With the exception of Doris Fein, most are not actually wealthy, but certainly they would be called upper middle class. They face no financial problems; money is rarely a consideration. For instance, when Don Sturdy is invited to Alaska, Africa, or Egypt, the question of his fare is never mentioned. Cherry Ames's father, a real estate broker, is able to send a check to the needy-patient fund at Cherry's hospital, a check large enough "to relieve that little Jane Smith's mind" (*Clinic Nurse* 116). Mrs. Bobbsey tells her family that the poor cannot afford to spend money on trips to the seashore (*At the Seashore* 5); since they are at the seashore, the implication is that they are not poor. Mrs. Bobbsey's sister is described as a former society belle, suggesting that her family was socially prominent. In *The Mystery at Devil's Paw* Frank and Joe Hardy "have saved several hundred dollars from odd jobs" in order to buy an outboard motor (4). By the 1980's the Boys could afford expensive luxury automobiles and music systems. "The Sturdys had considerable means" (*Among the Gorillas* 18); they lived in a handsome stone mansion; Don is given the casual gift of a motorcycle in *Port of Lost Ships*; and reference is made in *On the Ocean Bottom* to the trip planned by Don's friend, Teddy, and his father to Mongolia: the year is 1931 and the Depression was well under way. The first Tom Swift book describes his father as wealthy; Ned Newton remarks that "Tom would never think of robbing the bank. Besides, he has all the money he wants" (*Airship* 116). Tom Jr. is equally well off: at eighteen he has a car, motor boat, and airplane. The Rover Boys attend an excellent private school. Only Chip Hilton is an exception: his mother is a widow supporting herself and her son, yet even Chip's problems are only athletic and there is no question of financial difficulty.

By the 1980's Carson Drew could find his daughter "in bed in the luxurious suite they were sharing" (*Deadly Intent* 30). Nancy has a sportscar (even in the Depression, she always drove her roadster), and though in *The Case of the Disappearing Diamonds* (1987) she identifies herself as a private detective, she is never paid for her work: she has no need to be. The New Bobbsey Twins Series reveals that the children own expensive musical instruments and have their own musical group. In *The*

Camp Fire Mystery the Twins can spend unlimited time in New Mexico apparently on unlimited funds. All parents in the Sweet Valley Twins, Sweet Valley High, and Sleepover Friends series are professional people—doctors, scientists, professors. The most dramatic instance of superior financial status is found in the Doris Fein books. When her friend Harry Grubb dies, he leaves Doris $3.7 million, a huge estate with a manservant, a Mercedes-Benz 600 sedan, a 1936 model 316 Cord Phaeton, and a Triumph-7; she later buys a new 400 GT, "the Red Menace": "the key comes in a velvet jewel box and is 14 carat gold" (*Dead Heat at Long Beach* 35).

Juvenile readers are being asked to identify with characters who are, in general, in a much higher financial status than their own. Despite this fact, the series reveal a curiously ambivalent attitude toward wealth, curious in view of the financial position of their heroes, for a great many villains and evil characters are also wealthy. While no connection is ever made between the wealth and the good qualities of heroes, a definite relation is described between wealth and certain bad qualities.

Wealthy people are shown to be ill-mannered and underhanded; they are cowards, bullies, and snobs, as well as soft, lazy, and unhealthy. At least wealth has such effects on villains. Why it does not have a similar effect on heroes is never explained, though suggestions of hereditary influence are raised from time to time. As soon as Connie Halliday appears in *Sue Barton, Senior Nurse,* she is recognized as wealthy and immediately labeled a snob, without anyone's knowing her (20). Indeed, the assumption is tacit that readers will agree: she comes into the nurses' lounge with golf clubs and asks whether there is a links nearby. Though she later reveals admirable qualities, the image of the wealthy snob is taken for granted. Similarly, Marie Swift in *Cherry Ames, Senior Nurse* is a wealthy girl who found nursing "the most thrilling thing she ever tried" (25): the image of the dilettante is clearly formed. "Miriam Nesbitt was the richest of all the girls" in *Grace Harlowe's Plebe Year at High School*, and she wears "the costliest clothes" (15), yet she is presented as an "ill-bred girl" with a "rude and sneering laugh" (23), and she betrays her classmates' private party to a group of upperclassmen. Even Miriam's mother, "had seen with growing misgivings the innate snobbishness of her daughter's character" (128);

ironically, this revelation comes just ten lines after Mrs. Nesbitt has told Miriam that "your grandfather was a poor man too. He started his career as a merchant." How can Miriam's snobbishness be innate? Fats Ohlsen in *Touchdown Pass* has a "supercilious bearing as scion of the town's wealthiest citizen" (11). Emmanuel Rust, in *Don Sturdy on the Ocean Bottom* is "a multimillionaire... publicity seeker. Inordinately vain and likes the limelight" (26); later he is "arrogant, confident of the power of his immense wealth to accomplish anything" (84). Andy Foger, Tom Swift's constant adversary, is also a rich man's son: "money seemed to have spoiled him, for he was a bully and a coward" (*Motor Cycle* 5). Payson's Boy Scouts meet Mr. Hunt, who "regarded the wearing of jewelry as advertisements of prosperity, and wore them with the same satisfaction with which he regarded his new, gaudily-furnished house on the hill, and his automobile—also very new—and his numerous other possessions, all of which, like himself, seemed somehow to savor of veneer, and to nowhere have the ring of solid wood" (*Army Airship* 106). Hunt's description fits Doris Fein perfectly, yet, for some reason, she betrays none of his characteristics, tending rather to play down, even laugh at, her sudden wealth.

Frequently there is the suggestion that the wealth of villains has not been attained honorably. "In the course of years [Orrin North] had become wealthy and it had been hinted that not all of his riches had been honestly earned" (*Footprints Under the Window* 61). "There is something mysterious and shady about the sources of [Dwight Harrington's] wealth.... He is not an honorable businessman.... Honorable businessmen don't do that kind of work" (*Don Sturdy in the Land of Volcanoes* 33). Wealthy businessmen frequently conspire. In *Tom Swift and His Motor Cycle* "a syndicate of rich men try to steal Barton Swift's latest invention." The elder Swift remarks, "I know these men to be unscrupulous.... These men are rich and unscrupulous" (40, 42). Thirty-one volumes and eighteen years later, Tom faced similar villains, a conspiracy of wealthy theatre owners who try to steal and suppress his television camera in order to protect their own profits.

Strange to find such an attitude in books for young American readers. The United States economic system virtually depends for its functioning on business. A significant number of series readers will likely study business in public school and college; most readers will probably enter some aspect of business life. Many series are themselves products of "syndicates," though not in such a pejorative sense. Once again, considering the didactic potential of these books, why do authors and publishers seem committed to painting unflattering portraits of businessmen? Perhaps one can understand the feeling in books published during the Depression years. If anything, however, the strain has become more pronounced in the past decade. With unexpected consistency, villains in the Hardy Boys, Nancy Drew, and Bobbsey Twins series are "the wealthy"— bosses, owners of jewelry stores (as in *The Case of the Disappearing Diamonds*), owners of large automobile corporations (as in *Program for Destruction*), even entertainment entrepreneurs (as in *The Secret of Jungle Park*, where "Simon was always a money man. He didn't understand about having fun" [75]). Most of the villains in the Doris Fein Series are businessmen, though Harry Grubb is excused from blemish by being a friend of the heroine, who herself escapes censure, one supposes, because she is the heroine.

Moreover, the bitch goddess, success, is a dim figure in children's series fiction. In fact, even with the example of Horatio Alger breathing hard upon the early twentieth century and periodically afterward to inspire young Americans, any consideration of success is minimal in the series. In the first volume of the Happy Hollisters, Mr. Hollister is asked to address the Shoreham Businessmen's Club about one week after arriving in town; he says he will tell how his children helped to make his store, The Trading Post, a success. The implication is that about one week is all that is necessary to produce business success. Possibly because most occupations in series are treated for their potential for adventure, their ability to produce an unusual life, success is not an important concern. Yet in a country so fascinated by the attainment of "success," its lack of treatment is worth remarking.

In the same vein, only slight mention is made of materialism, and most occurs very early in the century. Tom Swift speaks of his servant, Koku: "Born in a savage country, he had not acquired an overwhelming desire for wealth" (*Undersea Search* 207), and Don Sturdy, in describing Egypt, says, "This is not a

Miscellaneous Aspects of Life & Society

land of hustle and push" (*Desert of Mystery* 28). The Doris Fein Series does make serious judgments about material success. In *Murder Is No Joke*, Doris observes, "In Southern California, what you drive determines your social status at a glance. Yes, I know it's silly and superficial. But you *are* what you drive. For example, Steven Sachs, being a wealthy young man from Southern California, would be expected to drive a luxury sportscar" (30–31). Almost identical language is found in *Dead Heat at Long Beach*: "It may sound shallow and materialistic, but here in Southern California, to a large extent, you *are* what you drive. And because dress is inevitably casual, what you wear is not important. Consequently, the symbol of your achievements, to those who don't know, is the automobile you own" (6). These few instances are about the extent of consideration given to what is surely an obvious American quality.

Nor is labor given any but passing notice. While tramps figure, especially in the early series years, as potentially sinister characters (they never actually do anything), no mention is made of labor conditions that might have produced tramps. Admitting that Tom Swift is a businessman, he is exempt from criticism as a hero. In *Undersea Search* he even looks like a benefactor to labor: he seeks a million-dollar treasure because "it will enable me to put into operation a plan to pension our workmen. I've long had that in mind, but I've never had the capital to carry it out" (38). Hence he comes off looking wholly altruistic.

The ambivalence in attitudes toward classes, wealth, business, success, and materialism is masked quite effectively by making an issue of the connection between wealth and villainy but deemphasizing the fact that heroes are also well off socially and financially.

THE CYCLE OF LIFE

Romance

Since most series before the 1970's were produced for the eight- to twelve-year-old age group, the lack of romantic involvement among heroes and heroines is understandable. Of one of his Boy

Scouts, Payson writes, "For his heart was so young and fresh that love affairs had as yet taken no particular grip upon him" (*Under Sealed Orders* 74); "Grace Harlowe and Tom Gray had been firm friends since her freshman year, and had entertained a wholesome boy-and-girl preference for each other, untinged by any trace of foolish sentimentality" (*Junior Year* 130). These passages give the overall picture of romance in the series books, though the words "fresh," "wholesome," "untinged," and "sentimentality" are stronger and more revealing than usual. Until the past two decades, romance is usually handled by not being handled: girls rarely appear in boys' books, and then only in minor roles, while boys are rare in series for girls. There are references to dates in the Nancy Drew books, but boys such as Ned Nickerson and Dick Jackson are dragged along to help solve crimes, rather than for a more personal reason.

No kissing occurs, and when Nancy comes home from a date with Dick, a high school tennis champion, she lies awake thinking of "the play, the excellent orchestra, how lucky she was to have Dick for a date, and what fun it had been" (*The Hidden Staircase* 6). Romance and in fact eventual marriages are set up in the first Grace Harlowe book; yet four years later, when Grace is a senior, she sees Tom Gray off to college and by way of farewell, they shake hands—fervently, to be sure. Tom Swift, Jr., is interested in Phyllis Newton, and his friend, Bud Barclay, dates Tom's sister, but basically they are "buddies" who swim and play tennis together. Tom does kiss Phyllis at the conclusion of *Tom Swift, Jr., and his Rocket Ship*, something his father a generation earlier would never have done to Mary Nestor. Mary appeared in the original series, but not until the twenty-third volume did the reader find that "Tom took Mary in his arms and—But I refuse to betray any secrets" (*Undersea Search* 217), despite the fact that Ned Newton has referred to her as "your friend and future wife" (40). Five books later and after eighteen years, Mary is "a beautiful girl to whom the young inventor was practically engaged" (*Talking Pictures* 16). Tom and Mary eventually did marry, an event which many readers felt was responsible for the decline of the series.

There is physical contact in the Rover Boys books between Dick and Dora Stanhope, "a girl of whom Dick thought a good deal" (*In the Mountains* 12). Later, Dick squeezes Dora's hand

and believes that she returned the squeeze (47), and halfway through the book, "he lingered long over the mental picture of sweet Dora and what she had last said to him. 'She's just an all right girl,' he said to himself" (150). Eleven years later, he gives her a hearty kiss "to which he felt his engagement entitled him" (*In New York* 29). Eventually all the Rovers married and had children, whose adventures became the subject of the second Rover Boys series.

The Hardy Boys, however, offer some of the more interesting opportunities to observe boy-girl relations over the years. The basic change can be seen in a comparison of volume 2, *The House on the Cliff* (1927) and the rewriting of the first book, *The Tower Treasure* (1959). In the former, "Iola Morton, a plump dark girl, was 'all right, as a girl,' in Joe's reluctant opinion" (74), while in the latter, "Joe thought she was quite the nicest girl in Bayport High and dated her regularly" (25); her plumpness is also gone in the revision. After 1959 there is consistent admiration expressed by both boys for Iola and Callie Shaw, Frank's girl friend: "Callie... whom Frank particularly admired" (*Footprints Under the Window* 114); "Joe made no secret of the fact that [Iola] was a very nice girl" (*The Melted Coins* 19).

A quite serious love affair develops in the Sue Barton Series, where, by volume 3, *Visiting Nurse*, the issue is to marry or not to marry. Judy Bolton also marries halfway through her series; in *The Yellow Phantom* a case of kissing and telling is found: "She was glad that Peter Dobbs had wanted to kiss her. It would be a new confidence to tell Irene when she came home" (171).

All in all, for the first three-quarters of the twentieth century, romance in the children's series is practically Platonic, a healthy relationship based on friendship and respect. Sex never appears and no intimacy beyond an occasional kiss is ever suggested. By the standards of the past two decades, the attitude is perhaps naive, but in comparison with the "have-it-all-now" contemporary scene, it exercises an undeniable charm.

By the later 1970's the picture had markedly altered. Writing in 1982 that "Joe Hardy, like his brother, is not much interested in the gentler sex," Louis Phillips was already out of date (176): Joe had become an inveterate womanizer. In *Revenge of the Desert Phantom* (1985), Joe thinks of Iola Morton, "knowing the strain their detective work put on a relationship" (21). Callie

Shaw tells Frank in *Dead on Target* (1987), "as soon as you're in a dark place, you get romantic" (99). At the end of *Hostages of Hate,* however, Callie admits, "I wondered how long you were going to wait before you kissed me" (149). Halfway through *The Case of the Disappearing Diamonds* (1987) Ned Nickerson, formerly only a means to a mystery solution, "reached out and trailed his fingers up her back. Nancy could feel the electric tingle in his touch" (82). A page later he admits, "I'd have to start wondering how much I love you. And Nancy, I do love you." By page 90 he "slowly leaned forward to kiss her." In *Deadly Intent* Bess and her date are "joined at the lip" (86), and Nancy herself concedes that "she'd been a willing victim of Daryl's sexy eyes and smooth personality" (82).

Alas, as with the Hardy Boys, for Nancy Drew mysteries come before romance, and in *False Moves* Ned, as a result, becomes interested in a ballet dancer; Nancy knows "she had no one to blame for breaking up with Ned but herself . . . their relationship always came second to Nancy's work as an amateur detective": Ned says that "he needed to see other girls" (2).

When Doris Fein meets Carl Suzuki at the airport, reference is made to "racially mixed necking" (*Phantom of the Casino* 15); later Carl proposes marriage, but Doris feels that she is not ready yet—at eighteen.

Even adults get into the act: Mrs. Tandy, housekeeper for the Woodland Gang, tells Police Chief Hemster, "Take me out for ice cream more often, John, and you'll find out a lot about me." It is, of course, gentle and overly cute, but Sammy teases her, saying, "Mrs. Tandy's got a boy friend" (*The Missing Will* 19, 20).

Characters in both the Sweet Valley High and Sweet Valley Twins series (aged, respectively, sixteen and twelve) think about little except romance. Though they rarely follow through on their promises, titles in these series are genuinely suggestive: *Double Love, All Night Long, Racing Hearts, Forbidden Love, Out of Control.* Covers also carry on the implications, with pictures of boys and girls embracing and teasing questions: "Is Jessica as grown up as she thinks she is?" (*All Night Long*); "Is Caroline's romance for real?" (*Love Letters*). Things have come a long way from the "fresh" and "wholesome" lives of Payson's Boy Scouts, their dreams as yet "untinged" with "foolish sentimentality."

Miscellaneous Aspects of Life & Society

Birth

Although the Rover Boys, Grace Harlowe, and Tom Swift all became parents, their offspring were born offstage. With one exception, no one is ever born in a series book, nor are birth, pregnancy, or related matters ever mentioned. Children begin series life at about four or five—at least none is younger—and their mothers seem to be through with childbearing. The exception is Sydney Taylor's *All-of-a-Kind Family* (1951), in the final ten pages of which Baby Charlie is born, after a long and tense night of waiting. Gertie, the youngest girl, protests lustily, "I don't want Mama to have another baby. I'm the baby!" (180). The other girls realize that they "had to give Gertie time to get used to the idea of being an older sister" (181). The incipient sibling rivalry is forestalled by the new baby's being a boy, though Ella complains that they are no longer an all-of-a-kind family. Except for this one birth, families are never added to in a series; they retain their size throughout.

Physical Impairments

Despite frequent threats of dangers, of injury, even of death, until the past decade such possibilities remained only verbal ones in the fiction series. Heroes have always managed to rescue themselves from their cliffhangings of whatever kind. Seemingly young readers were to be spared the experience of disease, illness, and crippling. A single exception is found in the 1950's and like the birth of Charlie, it occurs in the work of Sydney Taylor, *More All-of-a-Kind Family* (1954). In 1916 the family's favorite uncle, Hyman, becomes engaged to Lena, a Polish girl. Into their happiness comes "Epidemic in the City," chapter 11, when infantile paralysis strikes: "Regularly each summer the disease had made its appearance, but never before had it struck down so many ... there were empty seats in the classrooms, and the clang of the ambulance bell was heard more and more frequently" (113–114). Lena is among the stricken: "Lena's left leg is paralyzed. She'll have to wear a brace for the rest of her life" (124). She breaks the engagement and along with it, Uncle Hyman's heart, until Mama points out that "Hyman would rather have you with a bad leg than anyone else in the world"

(135). Although the two are married, there is no miraculous cure, and while readers learn to see such an affliction as permanent, they see as well that love and happiness do not necessarily vanish in the face of it.

Almost a generation passed before another such instance, but in the 1980's, crippled characters began to appear surprisingly often. In *The City in the Stars*, the initial volume of the third Tom Swift series, Anita Thorwald, a particularly unpleasant character (who became a series regular afterward), reacts strongly to Tom's reference to cyborgs; "Leaning down, Anita pulled up the right leg of her jumpsuit . . . just below the knee down, her leg was artificial, a smooth plastic housing around an intricately woven mass of wires and computer memory modules [and] some metal struts" (89–90). Bitterly, she tells Tom, "We can perform some remarkable technical feats . . . us cyborgs" (91). In fact, she can, having earlier beaten Tom soundly in a fast game of null-gravity ball. An extremely beautiful redhead to whom Tom is attracted, Anita is afflicted also with "venomous self-hatred" (93). Yet she asks no concessions and none are offered: Tom ultimately beats her, by seconds, in a space race, and they become close friends for the rest of the books. In later volumes her disability is also mentioned; indeed, in *The Astral Fortress*, readers have to face the possibility of such happenings in the golden world of childhood: "Anita had been the unfortunate victim of a childhood accident and her right leg was amputated below the knee. [However] a miracle of technology enabled her to lead a normal, active life" (24).

Other incidents of physical disabilities fill *The City in the Stars*. The villain, Dr. Grotz, suffers an accident and "they think they're going to have to replace his legs" (172); immediately after this scene, readers learn of a woman who "went into a lake a few months ago and they have still got her plugged into machines" (173). Greg Ellison, a victim of Grotz's attack, "came out of it okay"; the irony is severe, though, considering that he "got a lot of new parts. They had to give him a section of artificial spinal cord sheathing, and a couple of spare bits of innards, but he's alive" (183).

Much of the same kind of thing is found in the Bobbsey Twins adventure, *The Camp Fire Mystery* when Ginny Parsons is introduced: "The left sleeve of Ginny's blouse was tucked into her

Miscellaneous Aspects of Life & Society 141

jeans. 'I'll bet you never thought you'd meet a real one-armed bandit,'" Ginny jokes, adding, "I can do almost anything with one hand" (47). Questioned about her loss by Flossie, Ginny explains, "I was in a bad accident. But it could've been worse. I could've lost both arms, and then I wouldn't have been able to hold my kitten or eat or put on my clothes" (49).

One recognizes two strains. First, crippled persons can function in a relatively normal way: Ginny cooks, cleans up, climbs trees during a paper chase, and is accepted as a player in a ball game. No one will deny the value of showing such an attitude to readers, who may never have encountered a handicapped person. At the same time, there seems a desire to make light of the afflictions, almost to dismiss them. To do so is difficult for an older reader, especially in the light of Ginny's speech after Flossie hurts her own arm: "Mine bothers me, too, sometimes... I know it sounds strange, but... sometimes it feels as if my arm is still there. Isn't that silly?" (73–74). Here is genuine understanding of an experience unfathomable to most readers.

The Woodland Gang books present all four leading characters as, in a sense, crippled. Dave is handicapped physically: "My family was killed in the same car crash that hurt me" (*The Hidden Jewels* 20). The accident broke his neck: "I can't walk anymore" (19), yet he drives a car with special controls. Like Bill, who is Black, Dave senses possible prejudice against him; referring to an antique dealer, he remarks, "Maybe she thinks someone in a wheelchair is bad for her store" (11). Yet Kathy thinks he is the "nicest looking boy [she] had ever seen" (15). Other forms of "crippling" are noted. Bill is not only Black but also the shortest and fattest boy in his class; Kathy feels that "children always think I'm stuck up because I'm so shy. And these braces! Ugh!" (9). Sammy counters with his being "the tallest and fattest kid in the fifth grade... I'm a giant! And with eyes that cross!" (9). To similarly afflicted readers, none of these observations is likely to seem minor.

Crippling takes another form in *Revenge of the Desert Phantom*: the pretty African girl, Niki Jerusa, "was missing the little finger on her left hand!" Her loss seems almost gratuitous, "another point of identification; one [the Hardy Boys] wouldn't mistake" (23). Iola Morton expresses what must be the concern of many so afflicted: telling Joe about the upcoming beauty contest, she says, "there's this one girl who's doing better than everyone on the talent part, but I'll bet I got her beat on looks ... she's very pretty ... But one of her fingers is missing. How can you expect to win a beauty contest without all your fingers?!" (49) Niki, nonetheless, does win, and an important point is made for amputees.

Never before in nine decades of series history does one find such direct, even powerful, statements. Earlier arguments for a lack of realism in the series weaken in the face of this unexpected area.

Education

The suggestion that children's series often do not fulfill the clichés expected of them holds true in regard to education as well. Where a concerted attempt to convince young people of the benefits of education might be anticipated, nothing could be further from the truth. "College is a bore, unless you're planning a career," her friend Pauline tells Judy Bolton (*The Yellow Phantom* 5). During a conversation about college between the Hardy Boys, Joe says, "I'd rather go into detective work with Dad," to which Frank replies, "It certainly would be more exciting. Still, we'll have a good time at college, I imagine" (*The Great Airport Mystery* 2). His tone sounds as though he has not convinced even himself. Tom Rover had no doubts at all: "Well, you can't expect much fun when you're trying to get an education" (*In New York* 123), an opinion repeated exactly by the Bobbsey Twins' mother: "You can't play in the first grade like you did in kindergarten. You must study hard now" (*At School* 52). In the Don Sturdy Series there is no doubt either that experience rather than the classroom equips one more effectively for life. "The adventurous life you've been leading has developed courage of body and mind, and made you all the fitter for the battle of life" (*In Lion Land* 39).

There are some balancing ideas. Honey Bunch's uncle, Peter, is a college student who "worked very hard. But he seemed to find time to have fun" (*First Little Trip to the Seashore* 11). Mrs. Allison tells Grace Harlowe during her senior year in high school, "The years a girl spends in college are usually the happiest of her life. . . . Everything is rose colored. She forms high ideals that help to sweeten her life for her long after her college career is over" (23). Yet even in the "education series"—Grace Harlowe, Marjorie Dean, Beverly Gray, Chip Hilton—the chief emphasis is on nonacademic activities. The Grace Harlowe books illustrate the idea dramatically. Mrs. Gray, benefactor of Grace's class and donator of the prize for the best student of the year—a prize based on academic achievement—tells Grace, "the open air is much better than that of the classroom" (*Plebe Year* 25). During a sleigh ride in the same book, Tom Gray asks Grace, "Isn't this great! Wouldn't you rather do this than write an essay or study Latin prose composition?" (162). Grace herself may be expressing merely the wish of every sophomore in springtime when she sighs, "Oh, dear, I wish examinations and school were over.... I can't go to the woods alone, and I can't get anyone to go with me" (*Sophomore Year* 224). There is more than spring fever involved, however, when Dick Rover has to leave college to take over his father's business affairs: "In a way [Tom] envied Dick his opportunity to break away and get out into the business world" (*In New York* 124).

That education may be a totally useless expenditure of time is stated clearly in *The Clue of the Black Keys*: Nancy Drew, wishing to accompany a group of college girls to Florida (she is, of course, trying to solve a mystery), is told by Professor Anderson that he will allow her to go if she can pass the examination he is giving his students at three o'clock that afternoon; assigned areas are the Aztecs of Mexico and early tribes of Florida. Nancy, still a teenager, spends the morning and early afternoon in the library, certainly no more than six hours, and writes a successful examination.

The only reason for going to school is financial. Anne Pierson expresses her belief that "people like her can't understand that if a girl were allowed to finish her education, she could earn so much more in the long run than she could by working year after year in a mill" (*Grace Harlowe's Junior Year in High School* 58).

Clichés about education are found in series, however. "You'll notice that all the big bugs of professors don't seem to care a lickin' about the cash they gain. What they're after is fame and glory" (*The Boy Scouts at the Panama-Pacific Exposition* 79). In *The Clue of the Black Keys* Professor Graham is "a small, stooped man with beady eyes and wrinkled, leathery cheeks" (39); Professor Anderson wears "comfortable tweeds and smokes a briar pipe" (59). The best student in Grace Harlowe's class is shy, quiet, mousy, and lonely (*Sophomore Year* 147). Although Tom Swift has never seen the principal of the school whose roof he has crashed on, he is convinced that she will be an old maid (*Airship* 56). Really educated people never make an issue of the fact: Mr. Swift, for example, "has a degree, but he never uses it" (57). "College boys do all sorts of mean things. Make a boy swim an icy river and all that" (*The Bobbsey Twins at the Seashore* 70).

The current and very popular Sweet Valley High series, despite its "academic" implication, has almost no connection with education. Though Elizabeth and Jessica are often seen on school grounds and though Elizabeth is a serious student, it is extracurricular activities that engage them: shows, contests, sports, dances, personal problems. Nor is this series' clone—the Sweet Valley Twins for younger readers—any different: can Jessica get to a rock concert in spite of parental disapproval (*Sneaking Out*)? Can Elizabeth help her friend become a cheerleader without alienating her twin (*Choosing Sides*)?

Anyone looking to heroes of series for some positive statement about education will be disappointed. Nancy Drew, aged eighteen, has no work responsibilities and never considers college; since 1930 she has never been obliged to do homework. Nor have the Hardy Boys: as they are looking at television to see the disposition of their latest case in *Revenge of the Desert Phantom*, Aunt Gertrude demands, "Shouldn't you two be doing your homework, or are you such hot-shots now you can forget all about things like school and grades?" It is a fair question. Frank's answer is, "In a minute, Auntie.... We want to see this report" (152). Only the Woodland Gang consistently and conscientiously remind each other of their school responsibilities: "Dave said, 'Well, we'd better get to our homework so we're ready for tomorrow'" (*The Missing Will* 49).

An examination of the Bobbsey Twins books, the longest-running series (spanning almost the entire twentieth century—1904 to the present) reveals as it did to Phyllis Perry in 1978 that while the Twins attend church, both morning and afternoon services, despite a blizzard, and are allowed to make snowballs

Miscellaneous Aspects of Life & Society 145

and use their sleds, they are not permitted to go to school: to do so might be a health hazard! Looking back over almost a hundred years of series books, one finds that education is the last resort. Or it is simply background for terror, fantasy, and crime. An advertisement for "Private School—the chilling new series" indicates that aliens have taken over Thayer Academy, one of New England's most exclusive boarding schools; titles are *Nightmare Session*, *Academy of Terror*, and *Hostages of Hate*. Faced with such matters, education must obviously come second.

Death

Again until very recently, death occurred rarely in series, and when it did, never involved heroes, their families, or friends. Until the last decade, so far as a series reader could tell, life had no beginning and no end, only continuance. Hilda Van Stockum was right that fairy tales, in which both birth and death occur, are more real than series (135).

Ideas about presenting death changed markedly after 1980. The first chapter of *Dead on Target* (1987) reveals how greatly, as Iola Morton, Joe Hardy's taken-for-granted girl friend of sixty years, "erupted into a ball of white hot flame" (18), the victim of a terrorist bomb. All of the Westburg children in the Woodland Gang books, orphaned once by the deaths of their biological parents, are orphaned a second time after the deaths of their adoptive ones. A 1984 Sweet Valley High book, *Dangerous Love*, indicates that the rule in the Westfield family is no motorcycles, since a cousin was killed in a crash involving one. Only a year later in the same series, *Promises* opens with the death by leukemia of Tricia Martin, in a most tender, sensitive, and restrained scene.

Though heroes still do not die in series, their family and friends certainly do. There is no lingering over the deaths, however, all of which have positive results. In *Promises*, for example, Betsy Martin overcomes her alcohol, drug, and promiscuity problems after the death of her sister and because of it. Joe and Frank Hardy become devoted and successful terrorist hunters after Iola dies, and from time to time, Joe gives credit to her death, which seems to have accomplished more than she ever did in life. After the first pages of the first book, the

Woodland Gang never think of their lost parents again, pulling together with each other and Mrs. Tandy. Hence, though specific matters change in some series, the end result is still a generally happy ending.

IMAGES OF SOCIAL INSTITUTIONS

Science, Scientists, and Technology

Despite what Fred Erisman as recently as 1985 described as America's "fascination with technology" (23), science, scientists, and the technology they produce have received surprisingly little attention in the books most preferred by children—the series. Since the Rover Boys appeared in 1899 until the early 1980's, the major series devoted to such concerns can be counted on the fingers of one hand: the original Tom Swift (1910–1935), his offspring Tom Swift, Jr. (1954–1965), and occasional volumes of the Don Sturdy series (1925–1931) and Rick Brant series (1947–1964). Such series as the Moving Picture Boys, the Radio Boys, and the Railroad Boys were adventure stories in which one found applications of scientific inventions, not an interest in technological evolution itself. Publishers are quick to respond to a potential market, and it is hard to explain such a paucity in an America, which, since the eighteenth century, has been entranced by science and its products.

Even in the series referred to, the few mentions of science are arbitrary clichés. Don Sturdy's uncle, Professor Bruce is given to such utterances as "Another sacrifice on the altar of scientific research. Well, we could die in a worse cause, certainly" (*Port of Lost Ships* 108–109). In *Desert of Mystery* he said, "I'd back modern science against native experience and habit" (3), while in *Among the Gorillas* he cautioned, "In writing anything pertaining to science, one has to go very slowly and carefully in order to be sure of the facts" (30). The scientist, Parker, in *Tom Swift and His Wireless Message* assures that "science cannot deceive, madam" (210).

Actually scientists have more said about them than does their discipline. Rick Brant states that "one reason he so enjoyed his association with scientists was the dry sense of humor most of them seemed to have" (*The Egyptian Cat* 20). Again it is Don Sturdy who has most to say, albeit in stereotypes. Scientists have "a burning enthusiasm in the cause of science," which carried many, such as Professor Bruce, into "uncivilized countries where he had been in danger" (*Desert* 3). "I never saw anything like them for hard work.... When their enthusiasm is aroused, they never seem to tire" (*Ocean Bottom* 132). But Bruce is absent-minded, "walking around with his head in the clouds a good deal of the time" (*Lion Land* 64). He and other scientists are "middle-aged men... their shoulders stooped and their hair prematurely gray from their exacting studies" (*Lost Ships* 74), yet their conversation is composed of "discussions of abstruse matter" (*Lost Ships* 85). Tom Swift's father "had spent so many years investigating chemical and mechanical mysteries that he saw more clearly and more exactly into and through most problems than other people" (*Electric Locomotive* 97). "For a scientific man and a scholar," Captain Hardy says of Professor Bruce in *Among the Gorillas*, "you have an uncommon love of active adventure" (68); clearly most such men do not.

Occasionally one gets nearer to the bone. When his friend, Ned Newton, is held for ransom in *Tom Swift and His Television Detector,* the young inventor refuses payment, asking what his friend's life or his own matters compared to the safety of his country (178). In the third, 1980's, Tom Swift series, Tom, who verbally opposes violence, has just "disposed" of an opponent: "I don't like violence," he says, "but I couldn't think of anything else to do with the fellow" (*The Invisible Force* 140). Scientific absorption comes to breed a certain callousness. It may do worse. In spite of Tom's assertion that "I was not in this business so much for the work, as I was for the pleasure of it" (*Wizard Camera* 54), his father has been less fortunate: "long years of brainwork had made him nervous" (*Airship* 20), reducing him to "an aged man with a weak heart" (*Aerial Warship* 15).

As might be expected, among the literature devoted to children's fiction series, discussion of scientific concerns has been equally thin: there is little to write about. Phyllis Fenner devoted two pages to Tom Swift and the Rover Boys in 1935, when both series had ended, and Lucille Shanklin, another two pages to "Tom Swift's Last Stand" in the same year. In 1942 *Time* magazine related Tom Sawyer and Tom Swift in a single page, *The New Yorker* in 1954 spent another page on the arrival of Tom Swift, Jr. In all, comment stretches to a scant half-dozen pages.

To make the scientific picture even more vacant but to develop the technological one, note that the original Tom Swift was not a scientist at all, but an inventor; not Steinmetz but Edison was his progenitor. Titles of the first series indicate that Tom was working well within the realm of plausibility, not that of science fiction; his inventions were merely modifications or improvements of devices already in existence: the motorcycle, motorboat, airship, submarine, wireless, camera. Even when *His Talking Pictures* (i.e., television) appeared in 1928, Tom admitted that he was simply combining what radio and wireless had already been able to do (6). Basically the first volume reveals that he devises a new brake for Eradicate's wagon, a rubber washer to prevent dripping paint, and a repaired transmission for a motorcycle; he also fixes a churn, a lawn mower, and a mill. In fact, Tom's only real invention was his electric rifle in 1911.

What the series have done since the beginning of the twentieth century is encourage America's bewitchment with the machine. Grosset and Dunlap's blurb for *Tom Swift and His Motor Cycle* (1910) states that its purpose was "to convey in a realistic way the wonderful advances in land and sea locomotion and to interest the boy of the present in the hope that he may be a factor in aiding the marvelous development that is coming in the future." At the end of the same book, a general advertisement informs the reader that "every boy possesses some form of inventive genius. Tom Swift is a bright, ingenious boy and his inventions and adventures make the most interesting kind of reading." More than just ingenious, however, Tom was a technological genius, whose practical expertise served, Erisman believes, to "elevate technology to an adventure in itself" (25). Tom "passed a busy life," we read in *His Aerial Warship*, "making many machines and having some thrilling adventures with them" (14).

In fact, Tom Swift was an adventure series; much of its excitement either occurred in his laboratory or workshop or was a result of the work he did there. Any reader who felt some hesitancy about working in a factory or machine shop was assured that such labor had its interesting moments (villains were forever stalking Tom to steal his inventions or destroy them, often by bombs). By 1915 and *His Aerial Warship* Tom and his father were clearly industrialists; readers were asked to identify here with a hero who was faced with labor disputes, pension plans, and the like.

Moreover, like Edison, Tom was rich; though he often urged that he worked for the good of society and mankind, profits rolled in. Series villains were occasionally spies, but more often they were "a syndicate of rich men" or "unscrupulous men with plenty of money" (*Aerial Warship* 40), who were out to steal Tom's work for their own profit. Their defeat promoted Tom's financial success. The conclusion is that technological ability and training, not an education in the humanities, will guarantee material wealth, fame, and position; satisfaction will come, not from the arts or literature, but from technology. Indeed, technology seems able to ensure wealth, even if one is a financial incompetent: in *Tom Swift and His Electric Runabout*, Tom and Barton Swift are shown to be "proverbially poor businessmen, though they had amassed a fortune" (141–142).

Whether the fact that Tom's creator, Edward Stratemeyer, had not gone to college influenced such attitudes, the series is consistently antihumanities. "Mr. Swift was a very learned man. . . . Tom showed a taste for mechanics, and his father wisely decided that such training as his son needed could be given at home to better advantage than in a school or college" (*Motor Cycle* 54). Tom fairly gurgles with pleasure over an airplane he has developed in *His Great Oil Gusher*: "No grand opera prima donna has anything on her" (3). "Tom had a natural love of machines," we learn in *His Motor Cycle*, "and it hurt him almost as much to see a piece of fine machinery abused as it did to see an animal mistreated" (28–29). Even recreation is no match for the machine: in the same book we read that Tom "could no more pass a bit of broken machinery, which he thought he could mend, than some men and boys can pass a baseball game" (138). Standing over the wreckage of his airplane, Tom "felt almost as if he was talking to a living thing" (*Wireless Message* 74).

Furthermore, it is technology that will carry the world onward. In *His Electric Locomotive*, Mr. Swift tells his son, "Not only have you completed a marvelous invention and gained thereby a lot of money . . . but you have aided in the world's progress to no small degree. . . . You have, by your invention, shoved the clock of progress forward" (211).

Yet as early as the first volume in the series, a note of danger was sounded. The elder Swift's childhood is described: "One of his first efforts had been to arrange a system of belts and pulleys and gears so that the windmill would operate the churn in the old farmhouse where he was born. The fact that the mill went so fast that it broke the churn all to pieces did not discourage him . . . his father had to buy a new churn" (8). "The scientist lets nothing stand in his path," Professor Bruce says in *Don Sturdy Among the Gorillas* (86). Watching Eradicate Sampson whitewashing a wall, Tom tells him that "some day I'll invent a machine for whitewashing." The Black man cries, "Doan't do dat! . . . Dis, an' makin' dirt disappear, am de only perfession I got. Doan't go inventin' no machine, Mistah Swift!" (*Motor Cycle* 81–82).

Two decades after the demise of Tom Swift, Grosset and Dunlap tried to revive his success in a series devoted to Tom Swift, Jr., which ran for eleven years. Allowing another two decades to elapse, Simon and Schuster tried again with a third Tom Swift series (1981–1983). Neither group was liked by children; among those surveyed, the reasons are clear.

First, the language of both was a pseudoscientific jargon apparent in the titles and carried over into the texts: *Tom Swift, Jr., and His Electronic Retroscope; Tom Swift, Jr., and His Spectromarine Selector.* In *His Flying Lab*, Tom says, "The bulk of the object is a metal alloy of an isotopic composition not found on earth" (40); in *The Race to the Moon*, "My craft's power units will change this energy into electric current for running a super repelatron" (2). While the third series boasted titles somewhat more meaningful (e.g., *The Astral Fortress*), textual language was as bad: describing "a magnetic bottle," Tom tells Ben that "in theory, it's simple. . . . You freeze heavy hydrogen—deuterium—into a pellet. You fire this pellet into a spherical magnetic field. The two things are 'blind' to each other" (*The City in the Stars* 82). Children readily admitted they could not understand it; no more could an adult. Generally, it is the language found in such motion pictures as *Star Wars* and such television series as *Star Trek*. More recent series follow the trend. In *Batteries*

Miscellaneous Aspects of Life & Society 151

Not Included, part of the Not Quite Human Series, Chip, the robot boy, "has an internal interface radio" (1), "electrologic memory banks" (3), "dynakinetic circuits" (5), and an "internal gyroscope" (7). The Arcade Explorers entry, *The Electronic Hurricane*, finds Zera explaining, "I've been working for kiloyears to create the ultimate weather weapon. [It] will strike in exactly seven octal hours" (18). *The Cutlass Clue*, volume 2 of The A.I. [Artificial Intelligence] Gang Series, describes "a motorized, gyro-stabilized metal dog with four jointed legs operated by eccentric cams" (59).

Next, a young reader could identify with the technical know-how of the original Tom Swift, whose work was at least reasonable; no child is in the class of the eighteen-year-old Tom Swift, Jr., "the first earthman to reach the moon" (*Race to the Moon* 147), or with an even younger A.I. Gang, who in weeks construct and fly a rocket to outer space ahead of a group of adult scientists working on a similar project for months. The original Swifts located their workshop and laboratory, relatively crude affairs, in Shopton (i.e., Town of Shops); in *Tom Swift, Jr., and His Jetmarine*, "Swift Enterprises [had become] a gleaming four-mile-stretch of modern buildings and gleaming airstrips" (3) and had expanded as well to "a space station which Tom Swift, Jr., had built 22,300 miles above the earth" (*The Visitor from Planet X* 72). Thus the first series was earth based, the second occasionally left it, while the third took place entirely in outer space. The 1980's series Arcade Explorers takes a more limited scope: all of its action happens in "the Kingdom of Venturia [which] lies inside your computer" (*Save the Venturians* 3).

These points are significant: children prefer realism, or at least the appearance of reality. All the science series developed since the 1950's are pure science fiction with only a remote semblance of realism. From Shopton, U.S.A., with its earthly, businessmen villains, to the Maurevians and Brungarians of the second series and the Sansoths of the third is a long journey; they and the Venturians are the characters and worlds of Buck Rogers and Flash Gordon; even Dr. Luna of *The Astral Fortress* is simply Ming the Merciless trying to conquer the universe.

An intriguing wrinkle in the 1980's series is the fact that robots are found in all of them, and often as main characters.

"Aristotle, Tom's robot and favorite invention... has an inherent inferiority complex rooted somewhere in his complex circuits" (*The Astral Fortress* 17). The A.I. Gang have "Paracelsus, the computerized bronze head they had created and carried around in a leather bag and whom they had programmed to talk" (*The Cutlass Clue* 7). The Arcade Explorers have a robot named Digit. The acme is reached in an entire series devoted to an "electronic analog"—the Not Quite Human Series recounts the development and experiences of Chip (Microchip) Carson, a thirteen-year-old product of his science-teacher "father." Extremely limited, repetitious, and dull, the series works to death humor based on Chip's literal interpretation of words: "I've got my eye on you." "Which eye?" (*Batteries Not Included* 27), and its suspense on Chip's potential battery depletion. Even Anita in *The Invisible Force* sighs to Tom Swift, "The whole civilization thinks and acts like a machine. They already have billions of robots" (153).

Where the first Tom Swift simply enjoyed technology more than he did the arts, literature, or humanities in general, by the 1980's only technology offered a living. In *The Cutlass Clue*, "Dr. Marion Fontana... had turned to computer logic from her original major in medieval philosophy" (32). A knowledge of the humanities is abused in *The City in the Stars*: trying to break into Dr. Grotz's computer, Ben says that one must "psych out the quarry. History professors always use historical references, almost always classical, almost always trivial" (152). To ensure employment, science creates planned obsolescence: in *Robot Trouble* Roger tells Hap, who has just argued that something built right ought to keep working forever, "Boy, are you living in a dreamworld.... Long-term use is not the American way" (171).

The worst is yet to come. In the first Tom Swift series, villains were foreign spies or competing businessmen intent on stealing Swift inventions. By the 1980's anyone who favored the arts and humanities over scientific and technological development—indeed, anyone more concerned for the quality of life itself at the expense of technology—was a bad guy. This trend actually began in the 1928 *Tom Swift and His Talking Pictures*. The "pictures" are television: "Powerful moving picture and theater interests would not want to see such an invention... put on the market.... We're not going to let you make a machine that will permit folks to sit at home and see and hear a show without paying the admission price" (89). One of Tom's opponents argues, "If a man can sit in his own home and listen to a radio program, and, at the same time see the performers, he certainly won't put on a starched shirt and a stiff collar and pay ... for a seat in the theater ... he won't even come to a fifty cent movie" (184). All these economic fears have clearly come true, and one technological invention has destroyed others. But more significant are the implications, which have also come to pass—the dress and manners associated with theatre going, indeed, the culture and civilized behavior it used to inspire, have also vanished. One goes to the opera in jeans and sneakers. More than money has been lost.

The idea found its strongest expression in *Save the Venturians*:

> The kingdom of Venturia lies inside your computer. It was a beautiful and peaceful land until the brutal armies of the Technoterrorists launched a surprise attack. The terrorists hate all scientific advancement. Their plan is to turn Venturia's technological society back into a primitive wilderness. (3)

"Technoterrorists" focus on preserving the environment, indeed, life itself; by opposing machines, they are bad. Given the didactic potential of children's series, the idea is a frightening one; it was previewed in the 1936 film, *Things to Come,* in which a rocket designed for outer space exploration is attacked by an enraged mob of villains—philosophers, artists, teachers.

In spite of a consistent assertion that Swift Enterprises is involved only with "inventing things to benefit mankind," the first volume of the third series, *The City in the Stars,* documents the pollution of both earth and outer space by the work of science and technology. During the final race, Tom and Ben Walking Eagle pause briefly to look around them: "The sight of Earth as they came up over the rim of the Moon was still exciting to the young men.... From out in space it looked unpolluted, still fresh" (182–183). Yet they and many others are living permanently in outer space, escaping from the pollution of their own work. An earlier description of the space station, named

New America, indicates that in building the station, scientists had brought with them bees, earthworms, bacteria "that made the sterile Moon soil live"; Tom speculates, however, that "when mankind got to the stars themselves, cockroaches would somehow manage to tag along" (61). *Robot Trouble* in the A.I. Gang Series introduces an additional area of scientific pollution, that of space itself: Ray refers to "Space junk," adding that "we've launched so many satellites in the last three decades that heaven is getting cluttered" (57).

Perhaps there is one additional reason—and a finely ironic one it is—for the rejection of scientific series to be found in the Arcade Explorers volumes. The books are basically game plans for computer video games. One does not *read* the books, which are written on the primer level, in the first person, and in the present tense to match what is going on *now* on the video screen; one uses them to set up programs to play games (40 percent of the books are given to formulas to be typed into the reader's computer). At least the older series so disliked by their critics tried to encourage reading; Arcade Explorers discourages it, demonstrating that playing games is far more delightful. The implication is that science and technology themselves have become games, with the end of their efforts being toys for children. Television itself is an electronic marvel for the dissemination of vacuities. One comes to an inescapable conclusion, namely, that on the basis of what is revealed in the children's fiction series, civilization and its glory—the humanities—have lost the game to science and its offshoot technology in the final innings.

Law Enforcement Officers

"This case is too big for the police." So says Carson Drew in *The Mystery at Lilac Inn*, revealing an almost century-old attitude toward policemen in the children's series. This attitude is fascinating, considering the age level of most of their readers. Policemen are generally Irish (Lieutenant Collins and Chief Kelly in the Judy Bolton books, Patrick in those about Nancy Drew, Con Riley in the Hardy Boys Series). Until the late 1940's they were incompetent, ineffectual, stupid, and lazy; often they were cowards. Usually, as the Lone Ranger books demonstrate, indi-

Miscellaneous Aspects of Life & Society 155

viduals outside the police force, acting sometimes as vigilantes, must do their work for them. Striving always for law and order, the Lone Ranger nonetheless operates entirely outside the normal legal machinery; he even adopts the traditional appearance of the outlaw—the mask—and as the series makes unequivocally clear, he accomplishes results that for the police are impossible.

When trying to solve *The Mystery of the Moss-Covered Mansion*, the police overlook a crucial clue that Nancy Drew notices immediately (114), and her friends, Ben and George, are insulted when they are likened to policemen: "Don't put Ben and me in the same class as the police!" George says. "We're far more clever than they are" (155). Judy Bolton is contemptuous also. "Naturally the police want credit for finding it," she says in *The Clue of the Broken Wing* (91), when she has made a critical discovery herself. Don Sturdy's friend, Teddy, affirms the idea: "I wonder if there was ever a time when the police didn't cover up their ignorance by saying they'd soon nab the thieves?" "They're only human," Don replies; "I often think we don't give them enough credit for what they do" (*Port of Lost Ships* 71).

Despite Don's attempts to be fair, the series show policemen doing very little, and that, unsuccessfully. Perhaps the best examples come from the Hardy Boys, where Chief Collig, Officer Riley, and private detective Oscar Smuff appear in many of the books. This series also reveals the most dramatic changes in attitudes toward the police. For the first twenty-seven volumes, or from 1926 to 1949, police are shown in a consistently bad light. Helpless against bootleggers in *The House on the Cliff*, they are also cowardly; two books later, Riley is put to rout by children in a snowball fight and made to look the fool; in volume 6 he is arrogant and hostile to the Hardys' suggestions; by volume 11 Riley is practically an idiot: he is called "thickheaded" and a pickpocket steals his handcuffs (*Footprints Under the Window* 51). By 1944 Riley's "normal pace was about a half a mile an hour" (*The Melted Coins* 72); two years later he is "a slowwitted policeman who had been demoted for letting himself be robbed by a thief he had caught," and by 1947 he is so stupid that he is never given anything important to do (*The Phantom Freighter* 65). Riley's superior, Chief of Police Collig, had also "never been blessed with a superabundance of brains," and Chet

Morton is fond of remarking that if "you put their brains together, you'd have enough for a half wit" (*The House on the Cliff* 108-109). Louis Phillips in "Me and the Hardy Boys" admitted that "I sided with Joe and Frank, not only against evil, but also against the most inept and caustic police department in the world. . . . The Hardy Boys displayed a healthy disrespect for bureaucratic inefficiency. . . . [They solved the mysteries] without bothering to consult Bayport's comic book police force" (176).

The police could be far worse than stupid. In the Nancy Drew entry, *The Clue in the Diary*, they "rushed people to jail on the slightest pretext" (147), and one officer "ached to shoot that revolver so that he can get his name in the papers" (149). Carson Drew, earlier in the same book, notes the "merciless grilling that not infrequently caused the victims to confess to crimes they had not committed" (139).

As the series moved into the 1950's and unflattering racial and national stereotypes were being removed, changes in the image of policemen also began to appear. The character of Chief Collig changed completely. In *The Sign of the Crooked Arrow* (1949) he had a brief and inconsequential role but all the earlier hostility and envy were gone. For the next three books policemen did not play any part—as though the publishers wanted readers to forget the old image. When Collig reappeared in *The Crimson Shadow* (1953), he was "a grizzled veteran of many a battle with Bayport's criminal elements. He and the Hardys had often worked together in rounding up underworld characters" (12), a wholly preposterous statement. Thereafter whenever Collig was shown, he was cooperative, intelligent, and effective. Riley disappeared entirely, so far as his previous character was concerned, and he too was reliable and efficient. By 1960 Oscar Smuff too was an "old friend of the Hardys" (*The Mystery of the Chinese Junk* 13)

So drastic, sudden, and complete was the change that one almost suspects coercion. Phillips felt in 1979 that the series view of the police may have been a factor in keeping the Hardy Boys off library shelves. Whatever the reason, from the 1950's on policemen reveal a much different image, one more likely to create respect for law enforcement in young readers. By 1987 in *The Case of the Disappearing Diamonds*, Chief McGinnis

Miscellaneous Aspects of Life & Society 157

(still an Irishman) "was an old friend of both Nancy and her father. They liked and respected him. For his part, Chief McGinnis admired Nancy's enormous talent for criminal investigation" (99). In *The Missing Will*, Chief Hemster, "the strong-looking, kind, police chief of Bluff Lake" (13-14) is a great friend of the Woodland Gang. The following book showed Hemster as "the good-looking, kind police chief" (42). *The Secret of Jungle Park* presented Lieutenant Pike as "an old friend of the Bobbseys" (12) and an illustration shows Pike to have a beard, a far different conception of police officers from any seen earlier.

Nonetheless from the 1970's on, a parallel and competing view of the police persists from earlier days. Though the Hardy Boys admit in *Program for Destruction* that "Chief Collig was a good cop . . . they felt they could solve this case themselves" (69). While admitting that Lieutenant Pike is their friend, the Bobbsey Twins still feel that "maybe we can find out who's causing the accidents" (*Jungle Park* 13). They are able to do so, because "sometimes the police don't find everything" (14), especially a crucial eye patch the Twins find by simply looking around the floor!

By the 1970's and 1980's police were once more under attack, and a public view again carried over into the series. In the Hardy Boys Casefiles, the police are consistently called "cops" by both characters and author. *Hostages of Hate* presents Chief O'Neill, another stupid Irishman, unreasonable about both leads and facts. Inspector Sam Butler, the police officer in charge of protecting a presidential candidate in *Dead on Target*, is in fact the villain-assassin. The comic-fool returned in the person of Sergeant Brody, head of the Ancoteague Security Force in the A.I. Gang Series. Brody weighs "a hulking two-hundred pounds" and is "not notably fast on the uptake" (*The Cutlass Clue* 22). Later he is "huffing and puffing and trying to sound like he's on top of the situation" (100). In *Robot Trouble* he is called a "beef-head" (41); trapped on a floor covered with ball bearings, he goes through a series of Keystone Kops pratfalls. His discomfiture is acceptable because he was "no friend of the A.I. Gang" (36), and as shown in *The Cutlass Clue* would not take seriously the suspicions of a group of children. Moreover, he is a sexist, "so convinced of male superiority he would think anything thought up by a female was either harmless, or useless, or both" (38).

Thus the fortunes of law enforcement officers in the children's series have a seesaw appearance. For the first half of the twentieth century, police were portrayed in a negative light. Once the security-minded 1950's and 1960's arrived, they were shown much more favorably. Coinciding with critical attacks on Clint Eastwood's depiction of Detective Harry Callahan in *Dirty Harry* (1971) the status of policemen again became dubious. What exists at the moment is a kind of balance among the earlier comic view, a recognition of occasional venality and crookedness, and an attempt to deal fairly with police efforts to maintain social peace.

War and the Military

Except for the fiction series, war, for practical purposes, does not exist in children's literature. Montrose Moses during World War I indicated that the War had made its way into children's books, as had the Boy Scout movement and the Campfire Girls (135), but he gave no suggestion of how the War was dealt with. Just before the United States entered World War II, Frederick Melcher predicted that certain elements would appear in children's reading as a result of the War: he foresaw an interest in refugee children, South of the Border affairs (probably because of Roosevelt's Good Neighbor Policy rather than the War itself), manufacturing, United States history and its heroes, and aviation (always an important area of juvenile literature); he did not, however, say anything about the actual War (645). During World War II, Vernon Ives noted three main trends resulting from the War in children's reading: factual books about the armed services; books whose characters feel the effect of war; and books about the Allies which also interpret democracy (1592–1593).

None of these observers nor any others have examined war as an element in books for children, probably because, except for the series, few children's books contain views of warfare. The series have a great deal to say—in their titles. During World War I, the Brighton Boys might be active in *The Argonne Forest*, *At Chateau-Thierry*, or *At St. Mihiel;* during World War II, Dave

Miscellaneous Aspects of Life & Society 159

Dawson might be seen *On Guadalcanal, At Dunkirk*, or *In Libya*; but whether heroes were called the Boy Allies, Our Young Aeroplane Scouts, or the Red Cross Girls, they were still and always the Boy Scouts or Outdoor Girls that we had read about in countless other series. As was true when the Scouts visited the Rocky Mountains or the Maine woods, despite their titles, books in the various war series might have occurred anywhere and to anyone. A person who had been to Guadalcanal would recognize nothing of what happened there to Dave Dawson, while the account of Dunkirk in the same series is not even as full as that given in a brief newspaper article. Again, the series cash in on current interests in a titular way, but World War I is not fundamentally different from World War II: the heroes are Boy Scouts under fire. Neither Korea nor Vietnam found their way into a series.

As might be expected, the most prominent feature in books about military action and war is violence. Uncle Sam's Boys first appeared in 1910, when the army was still a peacetime activity; they continued until 1919, recounting the final victory of the Allies in the First World War. The early books are combined Boy Scout and cowboy adventure stories, with considerable violence. The first book, *In the Ranks* (1910) is chiefly an action against bandits, one of whom is "wounded in the right breast" (134), another is killed by the Major, and of a third, Hal, one of the heroes, says, "I'm afraid I've got to kill him, if he doesn't get me first" (228); the book ends with a running gun battle. Another such battle occurs in *On Field Duty* (1914), during which one crook has his wrist shattered by a bullet, another is wounded in the right forearm, and one of the heroes, Noll, subdues a criminal by putting his pistol in the villain's mouth.

Once the war actually began, there was a marked increase in violence, ugliness, and horror. During *With Pershing's Troops at the Front* (1919), a lecture explains how best to put a bayonet into an enemy's kidney (53); in combat, the hero, Greg, shoots one German through the heart and breaks the neck of another, laughing about both later because he cannot recall doing the acts (198). By the time of *Uncle Sam's Boys Smash the Germans* (1919), the series had assumed the full-scale proportions of Arthur Guy Empie's *Over the Top* and of other adult books following World War I. The first chapter finds several men buried by a shell: "a flying shell had torn off the top of his head . . . the second man was reached. He was dead, with both arms torn away. . . . The third man, dead, had part of his abdomen missing" (20). Later, Dick Prescott and Sergeant Kelly capture a German, who surrenders but tries to kill Kelly. " 'Don't take any chances, Sergeant,' Dick ordered, 'Spit him.' Utterly without emotion, Kelly drove his bayonet twice into the Hun's waist line. Then, dropping his rifle, he raised the stricken thing, hurling it into no man's land" (36). Only ten pages later, one German is bayonetted in the windpipe, another in the abdomen, the head of a third is crushed, and a fourth is spitted. Further on, a boy is put into a gunny sack, his head beaten to a pulp (95).

Ironies abound. Dick and three Indians creep into a German trench and kill fourteen of the enemy; the next chapter finds the group talking about "our humanity and their lack of civilization." Linton, a young private, puts his bayonet into one German's throat, then into another's. " 'Linton knows how the trick is done now,' Dick gleefully told himself" (114). The adverb is impressive. Trying to cross a river, the Americans find that barbed wire has been laid a few feet below the surface; they tangle in it and are machine-gunned by the Germans, forty dying (126ff.). Dick Prescott is himself shot six times on page 130, in the arm, shoulder, thigh, and wrist. The violence of this book is astonishing in a children's series, and unnecessary considering that the book was published a year after the War ended and presumably no further need existed for keeping high the pitch of civilian indignation. Worth noting also is the fact that the worst atrocities of the book are committed by Americans.

This series contains also the one instance of conscientious objection found in children's literature; it too is remarkable. *With Pershing's Troops*, chapter 8, titled "With the Conscientious Objectors," finds Dick Prescott interviewing men who have refused to bear arms. He asks, "coldly," whether they have conscientious objections to being hurt and any scruples against giving the enemy a chance to kill them (97); he calls them cowards and implies that they are frauds (98); discovering that the head of one man slopes upward into a point, Prescott says that this is the head of a real conscientious objector: "If a mule had a head like that our veterinarian surgeon would call it a fool mule and reject it" (101–102). Of the other two men he asks, "Have you been listening to Socialistic or other freak talk?" (101). Finally, he demands, "Are you men or are you dishrags" because "we cannot fight such a beastly enemy in any other way than by killing him" (101). Dick convinces two of the men to do "whatever Uncle Sam wants" (102), then goes into the barracks and orders every man there to write to his mother; one responds, "I'd do anything Capt. Prescott asked me to do" (104).

A related but less strong view is seen in *The Brighton Boys in the Argonne Forest*. Herb, one of the heroes, says, "I tell you, Don, there is nothing more harshly unjust than war!" To this idea Don replies, "I guess you're right . . . and yet, we wouldn't be called pacifists, Herb." "Pacifists? Never! Our cause is just; our country had to fight and it is the duty of those who could fight to get busy for her" (146). A chord almost of self-justification, even of embarrassment, seems to be sounding in both series, after the emotion of wartime experience has moderated to thought. The reader learns early in *The Argonne Forest* that "war is not a pleasant matter; there are few really happy moments even in victory" (41). Acceptance is difficult, since less than ten pages earlier the battle for the Argonne is described as "among America's most glorious deeds on the field of battle; among the most heroic annals of all warfare" (32). "It was a battle carried out for the glory of America . . . for the sake of justice and humanity and for the joy of smashing a foe that had not played fair according to the accepted rules of warfare. . . . And therein individual bravery and heroism enacted a very large and notable part in the victory over foes [the irony that follows is perhaps unconscious] numerically almost as strong" (33). Such a patriotic and idealistic view continues through the balance of the book and throughout the whole series. "Old Brighton labored to teach its lads altruism, charity, gentleness, and kindness" (41), but "if you don't kill or wound the enemy, so-called, he will kill or wound you. . . . As against aggression, injustice, injury . . . wars are, beyond argument, often most justifiable, even necessary" (42).

The enemy is described in the most flagrantly charged language. The German is "part fox, part snake, and more than half hog" (*The Argonne Forest* 101). Dave Dawson felt the same way about the Japanese in World War II: "They were Jap rats, and true to their rotten race they had struck their blow under false colors" (*On Guadalcanal* 109); earlier he has called them "you baby killers" (84). All such statements carry with them the tone and the code of the Boy Scout outraged by a villain that does not play fair. Retaliation thus is deserved and even enjoyable. Dave's Flying Fortress takes on six Japanese Zeroes, downing all of them: "Six for six. Not bad. It was almost fun while it lasted" (24).

Issues in the Korean war and that in Vietnam were, of course, less clearly drawn, more complex; simple patriotism was not sufficient justification for American actions. Most likely the absence of both these conflicts from series books is explained by these facts.

Religion

Except for the All-of-a-Kind Family, religion plays no role whatever in the lives of series characters. Heroes and heroines sometimes attend church, but attendance is as far as they go: religion has no influence on the life of any character. The Bobbsey Twins are not allowed to throw snowballs on Sunday (*Merry Days* 35); at assemblies before school, the principal "conducted the usual Biblical reading and patriotic songs" (*At School* 174), and at Christmas Mr. Bobbsey "read the Christmas story from the family Bible" (144); the family prays for sailors during a terrible storm at sea, and "surely the angels had listened to even the sleeping whisper of the little ones, who had asked for help for the poor sailors in their night of peril" (*At the Seashore* 197). When Grace Harlowe is a high school senior, a friend murmurs, "God is good . . . a higher power sure willed that Mabel should find true and worthy friends" (33). Echoing this sentiment, the child Sukey in *The Clue of the Broken Wing* tells Judy Bolton, "I guess God is the biggest thing of all" (174). Chip Hilton's friend Soapy says "a little prayer for help before a game" (*Buzzer Basket* 169), and Dick Rover "sent up an earnest prayer that Tom might be spared" (*In New York* 257). When the Rovers are shipwrecked (*On Land and Sea*), "the following day was Sunday. The girls thought that there should be some sort of religious exercises, and all went to the wreck, where Capt. Blossom read some chapters from the Bible and the others sang hymns" (140). The actual religious preference of none of these people is named.

The nearest any series book came to considering religion as a force was in *Tom Swift, Jr., and the Visitor from Planet X*. "Don't forget, Tom," his father tells him, "the mind of a human being or any other thinking inhabitant of our universe is based on a divine soul. No scientist must ever delude himself into thinking that he can copy the works of our creator." Tom Jr. replies soberly, "I know that, Dad. . . . Man's works will always be crude gropings, compared to the miracle of nature" (143). Later, his father assures Tom that "Providence protected us," but it was Tom's invention that saved the day. Religion seems dragged in, and neither this book nor any other supports the elder Swift's belief.

In the Grace Harlowe books, Nora is called "a good little Catholic," and *The Witch Tree Symbol*, a Nancy Drew title, deals closely with the Amish people. These two instances constitute the only specifically named religious faiths other than Judaism. The absence of such description is explainable perhaps on the grounds of publishers' reluctance to offend any group and to eliminate the possibility of, for example, a Catholic reader's unwillingness to identify with a Jewish or Protestant hero.

Judaism is the only religious denomination to play a significant part in children's series, and only three series—the Woodland Gang, Doris Fein, and the All-of-a-Kind Family—have Jewish main characters. Even in these three, religion is presented in its social aspects: it is not a motivating force. Only in the latter two can definite ideas about Jews be derived from the fiction series.

For the first half of the century, when Jewish persons appear, they are never referred to as Jews. Only on the basis of certain names conventionally assumed to be Jewish can one infer their presence. In *Nancy Drew and the Hidden Staircase*, the villain, Nathan Gomber, uses a false driver's license in the name of Samuel Greenman. Ollie Jacobs in *The Great Airport Mystery* is also found by the Hardy Boys to be a criminal. The villain in *Don Sturdy on the Ocean Bottom* is Rufus Gold, and the chief criminal in *Tom Swift and His Talking Pictures* is Jacob Greenbaum. *The Clue of the Broken Locket* presents a vulgar stage couple named Blair ("loud, cheap, unstable, and crude"), who had changed their name from Sellenstein. Their attorney, Abe Jacobs, is an "unscrupulous lawyer who made a living by questionable means" (47). Jacobs commits the ultimate indiscretion by chasing Nancy Drew and "leering" at her (195). Biggie Cohen, on the other hand, in *Touchdown Pass* is the close friend of Chip Hilton; Biggie's father is also an admirable figure, and the principal of Chip's high school is named Zimmerman.

Though Jews are not shown to be as readily recognizable as foreigners and Blacks, in *The Boy Scouts in a Trapper's Camp* Bernstein is a boy "whose features unmistakably stamped him as a Hebrew of the upper class" (48). The word "stamped" may carry a pejorative connotation almost of stigma.

Of the Woodland Gang, only Dave Stern is unquestionably Jewish by birth. The other children have been adopted by the Westburgs (inconsistently spelled Westberg in some of the books): their biological parents may or may not have been Jewish. The point is irrelevant, since the Jewish religion has no influence at all in the series.

Nor does it in the Doris Fein Series. Doris and her relatives are all stereotypical Jews—caricatures in the manner of Jackie Mason and Henny Youngman. As many clichés are attached to them as adhere to Blacks and foreigners. Though Doris describes herself in *Deadly Aphrodite* as "a nice middle-class Jewish girl from Southern California" (4), she is far from so mundane an image. She and all her family are well off financially (she herself has inherited $3.7 million). Her father is an ophthalmologist; before she became an heiress, Doris is able, by working in his office after school and during the summer, to earn enough to buy a Triumph sports car, yet she avers that she is not "a spoiled brat who has gifts lavished on her by rich parents" (*Phantom of the Casino* 12). Her mother is a nurse and her Uncle Saul, a dentist, "a Jewish Luciano Pavarotti" (10) who sings while he works. Aunt Ceil Doris sums up by saying, "You may have heard the expression Jewish American princess? Well, my aunt is too old to be a princess, but definitely acts like a dowager empress" (23); Ceil is a former professional ice skater with the Ice Follies, wears a mink cape though the weather is not cold, and is "the type who gets up in the middle of the night to go to the john but puts on makeup before she goes" (*Aphrodite* 25). When Carl Suzuki wants to marry Doris, Ceil remarks

Miscellaneous Aspects of Life & Society 165

that he is hardly Jewish. Dr. Fein replies, "He's got half the requirements: he's a professional man . . . a lawyer" (32).

All of them eat like lumberjacks and all are overweight; food is their besetting sin, and though Grandma Fein calls Doris *zoftig*, "a nice Jewish way of saying voluptuous" (*Phantom* 10), Doris is really fat: the dinner for Carl is referred to as "Nebuchadnezzar's Feast." Jerry Kobrin, a friend, feels that "we're the only Jews you can find in Santa Amelia Estates . . . the richest part of Santa Amelia [and] a WASP holdout area for years. Oh, nothing overt. No signs saying *KEEP OUT*" (20). Thus the exclusion of Jews from certain areas that prevailed in the 1940's and 1950's persists. None of the Feins shows its effects, however, and the Jewishness of the series lies in a string of Neil Simon–like one-liners. When Dave Rose hurries him, Jerry calls him a slave driver, "a regular Simon Levine" (26). In *Dead Heat at Long Beach*, Doris asks Ginsberg, the assistant director of IGO, the intelligence agency for which she sometimes works, "What's a nice Jewish boy doing working for this mother of deception?" (38)

Despite the Jewish names, jokes, and references, the Jewish religion is not found in the Doris Fein books. It is a major element in the All-of-a-Kind Family Series, a prime motivation in the daily lives of the characters. The Sabbath figures prominently in all the books, an event taken by the children as well as adults not only with seriousness but also with joy. The fifth chapter of the first volume is devoted to a full explanation of the day, all its aspects and meaning. Chapter 7 is "Purim Day," a holiday that reappears in *The All-of-a-Kind Family Downtown*. The ninth chapter begins preparations for Passover, and readers are informed about "the ceremonial feasts" during which "through reading parts of the Bible, singing religious songs, and eating special, meaningful foods, the Jews once again relive the days spent in Egypt so many thousands of years ago" (119): twenty pages are devoted to this holiday. Three chapters later one reads of Rosh Hashanah and of Yom Kippur, the subject of chapter 3 of *More All-of-a-Kind Family*, and we are shown how to build a sukkah in preparation for the coming of Sukkoth: as Sarah observes, "the Jewish holidays certainly come in bunches" (166). This "week-long holiday of rejoicing and thanksgiving" is allotted the whole of chapter 12 in *Downtown*, as Hanukkah is given an entire chapter in *More*. As is true of the Woodland Gang and Doris Fein series, food is a prominent feature of these holidays and the books; for people as poor as the Family, the festive boards groan under the weight of the meals. Most important, nonetheless, is the explanation that in these holidays and their meals is the "affirmation that the Lord is everywhere and the earth is full of his bounty" (*More* 169).

This series thus emphasizes the fact of being Jewish, both in religious and social areas, and both its seriousness and its pleasures. Although the books sometimes seem to resemble the Bobbsey Twins and the Happy Hollisters in their plots, it is important to note that the equivalent of the space of an entire book is devoted to events that are religious in origin and intention. These books belie the charge of a lack of substance often leveled at series; perhaps the underlying core is the reason. Moreover, unlike the series attitude which tends to maintain a separation between Blacks and Whites, foreigners and "native" Americans, this series makes understandable the customs of a particular group and tends to bring together people of many differing backgrounds and beliefs. Like the Woodland Gang, it is consistently admirable—and moving.

Attitudes Toward the United States and Travel

Both the Woodland Gang and All-of-a-Kind Family books make strong, carefully considered statements about U.S. ideals. They stand in remarkable distinction from the majority of other series, whose patriotism is elementary and chiefly verbal.

> "Three cheers for America!" cried Hippy. Mrs. Gray laughed.
> "Yes, indeed, my dears. America is a splendid country and every American should be proud to say so." (*Grace Harlowe's Plebe Year in High School* 146)

In general this attitude is consistently revealed in the various series.

> "Gee, it's a wonderful country, isn't it?"
> "You bet it is," replied Teddy. "There's nothing like it in the world. The fellow who advised everybody to see America first had the right dope." (*Don Sturdy in the Land of Volcanoes* 61)

Payson's Boy Scouts find the Rocky Mountains better than anything in Switzerland (*Panama-Pacific Exposition* 137–138). Meeting some foreigners on her trip west, Honey Bunch concludes that "the people probably wanted their children to grow up in a country where there was more room and a fairer chance to succeed than in the country from which they had come" (69). The Lone Ranger speaks of the "keen wits and cleverness that only a new, brave country can produce" (*The Lone Ranger* 120).

That the United States produces a special set of moral values is revealed in the assertion of Tom Swift, Jr., that "the Brungarians may mistreat prisoners in their own country, but we won't use their tactics" (*Race to the Moon* 46). After recovering his new explosive, Tom Jr. affirms that "this element can be of great help to mankind, but those rebels [i.e., non-Americans] probably would have blown us all to bits" (*Flying Lab* 207). When he tells Asa Pike from Maine, "You're a loyal American," Asa replies, "Anything to help Uncle Sam" (*Rocket Ship* 33). "Anything" can be a frightening word.

The great beauty and the values of the United States inspire a deep patriotism in all series characters, so deep, in fact, that it can wipe away personal animosities. Don Sturdy and Teddy undertake to save Brox and Rodent, villains and poor sports, who have been captured by natives that they have mistreated in *Don Sturdy in Lion Land*: "Of course we'll have to do something about it." "Naturally," said Captain Sturdy, "they're fellow countrymen of ours" (181). In *Desert of Mystery* Don says, "Do you suppose that I, an American, can let another American remain in the power of those rascally bandits if it's in any way possible to rescue him?" (21). As Fred Erisman noted, Tom Swift was an *American* inventor, his work being done for American use. Much of his effort produced weapons for the U.S. to use in war. When Tom traveled, he remained skeptical about foreign lands and foreigners. Well into the fourth decade of the century, Tom has to decide between the life of Ned Newton and giving up his latest invention as ransom. The answer, Tom concludes, is What is the life of his best friend or his own compared to the safety of his country? (*Television Detector* 178).

This general patriotism is all the more interesting in the face of a counterview, almost as strong: "Travel broadens the mind" (*The Rover Boys on Land and Sea* 5). The most geographic of series, Don Sturdy, makes many powerful statements about the worth of America, yet no adventure of Don's takes place in the United States, and in all twelve volumes, no more than fifty pages of any book occur on the North American continent. The series is filled with the romantic lure of the far-off. Although many of the Rover Boys' adventures do happen in the United States, Dick, Tom, and Sam spend considerable time elsewhere. In the series, travel of any kind is soul enriching. "Travel is the best kind of education," Don Sturdy says. "What you see with your eyes you'll remember far better than what you learn by rote" (*Land of Volcanoes* 6). Payson's Boy Scouts find that "during their western stay they had broadened and developed considerably; they had returned to Hampton better, mentally, physically, for the trip" (*Army Airship* 33). Travel has accomplished as much for Don Sturdy, whose uncle admits, "I never saw a lad who could show so much resourcefulness and courage in a pinch" (*Among the Gorillas* 3). Just such qualities did Dorothy develop, and they were all used to quit the wonderfully romantic Land of Oz and return to Kansas. Yet surely no one reads *The Wizard of Oz* for its Kansas sections.

From the late 1960's on, the series generally avoided any statements about the United States and travel, and hence avoided earlier value judgments altogether. The Bobbsey Twins may visit Jamaica, Knossos on Crete, or Africa, but their purpose is to solve mysteries, not broaden their minds. "You will enjoy the added flavor of a foreign land as the adventurous Bobbsey Twins stumble upon another mystery," the publisher's blurb for *The Greek Hat Mystery* informs us. "What a pretty place Nairobi," Nan remarks in *The Tagalong Giraffe* (12). Clearly, though, one is traveling "on business" and not for the good of one's soul. The United States may still be "God's country," but no reader could tell the fact from the children's series.

Nature and Animals

Again, in the series attitude toward nature, one finds ambivalence. On the one hand is a carryover from the Romantic and Transcendental movements. "When I step out of doors it is directly into the temple of God," says Dr. Merriam in a long lecture to Thornton Burgess's Boy Scouts (*In a Trapper's Camp* 102–103). He adds, "In nature one sees God made manifest."

Miscellaneous Aspects of Life & Society 169

His ideas are echoed by Sparrer Muldoon, the New York street urchin, after some weeks in the woods: "Bein' out here makes me feel just like Oi do when Oi goes to Church an' de sun comes trew dem colored winders and de organ plays." "Right, son," the trapper replies, "this is the great cathedral that God had built for himself and the littleness we feel is because of His own presence" (356). Sparrer resolves to leave the city and spend his life in nature. Virtually the same words are uttered by Anne Pierson in *Grace Harlowe's Plebe Year*: " 'It is beautiful,' said Anne, as she gazed up and down the wooded aisles carpeted in white.... 'It is like a great cathedral. I could almost kneel and pray at one of those snow-covered stumps. They are like altars' " (190). William Cullen Bryant expressed the idea in much the same way.

Perhaps under the influence of Theodore Roosevelt's doctrine of the strenuous life, the authors of various series argue that nature does more than reveal God: it makes a man a man. As Thornton Burgess puts it (with help from James Oliver Curwood and Harold Bell Wright),

> The red gods dwell
> 'Neath a mystic spell;
> The old flame glows,
> And the red blood flows,
> And a man's a man
> For a little span
> (*The Boy Scouts in a Trapper's Camp* 41)

The Scouts are told that "the fresh air of the woods will make a man of you in a week, more than New York could do in a lifetime" (89). Grace Harlowe also is told of Tom Gray, "If he has inherited [his uncle's] wholesome taste for the outdoors and nature, he must be a fine fellow" (*Plebe Year* 123). And Tom turns out to be just that: " 'He's like a breath of fresh air,' thought Grace, and indeed it was disclosed later that he intended to study forestry because he loved the country and the open air and taking long walking trips.... He was full of energy and ambition and infused such a wholesome vigor into whatever he did that the young people felt a new enthusiasm in his presence" (162). Smithy, one of Carter's Boy Scouts, refers to his father, "who had dearly loved to hunt and fish and spend his time in the woods, close to nature, as do all men who are worthy of the name" (*In the Rockies* 254). By contrast, in the 1987 Hardy Boys *Hostages of Hate*, the chief villain, the Dutchman, is described as having "the look of a man who spent too much time indoors" (95).

As certain series devoted to the natural life developed, they became ironically less and less concerned with the activities implied in their titles. *The Campfire Girls in After Years*, for instance, the sixth volume in that series, is concerned with political and domestic issues, the characters rarely venturing out of doors. While the cover shows three girls dressed as Indians paddling a canoe, no one in the story ever gets close to one. The Outdoor Girls Series followed the same path: *At Cedar Ridge* allots one half-page to the building of a fire and the cooking of a fish; otherwise the Girls are involved with distinctly indoor matters, such as dances, bowling, and bank robberies, and the book's subtitle is *The Mystery of the Old Windmill,* almost a Nancy Drew title. Apparently authors, publishers, and readers had lost interest in what had initially motivated the series.

"Nature is very kind," says Tom Swift, Jr., "if we'll only pay attention to what she has to offer. Everywhere she maintains a balance" (*The Caves of Nuclear Fire* 213). Although this idea is expressed in many series, ambivalence enters again, for nature even more frequently appears "red in tooth and claw." There is, for example, an astonishing number of storms and other natural cataclysms in the series. Storms have been used to create fear and suspense during the whole life of series books in the twentieth century. The Rover Boys faced storms continually, indeed, it seems, invariably; storms occurred not only in such logical places as the mountains, on land and sea, and in Southern waters, but also in New York City. When they went to the mountains, the Boys faced natural threats on six different occasions. Payson's Boy Scouts battle a storm for two entire days in *Under Sealed Orders,* a storm dominates the first two chapters of Shaler's *The Boy Scouts and the Prize Pennant*. Rick Brant is storm tossed in *100 Fathoms Under*. Storms seem equally inevitable in the Nancy Drew books, a relatively urban series. Storms bedevil the Hardy Boys in the opening chapters of *The House on the Cliff, Hunting for Hidden Gold,* and *The Hidden Harbor*

Miscellaneous Aspects of Life & Society 171

Mystery, and later in several others; in *The Sign of the Crooked Arrow* are found a flash flood and a forest fire. Grace Harlowe has to fight a sandstorm on the Great American Desert. Tom Swift is exercised by both a storm and a fire in *Tom Swift and His Airship*. Don Sturdy set some kind of record by battling a storm at least twice in every volume, occasionally three times. Tom Swift, Jr., following where his father led, weathered a storm in outer space (*Rocket Ship* 169ff.) and an earthquake and tidal wave in *The Visitor from Planet X*.

Nature, then, is shown as a consistent enemy and a constant danger, even in series which extol the beauties of the wildlife. In Thornton Burgess's purple-prose eulogies there is a recognition of this threat: "An overwhelming sense of littleness and insignificance swept over him. There was something sinister and threatening in the lowering hills. . . . It is a feeling which everyone who is alone for the first time in the wilderness experiences" (*Trapper's Camp* 247). Since he has just noted the beneficent presence of God in nature, one wonders what the "something sinister and threatening" can be.

Similarly irreconcilable attitudes are found in relation to animals. Despite persistent attempts throughout the twentieth century to foster a love of animals and a respect for their rights as fellow inhabitants of our planet, the series, almost without exception—and the exception lasted only two years, from 1986 to 1987, and produced only six books—denigrate animals, use them, and destroy them savagely. Few central characters have pets. Nancy Drew's dog, Togo, is seen two or three times; the Bobbsey Twins' cat, Snoop, and dog, Snap, also make brief appearances; the Hollisters have a cat and dog. All are sources of humor—cute, clumsy, and funny. They never have important roles and are never taken seriously.

More significantly, animals, like other natural phenomena, are objects of terror in most important series from 1899 to the present. The number of attacks by ferocious animals is surprising, and there is much repetition in the kinds of animals used to inspire fear in characters and readers: dogs, wildcats, snakes, bears, birds, wolves, fish, spiders, bulls, gorillas, even a rhinoceros. Many major endangered species are calculatedly shown as terrifying.

That a wolf might be met in the Rocky Mountains is not beyond belief, but that Grace Harlowe and her friends are attacked by a pack of wolves only three miles outside of a rather sizable city may strain one's credulity. In many other instances, wild animals attack characters under conditions that are at least unexpected and occasionally bizarre. Don Sturdy fights lions, leopards, and tigers in the Sargasso Sea, for example. Though many young readers may own a German Shepherd, *The Case of the Runaway Money* contains a picture of Freddie Bobbsey menaced by such a dog, who stands only a foot away from the boy's face, fangs bared to reveal the most frightening teeth (41).

Far more serious is the utterly violent, indeed sadistic, manner in which animals are destroyed. The woundings and death agonies of animals are recounted at length with unnecessarily vivid detail until one is compelled to believe that the characters and their authors enjoy witnessing and describing animal pain and suffering. Often the process is disgusting, frequently horrifying. The note is a decidedly unhealthy one in the books.

A snake is beaten to death over a long period in *The Bobbsey Twins in the Country* (46), a series for very young readers. Despite Thornton Burgess's many books about Reddy Fox, Longlegs the Heron, and others, and despite his avowed love for nature, he is frankly open to a charge of hypocrisy: in *The Boy Scouts in a Trapper's Camp*, Burgess writes about places "where the foxes and other critters with nice fur coats are sittin' around waiting to put their little footsies in our traps" (41). He goes further: "When I see the blood on the trail I kenned he was hit hard and would not travel far if left alone, so I sat down and smoked a pipe . . . he was getting weak and didna go far before he laid down again. This time I got another shot and broke his backbone but at that it took two more shots to finish him" (150). Later Burgess describes how a trapped bear "marches off with nineteen pounds of trap and the clog dragging from his foot" (170). Carter's Scouts shoot a sheep in the Rocky Mountains: "The big horn sheep fell over on the rock and kicked several times. 'There he goes now, and see him limp, will you, fellows? I hit him, tey, I sure did' " (130). The boys also kill a mother wolf and most of her cubs, "to rid the country of pests"; later a cub shows up, and one of the scouts says, "We'll have to knock him over the head, Aleck. . . . Well, the other must have escaped

Miscellaneous Aspects of Life & Society 173

somehow ... it doesn't matter to us, though, for the little beast will perish, without a mother to supply it food" (218). The scouts also enjoy killing animals. "Thereupon Bumpus picked up a long pole and aimed a vicious blow at the head of the snake. Taking the creature fairly across the neck, he sent it spinning away ... the fat scout raised his pole and brought it down several times with might and main on the head of the fearful looking reptile" (91). Uncle Sam's Boys kill a bear for the space of three pages; first the animal is stabbed with a bayonet, then shot, shot again, bayonetted once more, shot again, and finally "beaten severely over the head" (*In the Ranks* 91–93).

But it is the Rover Boys who excel at sadism. In the mountains they kill a wolf: "Tom swung his gun around by the barrel and hit the wolf a sharp rap on the head. ... Taking quick aim, he fired. The shot ... took the wolf directly in the neck ... he gave a yelp, and then began turning over and over in intense pain ... it managed to hide itself, and crawl away, seriously, if not mortally, wounded" (135–136). Previously they have left badly wounded wild turkeys to die slowly. Hemingway's Francis Macomber was told that such a thing is not done, but the Rovers do it. Jumped by a wildcat, "Dick brought around the gun barrel and poked it into the mouth of the wildcat. With a gurgle of pain, the beast fell back ... catching up a club, he aimed a blow which crushed the animal's skull" (152–153). "The charge of shot entered the bear's shoulder, making a number of painful, but not dangerous, wounds. ... Sam fired a second time, this time hitting the bear in the left hind leg"; they then set fire to the bear's face (185). Later, there is another bear attack: "One of the bears was hit full in the left eye ... the other was hit in the neck. Then Tom fired the shotgun ... and the bear Dick had hit was wounded in the side. ... Bang, went the piece ... the charge entered the beast's ear, and ... to make sure, John Barrow stepped in with a hunting knife in hand, and plunged the blade into his throat" (209–210). In *On Land and Sea*, Dick is attacked by a snake. "Old Jenny's aim was both swift and true, and the head of the reptile received a blow which knocked out one eye. 'Cut its head off,' Dick panted. It was no easy job ... but the head came off at last" (117). In only two books one can find thirteen such incidents; twenty-eight more volumes in the series makes the number staggering. Evidently the work of the naturalistic novelists affected even the children's series, for locations and details of wounds are given with the precision of Jack London and Theodore Dreiser.

The Don Sturdy books, also produced by the Stratemeyer Syndicate, contain much the same thing. When Don visits "lion land," he and his party catch an old lion in a net; "I'll put him out of his misery," says Don, though the animal is in no misery at all. Later they capture as many lions as they were ordered to do by a zoo in America, but "a few were old and were dispatched on the spot" (210); it occurs to no one to let them go. Through the entire series, Captain Hardy is described as just itching to get out and kill animals; most animals in this series are called "brutes," "monsters," and referred to as "ugly," "horrible," or "hideous." The same details of death are found: when Captain Sturdy kills a crocodile, "the bullet entered its right eye and penetrated the brain" (*Among the Gorillas* 110).

Lest one imagine that such treatment of animals is limited to earlier series, two later series (which in other ways are admirable) should be examined. In *More All-of-a-Kind Family*, Charlotte notices a swarm of flies eating from a garbage can; one lands on her nose. "Why, there was a fly swatter in her hand ... she raised it, bringing it down with a hard smack. ... Several flies fell to the ground." Speculating upon whether it is cruel to kill flies, she recalls her teacher's lecture on germs carried by flies. "'Ugh!' Charlotte shivered with disgust. 'I'm not going to eat any more of your old germs!' Whack! Whack! She laid about with the swatter furiously. ... She stopped for a moment. ... How many could she catch at one time? In the fairy story, the tailor killed seven at one blow!" She slams the swatter against the wall but kills only three. " 'You nasty old creatures! I'm going to keep right on swatting away till I smash even more than the tailor!' ... Triumphantly she held up the fly swatter. 'Ha, ha! Eight at one blow!' she whooped" (108–111). There is a relish in the scene, almost a blood lust; even in view of the need to prevent the spread of germs, the episode is unnecessarily ugly, almost egregious.

When the Woodland Gang goes to England, Bill asks one of their hosts, "How can you stand eating those cute animals [rabbits]?" Mr. Hill answers, "I figure the garden will feed either them or me. So I must get rid of them." With no more thought, Bill responds, "Then we will help you." Sammy is ecstatic at the prospect of a rabbit hunt: "Yippee! ... we're going to the Big Rabbit Round-up!" His words carry over as the title of chapter 9. Using a ferret, the hunters place nets over the rabbit holes or block them with stones. "Mr. Hill lowered the ferret into a hole. They heard it running down. In a few seconds hundreds of squealing rabbits began to run out of other holes, into the nets. ... Sammy said, 'I hate this. These rabbits are so scared!' " Lady Foot admits, "I do too ... but they have to go." The scene ends with a flat and frightening sentence: "They took the bags of rabbits down to the truck" (*Missing Will* 77ff.). To the imagination of young readers is left their ultimate destination.

In all the series only Tom Swift, Jr., is reluctant to kill, and consistently so. When attacked by a giant squid, Tom says, "I hate to destroy this creature" (*Jetmarine* 138); under attack by a leopard in *The Caves of Nuclear Fire,* he says, "I hate to shoot this beautiful specimen if I can avoid it"; and later, when a bear charges the Swift party, "In spite of the peril, no one wanted to shoot the handsome old fellow" (79).

Not until 1986 did a series appear dedicated to a genuine concern for animals. Doc Taylor is the proprietor of the Animal Inn, a clinic that gives its name to the series. The publisher's blurb for *A Kid's Best Friend* states, "It's not fair that animals don't have the same rights as people." While maintaining that stance, individual books in the series still emphasize unnecessarily the suffering of animals. In *Monkey Business* Zefferelli's Kosmic Karnival mistreats its animals. "A mangy bear [with] matted fur ... and a lot of bald spots" is found together with a young elephant whose "eyes were dull and listless" and "a small capuchin monkey [who] was huddled in the corner of its cage. Its eyes were bleary and filled with mucus" (27). Each entry involves the rescue or curing of sick, injured, or mistreated animals; their condition is fully detailed before the final restoration.

At least one assumed a decent motive. In *Scaredy Cat* (the title refers to a human) Doc Taylor's daughter, Val, makes an issue of not eating meat, though her veterinarian father does. She also delivers a diatribe: "I hate it when dogs have their ears cropped. Tails, too. It doesn't seem right that people cut off parts of animals just to make them look different. Poor dogs don't have any choice. Maybe [they] liked their ears the way they were" (27). When Toby tells her, "You're an animal nut. . . . You're not like most people" (28), he sounds a vivid social note. The usual attitude that animals are to be used for human satisfaction is eminently clear in *The Bobbsey Twins' Adventures with Baby May*, a 1968 rewriting of the 1924 *The Bobbsey Twins and Baby May*. In the earlier book, Baby May is an abandoned human infant; in the later, she is an elephant (some rewrites are curious). The Twins' friend, Nan, has entered a big photography contest. "You know what I'd do if I should win? I'd take pictures of animals . . . in every country and I'd have them published in a big book. Whatever money I made from it would go to help needy boys and girls" (15). Not, one notes, to help needy animals.

One last example: *The Blue Poodle Mystery*, a 1980 Bobbsey Twins entry, involves a young ballet dancer's dog, Eclair, who is painted blue before being stolen. Momentary concern is expressed that the dog could become sick if he licks the paint, but much amusement is found in "the polka dot poodle." The search leads to a group of thieves supplying animals for illegal experiments conducted by Dr. Westgard, who is "trying to establish a big name for himself in the medical world. . . . He really believes he's going to win a Nobel Prize [Tom tells the Twins]. . . . Ha-ha-ha! That's a joke!" (123). No other objection to animal experimentation can be found in any series.

Ironies abound. Throughout the twentieth century there have been persistent efforts to preserve the natural environment. The early work of John Muir and John Burroughs virtually coincided with the emergence of the modern children's series, marked by the Rover Boys' first appearance in 1899. Similarly, especially in the past three decades, much energy has been spent in educating humans, in particular children, to a concern for the rights and abuses of animals. Yet the most popular and best-selling children's reading has for the past ninety years remained for practical purposes oblivious of both environmental and animal rights efforts. Considering the didactic impact of such books on young readers, the picture is woeful.

Violence

What can be seen in retrospect as the major series—Tom Swift, Nancy Drew, the Bobbsey Twins, the Hardy Boys—as well as

Miscellaneous Aspects of Life & Society 177

many others totaling more than eight hundred books, were the products of the Stratemeyer Syndicate. To find fault with Edward Stratemeyer is not difficult: for example, if he did not directly foster racial stereotypes, he certainly perpetuated them. But as Christine Thorndill correctly pointed out in 1978, Stratemeyer was concerned that "desirable codes of social behavior be inculcated in the youthful readers"; consequently, his Syndicate encouraged respect for adults and authority and in particular "curtailed violence" (246).

Yet despite what would seem editorial policy on the part of Stratemeyer and other series producers as well, violence has been a consistent aspect of the series. In the earliest books, such as the Rover Boys, Grace Harlowe, the various Boy Scout series, the Bobbsey Twins, and Tom Swift, violence was largely composed of escapes from rampaging bulls and wolves, mechanical inventions that fail, or runaway boats on rapids. None involved more than suspense. After the first decade of the twentieth century, however, violence took on more serious overtones.

In *The Boy Scouts in a Trapper's Camp* (1922) the victim of an automobile accident has "one leg doubled under him in a way that denoted a bad break. His face was badly cut by the glass of the wind shield, and what was more, the crimson stream gushed in little spurts from a jagged gash on one arm" (65). In *Don Sturdy in the Land of Volcanoes* (1925), chapter 22, "A Night of Horror," deals with a sandstorm during which the party is bombarded with "flying pumice, some like needle points, others . . . as big as hickory nuts, with sharp, jagged edges that left blood behind . . . the razor-like pumice cut through the cloth and lacerated their flesh from head to feet" (186). Chapter 24, "A Lake of Fire," piles horror upon horror as Don and Brick fall into pits of molten lava; for almost thirty pages there is no letup of violence and terror. One of the villains in *The Lone Ranger* (1936) plans a murder: "I got a sheath knife . . . with a thin blade that will slide through two blankets as if they was cheesecloth. I'm not likely to miss Murch's heart the first time, but I'll run the knife into him three times quick just to make sure, and then I'll leave it there" (58). Later Glencoe is tortured in an Indian camp: "They stuck splinters into him, into his fingers and arms and feet, and set them afire one by one. They cut him with their knives about the face and chest. Then one of the braves came up to him with an iron bar, white hot at the end, and held it a few seconds close to Glencoe's eyes" (212). Virtually all the early Chip Hilton books contain a description of Chip's father, who was crushed to death under a brick kiln. Teenaged Rick Brant engages in considerable violence. During a fight in *100 Fathoms Under* (1948), "his tent stake was already swishing down in a vicious arc. His hand stung as his weapon caught the captain squarely on the forehead" (78). In the midst of an Arab attack in *The Egyptian Cat Mystery* (1961), Rick "squeezed the trigger and was rewarded by a choked yell.... He fired again, and a burnoosed figure grabbed the door frame for support.... He was lying on the floor with both hands clutched at his throat gagging and gasping for air" (160).

Surprisingly, in view of constant criticism of racial, sexual, and national attitudes expressed in the various series, there has been no marked objection to violence, perhaps because much of it during the 1930's and 1940's was that of the Saturday afternoon movie serial; certainly there were threats of physical violence and death, but they were not carried out. In these years, most of the Nancy Drew books dealt with injustice—a valuable property is stolen, someone is accused of a criminal act, money is withheld from its rightful owners. The 1984 series about the Woodland Gang still settled such problems. Until the late 1970's murder was not found in children's series, and death rarely occurred. In these later years, however, while there were not significant changes in the personalities of characters or their relationships, plots did begin to emphasize increased violence. In *The Case of the Disappearing Diamonds* (1987), a bomb is planted in Nancy Drew's mailbox (it goes off, almost killing her and Ned), a failing airplane engine forces the heroes to crash land, and a villain pushes Nancy out of a hospital window and beats on her fingers as she clings to the sill.

The Hardy Boys middle series stresses high-tech instruments, especially computers, and very contemporary events. *Revenge of the Desert Phantom* (1985), by way of example, involves the Boys with African politics as they try to get Niki Jerusa, daughter of an apparently assassinated president of a small African nation, home to take control. Jumped in Paris by six attackers, Joe finds "the salty taste of blood filled his mouth. He coiled his heel in a karate kick ... to the waiter's solar plexus" (32). He and his brother are "roughly strapped to cafe chairs, their waists bound by steel cables" (43). Once in Africa, they acquire the Rhino, a modified tank with a cannon and a machine gun; as they move toward Niki's home, they are attacked by six vehicles and there is gunfire on both sides. A clear revelation of the increase in violence is Frank's reaction to the battle:

> While his own life had been in jeopardy many times... until now he'd never actually fired a gun, much less a machine gun, on another human being. True, it was in self-defense and therefore justifiable, but it nonetheless was a jarring experience. Had he hit anyone? Had he killed anyone? (87)

Program for Destruction (1987), as its cover announces, pits the Hardy Boys against "a factory filled with crazed computers." There are death threats, time bombs, and "accidents" with computer-controlled automobiles. Toward the end they are trapped in a factory while the "computer-controlled assembly line robots had gone totally berserk!" (116). Most apparent in the book is the fact that one can destroy the world by introducing a computer virus into the world's computers: humanity is at the mercy of its instruments.

Still in the middle series is the feeling of the Saturday serial: one does not have serious concern for the fate of heroes. On the third level of the series, on the other hand, violence becomes unrestrained, and the children's fiction series have clearly taken a different and unexpected direction. The claim that the crimes involved in series do not include murder can no longer be sustained. By the 1980's murder has become a staple. While series with girls as heroines are less extreme in their violence than those with boy heroes, murder and violence have infiltrated them as well. Titles in the Nancy Drew Files series are *Murder on Ice, Smile and Say Murder,* and *Recipe for Murder. Murder is no Joke* is the seventh entry in the Doris Fein series. As a corollary, variations on the word "death" are frequently found in titles from the past decade: *Doris Fein: Deadly Aphrodite* and *Doris Fein: Dead Heat at Long Beach*; the Nancy Drew Files include *Deadly Intent, Never Say Die,* and *Very Deadly Yours*; the Hardy Boys Casefiles, *Dead on Target, Deathgame,* while the back cover of *Hostages of Hate* advertises the book as

"Double-edged death." Such words were never seen before the present decade. Previously the dominant words in the titles of children's series were "mystery," "clue," and "secret." Even if one admits that publishers have extended the age limits of readers to well into the teens, the level, type, and frequency of violence in such "children's books" is as appalling as it is in current motion pictures and television.

With its thirteen-year-old hero, Stephen Lane, the Race Against Time series was clearly intended to appeal to younger readers. Yet the gap between it and the "original" series intended for such an age group is vast indeed. The cover scene of *The Secret of the Third Watch* (1984), for example, shows a rescue from fire, smoke, and falling timbers. In the book itself are found four drawings, the first showing Uncle Richard being pushed from a subway platform into the path of an arriving train (the cover of *Blood Relations* in the Hardy Boys Casefiles series displays a similar scene); the second depicts the "ape man" preparing to administer a lethal anesthetic to Stephen. In the first three pages, Ralph is shot by a tranquilizer dart. Later the heroes are forced to back into a burning theatre and are trapped in a free-falling elevator in the Empire State Building. There are countless fights and threats from guns and knives.

The violence seems taken for granted. Halfway through the book, Uncle Richard suggests that Stephen respond to an inquiry: "Tell them there's been a bomb threat or a suicide attempt from the observation deck. . . . You know, something that any well-informed visitor would expect in this wonderful town [New York City]. . . . After you learn to survive here, the rest of the world is a cinch" (78–79). All the attacks from knives and guns, as well as what Barbara Moran and Susan Steinfirst call "other exotic forms of fighting" (115), are minutely described. The series also includes female characters who can fight as well as the males—evidently a mark of feminine distinction.

Nancy Drew is also proud of her karate skills, though they seldom work for her, and she has fights in virtually every entry in the Nancy Drew Files. Other matters have changed as well. As early as the second volume in the series, *Deadly Intent* (1986), Nancy narrowly escapes a knife thrown at her. The villain, James Li, menaces Nancy and her friends with a gun, then announces his intention of leaving them to die in a burning

Miscellaneous Aspects of Life & Society 181

warehouse. In *Murder on Ice*, as the blurb advertises, Nancy "finds herself matching wits with a dangerous killer."

But these beginnings quickly develop into more serious—and unusual—violence. In *Stay Tuned for Danger* (1987) death threats are leveled at TV star Rick Arlen from the first chapter (they are, incidentally, well-disguised clues to the potential murderer); one actually appears on the teleprompter and is read during taping by an unsuspecting actress. A klieg light is dropped on Rick during a performance; an insane fan tries to push him off a ferry; a taxi drives deliberately into Nancy and Rick; a bomb rigged behind his makeup mirror explodes, embedding glass in his hands—his face and eyes are saved only by a towel over them; finally acid is introduced into a tube of his makeup. In addition there are scattered gun and bomb threats against Nancy; the fact that they are unsuccessful does little to vitiate the seriousness of the intended actions.

In *Recipe for Murder* (1988) the violence is no longer only potential. At the end of chapter 1, Dr. Claude Des Pres is poisoned during his introductory lecture at the International Cooking School. After his recovery, Des Pres attacks Paul Slesak in the butchery room using a meat cleaver; Slesak fights back with a butcher knife. Nancy is attacked by the killer, who tries to strangle her. A doctored oven explodes, the flames engulfing Trent Richards. The next attempt on Trent's life is successful, when he is knocked out and left to freeze to death in the kitchen refrigerator.

Unusual forms of violence are common also to the Doris Fein series. In the first book in which Doris appears, *Dr. Doom: Superstar* (1978), Arnold Whitman tries to kill Danny Breckenridge from the lighting booth with a rifle he had taken from his father's arsenal; the elder Whitman is leader of the Sentinels of Freedom, "our local version of the KKK and the John Birch Society." His home contains "enough equipment to outfit an entire regiment! Rifles, grenades, anti-tank weapons" (135). As matters turn out, "the shot missed Danny Breckenridge all right. But it hit Mickey Lerner square in the chest. He's dead, Larry" (126). In yet another twist, Mickey was already dead, electrocuted by a cable attached to his guitar. Keith Jones, incidentally, a homosexual, had introduced Lerner to Danny; then he becomes jealous because Danny and Mickey are spending too much time in each other's company: "I thought," Keith says, "you were, you know, together. He was only using me to get into Danny's back up band . . . he called me a fat, slobbering faggot. That's when I decided to make things like they were before he ever came into our lives, Danny. I did it . . . for both of us" (150).

During *Phantom of the Casino* (1981) Helen Grayson backs Doris into a closet at gunpoint, telling the girl, "And if you move a hair, you get an extra eye" (130). *Dead Heat at Long Beach* (1983) finds Perez belting Doris and Major Alcala into a racing car, forcing whiskey down Doris's throat, and setting the throttle at full racing speed to make their deaths look like the result of drunk driving.

Opening the trunk of Steven Sachs's Cadillac, Doris finds that "Georgie Stark wasn't still inside the club. He was inside the trunk of the Cadillac. And he was very, *verry* dead" (*Murder Is No Joke* 57). Earlier, when he was drunk, Steven had killed a man and run from the accident. Georgie was with him and had been blackmailing Sachs ever since. As Steven explains the murder to Doris, he says, "I studied karate for three years. . . . I accidentally hit him in the throat and crushed his windpipe" (86). Steven also kills Karl Roman, who he thinks has a tape recording of Georgie's murder: "I chopped him from behind. But when he fell, he hit his head on one of those concrete bunkers" (87). Planning to get rid of Doris by faking an airplane accident, he finds the teenager fighting back. As Doris tells it, "I didn't respond. I knew if I did, he'd give me one of those chops to the windpipe that had killed Georgie. . . . Instead of screaming, I grabbed hold of his ear with my teeth and bit as hard as I could. . . . I felt part of it tear as I spun loose" (90). Only temporarily successful, Doris is left in the aircraft after Steven forces her to swallow drugs that will render her unconscious. She forces herself to vomit "the gush of fluids and half-digested pills onto my lap" (104).

Such graphic descriptions seem more suited to a Raymond Chandler novel than to one designed for children. But in *Doris Fein: Deadly Aphrodite* (1982) a different and stronger form of violence is worked on Doris. Always given to overeating, Doris has become, in her own words, "Mount Fein" (6). Her boyfriend, Carl Suzuki, left her when she became a wealthy heiress, and an old flame, Larry Small, is coming to see her; to get her weight down, Doris checks into the $1,000 a-day health club, Aphrodite's. There she is injected with what she is told is a special formula, JK-4; actually she becomes addicted to amphetamines—speed—shots during the day and sleeping pills at night. In the name of health, she becomes a drug addict, her body treated to a kind of violence one does not expect in a series book for young people—a kind one hopes not to see again.

If current movies contain an obligatory sex sequence, most of the new, or third, series contain obligatory fights. Their violence is impressive when first encountered; subsequently, one becomes inured to it. Perhaps the trouble lies in this fact: producers feel that violent shock is necessary to keep audiences coming back, when ironically just the opposite may be true. In any case, the third Tom Swift series (after the originals that stopped in the early 1930's and the Tom Swift, Jrs., that ended in the middle 1960's), despite its setting in some future time, has its share of attacks with karate chops, aluminum bars, and other hardware. In *The Astral Fortress* (1981) Tom confronts the villain, David Luna, "suddenly bringing up the box end of the wrench. It caught Luna under the chin and sent him flying backward.... Luna spat a mixture of saliva, blood, and chipped teeth onto the ground" (102–103).

Worse than actual revealed violence, which allows no room for reader imagination, is that which is potential or uncontrolled. Here is the reason that the Doris Fein books make such a strong impact: they suggest a kind of violence for which we are unprepared. Dr. Grotz in *The City in the Stars* (1981) is a genuine psychopath—one for whom normal rules and restraints have no meaning. "He rather enjoyed being heavy-handed at times. It tended to put fear in the hearts of his enemies, and fear was his most powerful weapon" (41). Grotz wants the Nobel Prize and rushes his findings into print without adequate testing, in order to beat any competition. When his assistant, Dr. Greg Ellison, is flying one of Grotz's untested crafts, he is the victim of an explosion: "Maybe it's better this way, Grotz thought. No witnesses to his failure" (98). A groan on the intercom, however, shows that Ellison is still alive. "Grotz swallowed quickly. He shouldn't be alive... spoiling all his plans" (99). When Ellison survives, his superior hires "two power-hungry thugs [who] loved their work.... He had never asked them to kill for him before. He knew they would want a lot of monetary compensation for that. He would pay it gladly. . . . Dr. Greg Ellison could not live" (102). The thugs fail, and Dr. Grotz muses, "They'd signed their own death warrants" (110).

Although Dr. Grotz's final conclusion can be anticipated, it is nonetheless shocking: "It was funny how, in the last few hours, he had begun to think of murder as a viable tool in the shaping of his destiny. It felt so natural, so right. . . . Why hadn't he considered murder before?" (111–112). He carries out his "logic" and attempts to kill Tom and Ben by tampering with their on-board computer, and toward the end of the book, he and his thugs administer another beating. All of it seems very strong medicine for young readers to swallow. One is dealing with genuine evil, the product of a man whose only concern is himself and whose ego sees only obstacles to be removed. Life is of no consequence.

It seems of no more consequence to the creators of the Hardy Boys Casefiles. This third and latest Hardy Boys series raises the level of violence to a par with the films of Charles Bronson and Clint Eastwood and the fiction of Robert B. Parker and Trevanian. In no other children's series—especially none of so long duration—does a consistently appearing character die. Yet after sixty years and almost ninety titles, on the first page of *Dead on Target* (1987), the first volume in the series, Iola Morton, Joe Hardy's girlfriend, is blown apart by a bomb planted in the Hardy's car. The eighteen-page chapter, a long flashback leading to the killing, ends, "But the car—and Iola—had erupted into a ball of white hot flame" (18). The title is thus almost mockingly obscene. In chapter 4, the Hardys are pursued through a shopping mall by a dart-shooting assassin, who, though he misses Frank and Joe, does kill a security guard, merely an innocent onlooker. On page 53 a terrorist commits suicide by biting a cyanide capsule. Here are three violent deaths in the first third of the novel.

Though intended for "older readers," the series is indistinguishable from purely adult books. The series is advertised thus at the end of a Nancy Drew entry, *False Moves:* "Computer whiz Frank and the charming, athletic Joe are deep into national intrigue and high-tech drama. The pace of these mysteries just never lets up. . . . Bond has high-tech equipment, Indiana Jones

Miscellaneous Aspects of Life & Society 185

courage and daring. . . . Only the Hardy Boys Casefiles have it all . . . a new action-packed series written for older readers." Throughout the Casefiles emphasis is placed on violence, threats of death, fights, injuries, bombs. One quarter of each book is devoted to scenes of specific violence.

Iola's death is the basic motive for much of the rest of the series, which focuses on terrorist activity throughout the world: she has been used up. Titles are quite different from *The Tower Treasure* (1927), *Hunting for Hidden Gold* (1928), or even *The Short Wave Mystery* (1945): *Evil, Inc.* (1987), *Death Game* (1987), *Cult of Crime* (1987). All of *Hostages of Hate* (1987) deals with the terrorist takeover of an airline, ironically during an antiterrorist convention in Washington, D.C. The Hardy Boys are involved because this time Callie Shaw, Frank's girlfriend throughout the series, is among the hostages. Frank tells Joe, "We're going up against a bunch of terrorists with machine guns. To top everything off, we're going in blind" (61).

There is much emphasis on TV violence. Fights average six pages in length, and since there are six of them on the average, a quarter of each book is given over to fights, each minutely described, with knives, guns, and other weapons and with exact details of bodily pressure points that render opponents unconscious. In the final scene of *Hostages of Hate*, the terrorists spray the airplane and its occupants with machine gun fire, and a live grenade is tossed about. In fact, Joe throws the grenade out of a window into the midst of surrounding police and government officials without looking to see where it may land or whom it may hurt. In *Dead on Target* darts are used to kill three times, once by the heroes. After he is stabbed in the hand during *Hostages of Hate*, Joe is unable to hang onto a villain because blood causes his hand to slip.

In earlier series, heroes never resorted to the tactics of villains. Not so in *Hostages of Hate*: the Hardys tie up the head terrorist, wire him with a bomb, and put the detonators in his mouth! Except for the fact that two teenage heroes accomplish a rescue that an entire seminar on counterterrorism and two government agencies fail at doing, the book cannot be differentiated from adult books on the same theme. In diction, characters, and plots, this series often deals with secret agencies of governments. Trevanian's *Shibumi* (1979), a very fine and serious adult novel, presents "Ma Perkins," a woman controlling the entire unofficial CIA within the official CIA; in *Hostages of Hate* "a dignified-looking elderly lady" is "head of the Network, running it from a mansion in Virginia" (6). She is the Hardy's friend because *they* had saved *her* from an assassination attempt in *The Lazarus Plot* (1987). In *Evil, Inc.* they also save "the gray man," their network contact, from an attack by two punks, who beat him to the rhythm of a rock song. In *Dead on Target* Police Inspector Butler is head of the terrorist group.

Much of the series is motivated by revenge for Iola's death (the original series had many kinds of crimes and mysteries). The fact legitimizes vigilantism, as do the rapes in the *Death Wish* films of Charles Bronson. Indeed, at the end of *Hostages of Hate* Fenton Hardy tells his two sons, "You run off like a pair of vigilantes" (146). Earlier he had asked them whether they do not feel that the United States government might be of some help; the Boys reply, "They haven't been much help up to now" (52).

Cult of Crime (1987) deals with a religious cult in the Adirondack Mountains: human sacrifice is one of their rituals; the leader, Rajah, ultimately invades Bayport and plans to set the whole town afire, and there is a human time bomb programmed to kill on command. The ugliest and most violent scene in *Evil, Inc.* subjects Frank to the truth machine, a device which calls for running electrical wires attached to electrodes fastened directly above Frank's eyes and other parts of his body. Reference is made to a hot new music group that simulates suicide on stage. Pierre takes the Hardys through his family's dungeon, displaying various instruments of torture, among which he says, "is my favorite—a cutting machine that will slice off fingers, toes, even whole arms and legs." The machines, he notes, "are in perfect working order" (119).

One concludes that the children's fiction series have degenerated from relatively innocent mysteries and adventure to a highly serious and cynical stressing of violence and shock for their own sakes. In this one additional way children are thrust into so-called adulthood and bereft of innocence. Also significant is the fact that objectors to the series have aimed at their poor literary quality and repetitiveness and at their racial, national, and sexual biases. There has been no real objection to

Miscellaneous Aspects of Life & Society 187

their violence. Television and theatrical films seem to have created a callousness that makes their graphic violence acceptable also in children's reading matter. The phrase "rape of the innocent" was coined to describe the comic books of the late 1930's and 1940's; it seems justifiable to apply it as well to children's fiction series of the 1980's.

8 RECOMMENDED AND UNACCEPTABLE ELEMENTS

JUSTICE

WITH NO SINGLE EXCEPTION, all series books contain exact demonstrations of justice. Readers are assured that good is rewarded and evil punished. If one acts well, one can expect to benefit: Bill Tagg, the helpful tramp of *Tom Swift and His Talking Pictures*, we are told, will be "suitably rewarded" (216). If he does not act well, appropriate retribution will follow. Often punishment is humorous and embarrassing: when Alvin Beck, a bad boy whom Honey Bunch and Norman meet on their trip to Niagara Falls, tries to steal Norman's ice cream cone, he trips and falls face first into it. Punishment can be more violent: Josiah Crabtree, a villain of the Rover Boys Series, has his leg broken all to pieces and will be a cripple for life; "Mr. Crabtree was particularly mean," says Mr. Rover, and Dick adds, "Well, he is suffering for it" (*In New York* 267).

A clear relationship exists between action and result: a person performs a given action and receives the reward one would expect. No counterpart of Job is found in any series; readers and characters always know the reason for what is happening. When the evil Joshki of *Don Sturdy in the Land of Volcanoes* is killed "by a high wind" (205), the implication is obvious. More often, human agencies carry out justice. Sue Barton and her friends punish Francesca Manson, who has been tormenting Hilda Grayson, by allowing her to believe that Hilda has committed suicide (*Student Nurse*, chapter 5). Julia Crosby lies in order to keep the sophomores from using the gymnasium in *Grace Harlowe's Sophomore Year in High School*; as a result she is forbidden to use the gym herself and has to recite an extra page of history for two weeks. She weeps "tears of rage and mortification" (26).

The most notable agent of justice in a series is the Lone Ranger, who is introduced in the first volume by the statement that "his appearance on the scene of lawlessness and danger was always followed by the rescue of the unfortunate and the just punishment of guilty persons" (1-2). Usually working through legal channels, occasionally he steps into the realm of the poetic. In *The Code of the West*, for instance, he arranges to shanghai Mag Dolan, who has herself been responsible for the similar fate of many others: "You've sent hundreds of men on trips they didn't want to take.... Now it's your turn" (125).

In the area of justice, then, juvenile readers are presented with an assured moral universe where one gets one's just deserts. The reality of such a view is at least questionable.

OPTIMISM

Lest a young reader have temporary fears about the triumph of justice, he is offered a consistently optimistic tone in the series. Outright statements affirm a favorable outcome for all the actions of heroes. "Everything will come out all right in the end, I'm sure," says Cherry Ames in *Clinic Nurse* (78); "I'm sure everything will come out all right for everybody," Nancy Drew reiterates in *The Hidden Staircase* (11), adding in *The Mystery at Lilac Inn*, "I just know things will come out all right" (115). Tom Swift's friend Ned Newton looks back rather than ahead: "Everything came out all right, didn't it?" (*Talking Pictures* 216). During the Bobbsey Twins' trip to the Land of Cotton, "everything ended happily" (206).

The confidence of characters to make everything come out right is also very common. Faced with a storm during an airplane flight, Tom Swift, Jr., assures, "We'll pull out of it somehow" (*Jetmarine* 75); during a similar scene in *The Race to the Moon*, Tom is asked, "Have we any chance at all?" He replies, "Sure, we have" (68), and of course he is right. "I won't admit defeat," says Nancy Drew (*Lilac Inn* 85), and her friend Helen affirms her belief three times in two pages: "You'll discover something one of these days" (72), "you'll do it, too," and "you'll find a way out of this tangle" (73). A few pages later Nancy is reminded that "you've never failed to solve a mystery yet" (115). More than half a century later, nothing had happened to shake Nancy's confident optimism; in *Deadly Intent* (1986) checking out a dressing room, she assures Roger that its occupant evidently did not plan to go anywhere: "You're sure?" he asks, and Nancy replies, "There's no question about it" (14).

In general, the series feel that where there's life, there's likely to be hope as well. Don Sturdy literally quotes the platitude in *The Port of Lost Ships* and also in *The Desert of Mystery*. "Don't despair, Sam," Tom Rover tells his brother as they are faced with a usual predicament, "we've been in worse holes, remember, and always managed to escape with a whole skin" (*In the Mountains* 169). One suspects Don Sturdy of reading over his shoulder when he says in *Among the Gorillas*, "Cheer up, Brick . . . It's a mighty tight place, but we've been in tight places before and got out of them. We're far from dead yet" (203). Again after fifty years, Nancy Drew is still assuring Karen in *The Case of the Disappearing Diamonds*, "there's always hope" (22).

Once danger, difficulty, and despair have been faced, heroes forget them and go on to better things. "Having recovered from the effects of the storm, the Rover Boys became as light hearted as ever" (*On Land and Sea* 58). The reader is shown a world which, regardless of present darkness, is bound to lighten, and where everything that happens will have a successful and happy ending.

TRAITS OF CHARACTER

Proponents of "serious" juvenile literature condemn the series for indoctrinating children in undesirable personal qualities. As has been shown, several unfortunate views of human relations and institutions do exist in these books. In general, however, the virtues they recommend are frequently worth possessing, while the proscribed qualities are often worth avoiding. Nearly a half-dozen attitudes appear regularly and consistently.

Reason vs. Emotion

First, reason is preferable to and more productive than emotion. This idea is stated directly in innumerable series and illustrated in virtually every major hero and heroine. Exceptions are Beverly Gray, whose "quick temper was the only drawback to an otherwise sweet nature" (*Beverly Gray, Freshman* 16), and Cherry Ames, who is also said to be quick-tempered, though little evidence of the fact is seen. "Had Stonington Hunt possessed control of his rage," Payson tells us in *The Boy Scouts and the Army Airship*, he might have been many times a millionaire, but his ungovernable temper had lost him many a good chance" (118). The elder Tom Swift tells his son, "But there's no point in letting it upset us. If we do, our enemies have secured another advantage." Tom Jr. replies, "You're right, Dad.... I just wish I could take things as calmly as you do" (*Race to the Moon* 112). Usually he does. For example, when his sister puts their plane into a dive and cannot pull out, Tom takes the controls: " 'I have it,' Tom said quietly" (*Flying Lab* 44). Faced with an excited reporter, Nancy Drew remains calm; only her "flashing eyes betrayed her anger" (*Disappearing Diamonds* 33), since "Nancy didn't lose her temper very often" (122). Such calm, clear thinking and behavior "had earned her her reputation as a detective" (*Deadly Intent* 15). As noted in *Revenge of the Desert Phantom,* Frank Hardy "tended to think things through before acting. Joe tended to act first and think later" (8); in *Evil, Inc.*, Frank warns Joe of this defect, saying, "It demands a cool head, not a hothead" (17–18). The A.I. Gang resorts occasionally to physical means, but they are shown to be "brain children," who outthink their opponents.

Typical American pragmatism is involved—reason produces advantage and money. Nonetheless the principle is probably a good one to inculcate in young readers and in the books it seems possible to attain. Rob Blake in Payson's Boy Scout Series "could be cool and deliberate ... for quick thinking, as well as prompt action, always proves a good asset in emergencies" (*Under Sealed Orders* 51). Mention is made often in the Lone Ranger Series of "the iron control with which the Lone Ranger curbed his anxiety and impatience" (*The Lone Ranger* 196). Jasper Grinder loses his job in *The Rover Boys in the Mountains* because of an ungovernable temper. Despite his name, Tom Swift was probably the calmest of all series heroes. "Characteristic was it of Tom Swift to act calmly in times of stress and danger ... only for an instant did he show any signs of perturbation. Then with calmness and deliberation the young inventor quickly did a number of things still almost as cool as the proverbial cucumber" (*Undersea Search* 69–70). When his submarine breaks down at the bottom of the sea, "there was a look of alarm on the faces of Ned Newton and Mr. Damon. But Tom Swift smiled. 'This is annoying and will cause us delay,' he announced, 'but there is no danger' " (165). After the motor of his new airship fails in mid-air, his companions ask whether there is any danger; Tom answers, "I've done this same thing before and from greater heights" (*Wireless Message* 50). The words "quiet" and "quietly" are used innumerable times to describe how Tom reacts in emergencies.

Heroes, in fact, seem to thrive on emergencies. Danger apparently produces the self-control and calmness so much admired. Don Sturdy's various adventures have taught him "coolness, quick-thinking, and self-possession" (*Port of Lost Ships* 35). In an emergency, as his uncle observes, "He'll be as cool as an iceberg" (*Among the Gorillas* 133); in *Lion Land* Don decides that he "would not tamely succumb to horror" (138).

Finally reason is preferable to brawn. As a sophomore, Grace Harlowe avers, "It is better to retire with dignity than to indulge in a free-for-all fight" (19). Both the Sturdys and Swifts prefer not to use force. "I suppose we could apply some third degree methods," Captain Hardy says in *Desert of Mystery*, "but I don't like to do that except as a last resort" (175). The Swifts "were always opposed to arming any of their craft, and preferred to outwit their enemies by strategy rather than bloodshed" (*Jetmarine* 125). "We won't start hostilities," Tom Jr. says. "That's against everything Dad taught me and everything the Swift name stands for in science" (*Race to the Moon* 157). Even in the recent Hardy Boys' *Hostages of Hate*, Frank tells Joe, "When you have brains, you don't need muscle" (105), yet it is muscle that continually wins the day for them.

Overall, young readers are urged to use their heads, to control themselves, to remain calm. When heroes resort to physical means, they do so only under pressure and never provoke situations that result in fighting or violence. Children could be given worse recommendations.

Honor

A sense of honor ranks next among the highest attributes a person can have. Unlike the application of reason, honorable behavior does not produce pragmatic dividends; it does, however, produce great rewards in one's conscience. In the series, honor takes various forms.

No series illustrates the point more emphatically than the Lone Ranger. Invariably, "the masked man hesitated. He did not like to attack from the rear" (*The Lone Ranger and Tonto* 78). "It was against his code to use any of the familiar means of making an unwilling man talk. Even though Dave Walter's life depended upon what the gambler might reveal, the masked man found himself incapable of resorting to physical torture" (94). The Ranger's code involves more than himself: "No honest public official," he says, "is ever under any obligation except to carry out his duties" (*The Code of the West* 5). Sometimes his honor works hardships on others. When his horse is killed by escaping desperados, he says to the dead animal, "I could have emptied three saddles . . . one bullet apiece, and they wouldn't have had a chance. But I'm not built that way. So you and I had to take the chance, and you lost, pony!" (*The Lone Ranger* 22). What the horse might have advised if consulted, one can only imagine.

Fenton Hardy jeopardizes his life for the sake of honor in *The House on the Cliff*: asked to sign an agreement not to inform on his captors, Hardy wonders what is to prevent his signing and then telling the police anyway. "We know you too well, Hardy," he is told. "We know that if you signed that promise, you would keep it." "Exactly," he replies. "And that is why I won't sign it" (160). That there may be practicable limits to honor is never considered. Though he has legal recourse to avoid financial disaster, Carson Drew knows that "my conscience would give me no peace if I try to be excused by the court" (*Moss-Covered Mansion* 194). Young readers surely noted that it was the heroes' parents who set such examples. Judy Bolton agreed with the principle. Told that there are tricks to all trades, she replies, "not dishonest tricks," and she briefly states her scruples against deceit and treachery (*The Yellow Phantom* 80).

Bert Bobbsey, bullied at school, says, "I won't hit first, but if he hits me—" (54). This code is used consistently by Tom Swift, who gets hit quite frequently as a result, but who invariably wins, presumably because of his honor.

Another aspect of honor can be seen in *The Rover Boys in the Mountains* when Sam is accused of beginning a fight. Fred Garrison admits that "It was Larry Mason. But I shan't give Larry away." "Neither will I," Sam adds (17). One does not squeal, even if keeping silent threatens expulsion, as it does for Sam. In the books about the Bobbsey Twins, Danny Rugg invariably accuses others of misdemeanors and writes informing notes, but "Bert and Charlie ... did not wish to be 'squealers'" (*Horseshoe Riddle* 63).

Honorable behavior pays dividends. "Best of all [Grace Harlowe] had the reward of her own conscience. In being true to Anne she had been true to herself" (*Sophomore Year* 162). Carson Drew would have concurred. Moreover, honorable people are always believed. When Captain Putnam asks for the truth, Dick Rover replies, "I have never told you anything else" (*In the Mountains* 17); his answer is instantly accepted and he is relieved of suspicion. Only psychic rewards are permitted to heroes, however. Nancy Drew "has made it a point never to accept a reward" (*Lilac Inn* 198), and the Lone Ranger slips away before even thanks can be extended. However dangerous some attempts to maintain honor may seem, no one would argue against the effort to teach it to children. "Why is it some fellows can't learn that crookedness doesn't pay?" Don Sturdy asks (*Port of Lost Ships* 57). Less desirable standards of behavior can be conceived.

Good Sportsmanship

A third recommended character trait, good sportsmanship, is treated from four points of view. First, rules must be followed; winning by unfair means is contemptible. "So he hid behind a tree and hit me before I could see what was coming. That's a fine way to fight!" says Bert Bobbsey (*Land of Cotton* 14). Rob is asked whether his Boy Scout troop wants to claim the win because of being fouled; he replies, "We don't wish to take advantage of anything like that" (*Army Airship* 22). It is mildly ironic that, as his troop does win, " 'Good boy!' shouted the impartial referee" (26). "You aren't playing fair!" Pam tells Joey Brill, who has forged the winning ticket in *The Happy Hollisters* (77); and Grace Harlowe tells Julia, "You never win anything honestly. I see that it is useless for me to appeal to something that you cannot give" (*Sophomore Year* 97). Villains in general do not follow rules.

As expected, the Chip Hilton sports series places great emphasis on good sportsmanship and fair play. In *Touchdown Pass* Chip feels "sharp anger against the dirty playing to which he had been subjected all afternoon" (4). Implicit disgust is strong in *The Lone Ranger and Tonto* when a villain is described simply thus: "Fair play was a thing unknown to Higgy" (200).

Second, one must be a good loser. "The little Frenchman was a good loser" constitutes Tom Swift's highest praise of an opponent (*Airship* 85). Both sides are shown in *The Haunted Bridge*. Nancy Drew plays three golf matches. When she beats Miss Gray and Miss Howard, both congratulate her; when she beats Miss Allison, she is accused of cheating. In context, no reader can doubt what response is expected. Exactly a half-century later, Nancy was just as fair; while playing tennis, George sends a ball that Nancy cannot return: "Nice shot, George!" the detective shouts. "That's the match" (*Disappearing Diamonds* 56).

Third, it is axiomatic that bad sports lose. There are no exceptions, which fact illustrates the strong sense of justice in the series. Losing a sled race to Bert Bobbsey, Charlie claims, "Nellie is heavier than Nan. Let us try it alone next time" (*Merry Days Indoors and Out* 65). They do, and Charlie loses. At school, Danny Rugg fouls Bert in a race and also loses. In *Buzzer Basket* the Northern State team loses, naturally, because their coach calls plays unfairly from the bench and because they foul Chip Hilton's team. Fats Ohlsen is kicked off the team in *Touchdown Pass* for being a bad sport.

Not until 1984 in *The Secret of the Third Watch* did one find an example of bad sportsmanship on the part of heroes: Uncle Richard takes a taxi before the man who had signaled for it first is able to get in; all the main characters have a huge laugh at this man's expense. They also knock out and tie up hospital attendants, whose clothes they want as a disguise; their action is "justified," because "it's time to take shortcuts" (66). Such poor sportsmanship is almost expected in the series—the Race Against Time—which was a poor one: repetitious and violent.

Equally comforting in the fourth place is the fact that good sports usually win. Grace Harlowe notes that "people who give a square deal ... always win out" (*Sophomore Year* 191). "Always" may be too sweeping a term, but certainly in series good sports do much better than poor ones.

As a final clinching argument for good sportsmanship, Don Sturdy offered one of the subtlest statements anywhere in a series: "Once in a while you run across fellows who are neither sportsmen nor gentlemen" (*Lion Land* 102), which makes those who are not all the more obvious and reprehensible.

Modesty and self-effacement characterize people of genuine ability; pride and conceit indicate inadequate people. In *The Clue of the Broken Wing*, Judy Bolton recognizes that although Irene is a famous singer and television personality, "she still had the same shy smile and elusive manner that endeared her to Judy when she first came" (105). "Both Captain Sturdy and Professor Bruce disliked publicity and avoided it as much as possible" (*Lost Ships* 67). Boy Scout Rob Blake is "as humble as he is great, and that's the limit of a boy's vocabulary when speaking of a chum" (*Under Sealed Orders* 12–13), In *Program for Destruction* the Hardy Boys respond to praise for their ability by saying, "We've been known to crack a few cases" (5): this one is their 87th. Similarly, Nancy Drew is praised in *Deadly Intent*, her 102nd case; "I am beginning to make a name for myself," she says (10). Tom Swift liked conceit no better: "I don't especially care for him ... too fond of himself" (*Undersea Search* 54). As the series are dedicated to showing that poor sports always lose, they are equally eager to prove that a haughty spirit goeth before a fall.

Kindness

Also urged on readers are kindness and its attendant qualities of generosity, unselfishness, and self-sacrifice. What was said earlier about the almost sadistic enjoyment of animal suffering limits the application of kindness to humans. Scarcely a word about kindness to animals is to be found in any series. Sue

Barton, as a Visiting Nurse, describes her admiration for the Henry Street House as "an organization that functions, not for gain, but solely for the benefit of other people. . . . Its policy is based on kindness and understanding and justice" (192). Kindness is preached throughout the Bobbsey Twins. " 'We must never forget to do a kindness when we can, Nan,' said Mamma" in the very first book (158). Visiting the country, the Twins volunteer to pick the crop of Mr. and Mrs. Burns, after he has had a shock and cannot work. They refuse pay, saying, "Mother wouldn't like [us] to take the money" (91). Kindness not infrequently has practical results, but in general, like virtue, it is its own reward, and the Twins have no ulterior motive for performing the kind act. During Honey Bunch's *First Little Trip to the Seashore*, her friend Grace tries to take the heroine's cherry and drops her own ice cream cone; Honey Bunch not only gives her the cherry but adds her own cone to make up the loss. Rick Brant is told by his father that "our own treasury is getting low, since we turn our experiment results over to the public without profit" (*100 Fathoms Under* 187).

Pluck, Fortitude, and "Sissiness"

Pluck and fortitude are important and desirable qualities of character. Although the words "pluck" and "plucky" were used in the series well into the 1930's, since then they are seen rarely. The quality described, however, is one of the most admired in these books. Basically, pluck implies a strong heart in the face of danger. When Grace Harlowe is given a wild horse to ride, it "was only by the exercise of sheer pluck that [she] held her seat in the saddle" (*Great American Desert* 30). Later her friend Elfreda is dragged behind a horse. "Elfreda was taking severe punishment, but she was enduring it pluckily" (30). When Nancy Drew swears not to give up trying to solve the mystery at Lilac Inn, her friend Helen says, "I certainly admire your pluck" (72). Don Sturdy refers to his uncle as the pluckiest man alive (*Among the Gorillas* 133), and Payson's Boy Scouts are told, "You boys certainly have plenty of pluck" (*Army Airship* 143). The quality, then, is not limited to either sex, but found in both. In later series, when the word ceased to be used, keeping up one's courage though faced with terrible odds remained an enviable trait. Long before Hemingway made it fashionable to be tough and uncomplaining while enduring pain, suffering, and misfortune, the ability to do so was highly admired in the series. It is actually an extension of pluck. Some series, in fact, would do credit to Hemingway. In *Uncle Sam's Boys in the Ranks*, for example, two regulars are hit before they can find cover. "These men, however, made no outcry, but . . . lay quietly where they had fallen until the time came for them to have attention" (241). One of the Scouts visiting the Rockies is injured, but "Thad did not believe in any display of weakness in Scouts" (204). Step Hen, another Boy Scout, is also injured, "but they would not hear a single groan from him, if he had to make his lips bleed, biting them with his teeth . . . it was the spirit that makes heroes" (168). From another angle, the injured villain Josiah Crabtree "showed his cowardly nature by groaning dismally every time he moved" (*The Rover Boys in New York* 259).

Such fortitude is not the prerogative of males. When Beverly Gray is a Freshman, she almost perishes from being lost in a blizzard; she is held captive for three days by an insane hermit; and she is attacked by a grizzly bear. Finally rescued, her only comment is, "It's great to be back!" (128). Hemingway would have loved it.

Nonetheless, while pluck and fortitude are not denied to girls and women, they are expected qualities in boys and men. To lack them implies cowardice, or worse, sissiness. In this respect, the series establish some very specific attributes for boys to aim at. In *The Bobbsey Twins at the Seashore,* "Hal was a real boy, the greatest compliment that could ever be paid to him" (82). What constitutes a real boy is never vague or indefinite. Pluck and fortitude he must have. *The Boy Scouts in the Rockies* reveals other qualities. Smithy is first described as a "dudish-looking boy" (6) and later as "the dude scout" (11). Since a dude is one too much concerned with his manners and appearance—a fop and a dandy—such qualities are to be avoided. Furthermore, Smith's "nature seemed too mild and sissy-like . . . his father used to be a great hunter years ago; but he guessed he'd inherited his mother's gentle disposition . . . he had always been given too much to dress, and the little things of life, at which most fellows look with scorn and contempt. He must have the edges roughened a little if he was ever going to hold his own when he went to college, or out into the wide world where 'sissy' boys are held up to derision" (81). Later the reader is told that "it would be some time before Smithy could so far overcome his former gentle traits of character to feel the hunter's fierce lust for his quarry" (134). In short, Smithy is being derided for not enjoying killing and perhaps inflicting pain on animals. One feels the influence of Theodore Roosevelt and the doctrine of the strenuous life throughout the Boy Scout series, if not indeed in the entire movement. Even the Grace Harlowe books are an argument against the effete life and for a vigorous, outdoor one.

Fortunately, Smithy is able to reform by discovering "that he had the red blood of his father running in his veins. . . . Never again would he sit at the feet of an old lady and learn to make fancy work" (252). The statement is overdone but revealing. The passage continues: "After this, the baseball and football fields would claim a goodly share of his attention, for Smith was bent on making himself *manly*, a credit to his father . . . who he knew had once loved dearly to hunt and fish and spend his vacations in the woods close to nature, as do all men who are worthy of the name" (252). Comment is superfluous.

Occasionally a mild counterargument can be found, as in *Merry Days Indoors and Out*: Danny Rugg is seen as "very rough and ungentlemanly" (71), and Bert is urged to avoid him. Interestingly, the Chip Hilton sports series, which began in 1948, affirms the idea that strength may involve more than the hypermasculinity implied earlier. In *Buzzer Basket* (1962), "Like most strong men, Dad Young possessed a gentle manner" (30). The word "most" displays an attitude that author Clair Bee, himself a coach and sportsman, manifests throughout the series. The majority of series would not endorse such an idea, yet it is a time-honored one. Whether it is a reaction to what many social critics term a "blurring of the sexes" and their characteristics after the 1950's is doubtful. Certainly the idea is found with no frequency in the children's series.

Early in series history, Ella Lyman Cabot considered "Children's Reading as a Help in Training Character" (1916): "We want our children to be truthful, reasonable, brave, open to the blessings of work, play, and love, and above all passionate to serve the ideal through service to the state" (209). Her article is well intentioned, though astonishingly naive and moral: she suggested organizing a public school around such areas as ethics, love of animals, and self-control, and using books to illustrate these qualities. The series books clearly do effective service along these very lines and equally clearly are intended to do so.

AFTERWORD

HENRY STEELE COMMAGER, IN his Introduction to *A Critical History of Children's Literature*, sets up a composite English and American character, based upon elements found in the juvenile literature of both countries. Almost half of the American qualities he lists are not borne out by the series books.

1. Equalitarianism, not class consciousness. (There is a definite class consciousness in series.)
2. Democracy and humanitarianism. (Democracy is talked about but class consciousness is certainly present; humanitarianism is not an issue.)
3. Strong family feeling. (Most series children have no family feeling and leave the family regularly.)
4. Work and the gospel of work. (Except perhaps for Tom Swift, no series hero or heroine leads a normal working life or, indeed, works at all.)
5. Adventure, but in the American West, not in distant lands, adventure that makes not for imperialism but as often as not for provincialism. (To an extent true; but most series spend only an occasional volume in the American West and much more time abroad; provincialism is extreme in series.)

His remaining qualities are found in the series:

6. Courage and hatred of a bully.
7. Self-reliance.
8. Nature in the raw, not tamed.
9. A feeling for fair play and the underdog.
10. Ingenuity and mechanical skill.
11. Humor that is boisterous and based on the tall tale, not whimsy.

12. Simplicity and morality.

As has been shown, in the past librarians, along with critics of children's literature and teachers, took arms against the series and their values. While series attitudes toward race and nationality, for example, were obviously unacceptable, many of their recommendations were, in fact, moral and desirable.

Since the 1970's, although many series have become almost amoral, libraries have capitulated to public demand and allow these books shelf space. Series publishers have become cynical (perhaps they always were, but not so blatantly so): whatever will sell seems their only criterion. Edward Stratemeyer, however much one may object to his acceptance of racial stereotypes and other such beliefs, nonetheless sought to teach moral and social values. Series now pander to attitudes already in place— they do not seem disposed to create any or to encourage better ones.

Reading is more affecting than television; when a child watches TV, he or she is at home, more or less surrounded by family, who may occasionally make judgments. In any case, imagination is only minimally required, if at all. But imagination is a most powerful instrument. As the child reads, he or she is in a small cocoon, imagining happenings far more "real" than what the eyes can reveal. Twenty-five years ago, I was a supporter of the series against advocates of "the list" of books not to be circulated. I was opposed to censorship; my research convinced me that the series were not poorly written in general; the original series were, and are, fun to read. I find myself now an ardent opponent of the "new" series, especially those that have emerged since the 1970's. Publishers supply what children ask for, not what they necessarily should have, in order to sell their product. So do libraries. So do schools and education in general. At the Rameses exhibition appearing at Boston's Museum of Science, it was determined that the attention span of visitors was twenty-five minutes; no performance or tour would last longer. That time is exactly the length of a television situation comedy or cop show (excluding commercials).

Devolution is inevitable, thus, and has occurred. I could, and did, read *Robinson Crusoe* in the third grade at the age of eight; my college students cannot read it now, at the ages of eighteen

Afterword

to twenty-two. Series books become shorter and shorter, simpler and simpler, and more and more they resemble television in method, plots, dialogue, and structure. If one considers the Hardy Boys Casefiles, the Nancy Drew Files, Doris Fein, the Sweet Valley High and Twins, even the New Bobbsey Twins with their garish covers and faces that make *The Children of the Damned* seem warm and friendly, one will find that these books are no longer fun. They are, I think, dangerous, in that heroes and heroines so often get away with objectionable behavior (as they do on TV). Morality is unknown—the heroes are good because they are the heroes; right and wrong blend and become indistinguishable. Casual references to drugs and drinking are found, as is profanity. A good deal of cynicism about the United States, its officials, law enforcement officers, and education is to be found also, and while, like Don Sturdy's father, I am not in favor of wrapping children in cotton wool, much of the cynicism in the Hardy Boys Casefiles, the Race Against Time Series, and Doris Fein is egregious.

Tom Swift had a hard, uphill climb to some sort of acceptance; his slide down the other side was quicker. The vast majority of new series are aimed at girls—Sweet Valley High, Sweet Valley Twins, Sleepover Friends, Babysitters Club—and publishers claim that they cannot move mystery series with boys as heroes (the Hardy Boys Series is an obvious exception). Hence the ancient stereotypical assumption that girls are readers, as well as better students, is reaffirmed. As a child growing up in the Depression, I found that everyone read, all the time, even though we lived in a slum. When I walk into the backyard shed that serves as a library, I cannot help but smile at the one wall that holds the Rover Boys, Honey Bunch, and Don Sturdy; the opposite wall holding books about Sweet Valley and the like provokes a frown and a sense of distaste. They sell. But so does fast food.

BIBLIOGRAPHY

SECONDARY SOURCES

Adams, Bess Porter. *About Books and Children: Historical Survey of Children's Literature.* New York: Henry Holt, 1953.

"Adventure Stories Preferred by Boy's Club Readers." *Publishers Weekly* 160, July 28, 1951: 297–298.

"Age Does Not Dim the Glory of the Rover Boys." *Literary Digest* 117, April 21, 1928: 38.

"America's Children Meet a Fresh Crop of Heroes." *Newsweek* 40, September 1, 1952: 67.

Ames, Pauline. "Revaluing Children's Fiction." *Wilson Bulletin for Librarians*, January 11, 1937: 314.

Arbuthnot, May Hill. *Children and Books.* Chicago: Scott, Foresman, 1947.

Armstrong, Judith. "In Defense of Adventure Stories." *Children's Literature in Education* 13, Fall 1982: 115–121.

Ayres, Ernest F. "Not to Be Circulated." *Wilson Bulletin for Librarians* 3, March 1929: 528–529.

Baruck, Dorothy. "Trends in Children's Literature Today." *Elementary English Review* 12, October 1935: 187–191.

Beck, Warren. "Huckleberry Finn vs. the Cash Boy." *Education* 49, September 1928: 1–13.

Beckman, Margaret. "Why Not the Bobbsey Twins?" *Library Journal* 89, November 15, 1964: 4612–4613, 4627.

"Bedtime Man." *New Yorker* 16, October 26, 1940: 16.

Biemiller, C. L. "A Series Can Creep Up on You." *Publishers Weekly* 204, July 16, 1973: 62.

Bixler, Phyllis, and Lucien Agosta. "Formula Fiction and Children's Literature: Thornton Waldo Burgess and Frances Hodgson Burnett." *Children's Literature in Education* 15, Summer 1984: 63–71.

Bjorklid, Ase. "Deichman Library and Series Books for Children." *Library and Information Science Abstracts* 1980: 112–115.

Bowman, K. Irene. "Why the American Library Association Does Not Endorse Serials for Boys and Girls." *Iowa Library Quarterly* 9, July–August 1921: 212.

Bridget, Sr. "Divorce and Children's Literature." *Catholic Library World* 34, December 1962: 202–204, 223, 227.

Brown, James Oliver. "Writing Realistic Books for Children." *Library Journal* 69, June 15, 1944: 560.

Brown, Janet E. "The Saga of Elsie Dinsmore: A Study in Nineteenth Century Sensibility." *University of Buffalo Studies* 17, July 1945: 71–131.

Brown, Spencer. "The Dilemma of Liberal Censorship." *Education Digest* 30, September 1964: 4–6.

Bruce, J. "From 8 to 14." *Tablet* 217, December 7, 1963: 1333–1334.

———. "Mostly for Boys." *Tablet* 217, November 9, 1963: 1212.

Brynes Asher. "Boy-Men and Man-Boys." *Yale Review* 38, December 1948: 223–233.

Butcher M. "Around Eight." *Tablet* 217, December 7, 1963: 1332–1333.

Cabot, Ella Lyman. "Children's Reading as a Help in Training Character." *Religious Education* 11, June 1916: 207–220.

Secondary Sources

Cariou, Mavis Olive. "Syntax, Vocabulary and Metaphor in Three Groups of Novels for Children in Grades Four to Six." (Ph.D. Dissertation) University of Michigan, 1983.

Carringer, M. A. "The Ten Year Old Boy and His Books." *Education* 33, November 1912: 166–169.

Character Formation Through Books. Compiled by Clara J. Kircher, q.v.

"Children Want Realism in Books, Authors Guild Told." *Publishers Weekly* 156, October 29, 1949: 1895–1896.

"Children's Corner." *Publishers Weekly* 118, October 26, 1935: 1546–1548.

"Children's Hero: Rebel or Conformist?" *Wilson Library Bulletin* 38, October 1963: 154–164.

"Chip Off the Old Block." *Time* 63, January 4, 1954: 66.

Chira, Susan. "Harriet Adams Dies; Nancy Drew Author Wrote 200 Novels." *New York Times*, March 29, 1982: 1, B1 col. 4.

"Citizenship Stories." *Religious Education* 12, April 1917: 165–167.

Colby, Joan Poindexter. *The Children's Book Field.* New York: Pellegrini and Cudahy, 1952.

Cole, Doris M. "Bad Boys and Their Books." *Wilson Library Bulletin* 16, March 1942: 532–536.

Commager, Henry Steele. Introduction, in Meigs et al., *A Critical History of Children's Literature*, q.v.

Coryell, Hubert V. "When Boys Read the Books They Like." *Publishers Weekly* 128, October 19, 1935, 1463–1466.

Curry, Charles, and Erle Elsworth Chippinger. *Children's Literature.* Chicago: Rand, McNally, 1920.

Dalgliesh, Alice, and Annis Duff. *Aids to Choosing Books for Your Children.* New York: Children's Book Council, 1964.

Daniels, Lee. "Hardy Boys Named in Literary Suit." *New York Times*, June 10, 1980: 1, C1 col. 3.

Day, Clarence. "Noble Boys." *Saturday Review of Literature* 15, November 14, 1936: 3–4.

Deane, Paul. "Black Characters in Children's Fiction Series Since 1968." *Journal of Negro Education* 58, Spring 1989: 153–162.

_____. "A Century of Xenophobia in Fiction Series for Young People." *Journal of Youth Services in Libraries* 3, Winter 1990: 117–127.

_____. "The Persistence of Uncle Tom: An Examination of the Image of the Negro in Children's Fiction Series." *Journal of Negro Education* 37, Spring 1968: 140–145.

_____. "Science and Technology in Children's Fiction Series." *Lamar Journal of the Humanities* 16, no. 1, Spring 1990: 20–32.

_____. "Tom Swift and His Uphill Climb." *Opinion* 1, no. 2, Summer 1968: 1–3.

_____. "Violence in Children's Fiction Series." *Journal of Popular Culture* 4, no. 2, Fall/Winter 1990:67–81.

_____. "Who Speaks for Nancy Drew?" *Opinion* 4, Winter 1972: 1–4.

Dohm, Dorothy G. "Father Joins the Family." *Horn Book* 15, October 17, 1939: 397–401.

Donelson, Kenneth, and Alleen Pace. *Literature for Today's Young Adults*. New York: Scott, Foresman, 1980.

"A Dozen Years of Improvement." *Publishers Weekly* 130, October 17, 1936: 1581.

Eakins, Mary K. "Trends in Children's Literature." *Library Quarterly* 25, January 1955: 47–57.

Eakins, Mary K., and Blanche Janecek. "Reports of Children's Books in Series and Editions." *Library Journal* 73, April 15, 1948: 624–635.

"Editor Makes Plea for Fantasy and Action Stories." *Publishers Weekly* 154, November 13, 1948: 2053.

Ellis, Wilmot E. "Juveniles of the Recent Past." *Saturday Review of Literature* 14, August 8, 1936: 9.

Erisman, Fred. "Two Versions of Technology: Howard Garis's Science-Adventure Series Books." *Lamar Journal of the Humanities* 11, Fall 1985: 23–29.

Evans, Ernestine. "Trends in Children's Books." *New Republic* 48, November 10, 1926: 336–339.

Evans, Eva Knox. "The Negro in Children's Fiction." *Publishers Weekly* 140, August 30, 1941: 650.

"Explain Opposition on Ban in Library of 'Series' Books." *Daily Herald* (Provo, Utah), January 31, 1965, page unavailable.

Fearn, Margaret, editor. *Only the Best Is Good Enough: The Woodfield Lectures on Children's Literature, 1978–1985*. London: Rossendale, 1985.

Felder, Deborah. "Nancy Drew: Then and Now." *Publishers Weekly*, 229, May 30, 1986: 30–34.

Fenner, Phyllis. "Tom Swift and the Rover Boys." *Wilson Bulletin for Librarians* 9, June 1935: 542–543.

Fisher, Helen H. "Family Life in Children's Literature." *Elementary School Journal* 50, May 1950: 516–520.

Foster, Marie F. "Concerning Authors for Young People." *Wilson Bulletin for Librarians* 11, November 1936: 186–187.

Frank, Josette. *What Books for Children?* New York: Doubleday, Doran, 1937.

"A Further Statement on Negro Dialect in Children's Books." *Publishers Weekly* 141, January 10, 1942: 104–105.

Gardner, Emlyn E., and Eloise Ramsey. *A Handbook of Children's Literature: Methods and Materials*. Chicago: Scott, Foresman, 1927.

Gardner, Martin. "Why Librarians Dislike Oz." *Library Journal* 88, February 15, 1963: 834–836.

Garis, Roger. "My Father Was Uncle Wiggily." *Saturday Evening Post*, December 19–26, 1964: 64–66.

Gesell, Arnold, and Frances Ilg. *The Child from Five to Ten*. New York: Harper and Brothers, 1946.

Golumb, Bernard. "A Defense of the Oz Books." *Junior Libraries* 4, October 15, 1957: 137–138.

"Good Dollar Children's Books." *Publishers Weekly* 131, April 24, 1937: 1751.

Green, Jenny Lind. "When Children Read for Fun." *School and Society* 17, April 7, 1923: 390–392.

Hall, C. Stanley. "What Children Do Read and What They Ought to Read." *National Education Association* 1905: 868–871.

Hanna, Geneva, and Mariana McAllister. *Books, Young People, Reading Guidance*. New York: Harper and Brothers, 1960.

Harriman, Margaret Case. "What Do You Remember About Your Favorite Childhood Books?" *Good Housekeeping* 119, November 1944: 36, 174–175.

Harvey, John Frederick. *The Content Characteristics of Best-Selling Novels*. Chicago: University of Chicago Press, 1949.

Heins, Ethel L. "Brand Name Fiction." *Horn Book* 58, June 1982: 254–255.

Hess, Fjeril. "Girls Like Stories Which Have Lots of Action." *Publishers Weekly* 121, March 26, 1932: 1477–1478.

Hollowell, Lillian. "Series in Children's Books." *Wilson Library Bulletin* 27, May 1953: 736–738.

Hughes, Helen Sard. "Literature for Children: A Protest." *English Journal* 2, September 1913: 494–499.

Secondary Sources

Hunt, Clara Whitehill. "The Child and the Book in Wartime." *English Journal* 7, October 1918: 487–496.

———. "Good Taste and Bad Taste in Girls' Books." *Ladies Home Journal* 27, April 1910: 679–680.

Ilg, Frances, and Louise Bates Ames. *Child Behavior*. New York: Harper and Row, 1955.

"Inventory of What Children Voluntarily Select to Read." *Elementary School Journal* 39, September 1938: 11–12.

Ives, Vernon. "Children's Books and the War." *Publishers Weekly* 144, October 23, 1943: 1592–1593.

Jennings, Joe. "Leisure Reading of Junior High School Boys and Girls." *Peabody Journal of Education* 6, May 1929: 335.

Johnson, Elizabeth. "Reading for Pleasure Is Not the Main Thing." *Wilson Library Bulletin* 3, June 1929: 679–680.

Jordan, Arthur Melville. *Children's Interests in Reading*. Chapel Hill: University of North Carolina Press, 1926.

Jordan, Charles J. "... So Who Wrote Poppy Ott and the Pedigreed Pickle?" *Yankee* May 1971: 140–146, 161–164.

"Judge Rules in Dispute of Nancy Drew, Tom Swift, et al." *Publishers Weekly* 217, June 27, 1980: 14.

"Juvenile Books During Twenty-eight Years." *Literary Digest* 57, April 27, 1918: 39–41.

Kellison, Dorothy. "Mr. Gardner, Meet a Librarian." *Library Journal* 88, April 15, 1963: 1708.

Kennerly, Sarah Law. "Confederate Juvenile Imprints: Children's Books and Periodicals Published in the Confederate States of America, 1861–1865." (Thesis) University of Michigan, 1957.

Kiefer, Monica. *American Children Through Their Books, 1700–1835*. Philadelphia: University of Pennsylvania Press, 1948.

King, Martha Bennett. "Human Relations in Children's Books." *Wilson Library Bulletin* 22, May 1948: 675–678.

Kinlock, Lucy M. "The Menace of the Series Books." *Elementary English Review* 12, January 1935: 9–11.

Kircher, Clara, compiler. *Character Formation Through Books: A Bibliography.* Washington, D.C.: Catholic University of America Press, 1952.

Kleech, F. "A Comparison of the Reading Preferences of the Eighth Grade Rural and Urban Children with Regard to Books and Magazines." *Christian Educational Review* 61, November 1963: 552–553.

Kristensen, Kurt. "The Hardy Boys and Girl Detective in Perspective." *Library and Information Science Abstracts* 47, no. 4, 1980: 286–287.

Lancaster, Thomas J. "A Study of the Voluntary Reading of pupils in Grades IV–VIII." *Elementary School Journal* 28, March 1928: 525–527.

Larrick, Nancy. *A Parent's Guide to Children's Reading.* New York: Westminster, 1964.

Lazarus, Emma. "The New Colossus." (Sonnet at base of the Statue of Liberty) 1886.

Lind, Katherine Niles. "The Social Psychology of Children's Reading." *American Journal of Sociology* 41, January 1936: 454–469.

Littlefield, Henry M. "The Wizard of Oz: Parable of Populism." *American Quarterly* 16, Spring 1964: 47–58.

Livsey, Rosemary. "Modern Career Stories for Girls." *Horn Book* 19, January–February 1943: 50–55.

Long, Harriet. "The American Scene in Recent Children's Books." *Wilson Library Bulletin* 15, October 1949: 122–126.

MacDonald, J. F. "Foreigners in Juvenile Fiction Series, 1900–1945." *Journal of Popular Culture* 8, Winter 1974: 534–548.

Mandel, Richard C. "Children's Books: Mirrors of Social Development." *Elementary School Journal* 64, January 1964: 190–199.

Margaret, Miriam, Sr. "Children's Books That Have Shaped the Past." *Catholic Library World* 34, March 1963: 348–352.

Master, Helen S. "Fiction in the Elementary Grades." *Elementary English Review* 12, October 1935: 178–184.

Mathiews, Franklin K. "Fashions in Fiction for Boys." *Publishers Weekly* 116, August 31, 1929: 847–850.

McGraw, William Corbin. "Pollyanna Rides Again." *Saturday Review of Literature* 41, March 22, 1958: 37–38.

Meigs, Cornelia, Anne Thaxter Eaton, Elizabeth Nesbitt, and Ruth Hill Viguers. *A Critical History of Children's Literature*. New York: Macmillan, 1953.

Melcher, Frederick G. "The War and Children's Reading." *Publishers Weekly* 138, August 31, 1940: 645.

Mellon, Constance A. "Teenagers Do Read: What Rural Youths Say About Leisure Reading." *School Library Journal*, February 1987: 27–30.

Mercier, Jean F. "Starting Young." *Publishers Weekly* 213, March 13, 1978: 65.

Miller, Edwin. "The Boy and His Book." *English Journal* 7, December 1948: 644–647.

Mitchell, Lillian Herron. "Not to Be Circulated." *Wilson Bulletin for Librarians* 3, April 1929: 580.

Molson, Francis. "Three Generations of Tom Swift." *Children's Literature Association Quarterly* 10, Summer 1985: 60–63.

Moore, Thomas Verner. Introduction, in Kircher, *Character Formation Through Books*, q.v.

Moran, Barbara, and Susan Steinfirst. "Why Johnny (and Jane) Read Whodunits in Series." *School Library Journal* 31, March 1985: 113–117.

Moses, Montrose J. "Children's Books in Wartime." *Good Housekeeping* 65, December 1917: 135–136.

"Mr. Frank Merriwell." *Newsweek* 25, January 29, 1945: 44–46.

Mussen, Paul Henry, and John J. Conger. *Child Development and Personality*. New York: Harper and Brothers, 1956.

"Negro Dialect in Children's Books." *Publishers Weekly* 140, October 18, 1941: 1555–1558.

Nesbitt, Elizabeth. "Juveniles Give Meaning to Life." *Library Journal* 73, January 1948: 75–80.

"New Writers for Girls." *Literary Digest* 48, January 31, 1914: 205–206.

Nolan, Eleanor Weakley. "The Colored Girl in Contemporary Literature." *Horn Book* 18, September-October 1942: 348–355.

"Not to Be Circulated." *Wilson Bulletin for Librarians* 3, January 1929: 446.

"Orange, N.J. Honors Nancy Drew." *School Library Journal* 22, November 1975: 10.

Packard, Edward B. "Interactive Fiction for Children's Books: Boon or Bane?" *School Library Journal* 34, October 1987: 40–41.

Parson, M. S. "Stabbed to the Heart." *Library Journal* 88, March 15, 1963: 1196.

Patte, Genevieve. "Let 'Em Read! Reality and Fantasy in Children's Literature." In Fearn, *Only the Best Is Good Enough*, q.v.

Pease, Howard. "Technically Speaking." *Horn Book* 19, March-April 1963: 90–97.

Perry, Phyllis J. "Looking Back on the Bobbsey Twins." *Language Arts* 55, February 1, 1978: 202–203.

Phillips, Louis. "Me and the Hardy Boys." *Armchair Detective* 15 (2) 1982: 174–177.

Pilant, Elizabeth. "The Place of Children's Literature in the Cultural Scale." *School and Society* 77, August 8, 1953: 36–38.

"Platitudes Every Child Should Know." *Scribner's Magazine* 55, January 1914: 130–131.

Secondary Sources

Pothier, Dick. "Nancy Drew: First Libber?" *Boston Globe*, January 6, 1976: 1, 17.

Praeger, Arthur, "Edward Stratemeyer and His Book Machine." *Saturday Review* July 10, 1971: 15–17, 52–53.

Preer, Bette Banner. "Guidance in Democratic Living Through Juvenile Fiction." *Wilson Library Bulletin* 22, May 1948: 679–681.

"Provo Library Board Gives Stand." *Daily Herald* (Provo, Utah), February 10, 1965, page unavailable.

Rankin, Marie. "Children's Interests in Library Books of Fiction." (Thesis) Teachers College, Columbia University, 1944.

"Replacements for 'Blacklisted' Series by Small Libraries Project." *Library Journal* 89, December 15, 1964: 4996.

Rosenberg, J. K. *Young People's Literature in Series: Fiction, Non-fiction, and Publisher Series, 1973–1975*. Littleton, Colo.: Libraries Unlimited, 1977.

Scott, Polly Ann. "Children's Books Through the Eyes of the Dealer." *Publishers Weekly* 117, June 28, 1930: 3147–3150.

Seaman, Louise. "Children's Books and the Depression." *Wilson Bulletin for Librarians* 7, March 1933: 413–417.

"Series Library Dispute." *Daily Herald* (Provo, Utah), January 13, 1965, page unavailable.

Shanklin, Lucille. "Tom Swift's Last Stand." *Wilson Bulletin for Librarians* 9, June 1935: 588–589.

Shepard, John P. "The Treatment of Characters in Popular Children's Fiction." *Elementary English* 39, November 1962: 672–676.

Simonson, Ida. "The Child's Outlook upon Life thru [sic] Literature." *Library Journal* 53, January 1, 1928: 17–23.

_____. "Literature for Children: A Course for Normal School Children." *English Journal* 2, May 1913: 305–311.

Sisk, John P. "The Rover Boys Revisited." *Commonweal*, May 8, 1959: 143–146.

Smith, Dora. *Fifty Years of Children's Books, 1910–1960: Trends, Developments, Backgrounds, Influences*. Champaign, Ill.: National Council of Teachers of English, 1963.

Smith, James. *A Critical Approach to Children's Literature*. San Fernando, Calif.: San Fernando Valley State College, 1967.

Smith, Irene. *A History of the Newbery and Caldecott Medals*. New York: Viking Press, 1957.

Smith, William J. "The Bobbsey Twins at an Orgy." *Nation* 198, June 27, 1964: 633–635.

Smyers, Richard Paul. "A Librarian Looks at Oz." *Library Occurent* 21, December 1964: 190–192.

Soderbergh, Peter. "The Stratemeyer Strain: Educators and the Juvenile Series Books, 1900–1973." *Journal of Popular Culture* 7, Spring 1974: 864–872.

"Some Children's Books." *Harper's Weekly* 49, December 9, 1905: 1768.

Spock, Benjamin. *Baby and Child Care*. New York: Pocket Books, 1959.

Stang, K. J. *Series Books for the American Girl, 1910–1940* (A.M. Thesis) University of Chicago, 1980.

Stebbins, Hilda Brace. "Youth Needs Red-Blooded Books." *Parents Magazine* 5, August 1930: 19.

Stockum, Hilda Van. "Today's Problems in Children's Books." *Horn Book* 21, March-April 1945: 135–136.

"Stratemeyer, Author, Is Dead." *Publishers Weekly* 117, May 24, 1930: 26–27.

Strauss, Flora. "Let Them Face It: Today's World in Books for Boys and Girls." *Horn Book* 21, January-February 1945: 63–64.

Secondary Sources

Terman, Lewis M. *Children's Reading: A Guide for Parents and Teachers.* New York: D. Appleton, 1927.

Thirty Twentieth Century Children's Books Every Adult Should Know. Boston: n.p., n.d.

Thom, Douglas A. *Everyday Problems of the Everyday Child.* New York: D. Appleton, 1929.

Thorndill, Christine Maltby. "Skeletons in the Closet: Revision of Racial, Ethnic, and Sexual Stereotypes in Series Books." *Top of the News* 34, Spring 1978: 245–248.

Thurber, James. "The Wizard of Chitenago." *New Republic* 131, December 12, 1934: 141–142.

"Tom, Jr." *New Yorker* 30, March 20, 1954: 26–27.

"Tom Sawyer vs. Tom Swift." *Time* 39, February 23, 1942: 44.

True, John Preston. "Juvenile Literature (So-called)." *Atlantic Monthly* 62, November 1903: 690–692.

"Twenty-one Years of Juveniles." *Publishers Weekly* 130, October 17, 1936: 1583–1584.

Viguers, Ruth Hill. Introduction, in *Fanfare . . . 1958–1962: The Horn Book's Honor List of Children's Books.* Boston, n.d.

⸺. Letter to Paul Deane, May 5, 1965.

Wagenknecht, Edward. *The Movies in the Age of Innocence.* Norman: Oklahoma University Press, 1962.

Walker, Joan MacWillie. "On the Other Side of the Counter." *Publishers Weekly* 138, August 31, 1941: 677–679.

Wallace, Robert. "Kids' Books: A Happy Few Amid the Junk." *Life* 57, December 11, 1964: 112–130.

Ward, Pearl. "College Classes Choose Favorite Children's Books." *Elementary English* 39, November 1962: 680–684.

Wattenberg, William E. *The Adolescent Years*. New York: Harcourt, Brace, 1955.

Weeks, Edward A. "Children Who Live Forever." *Saturday Review of Literature* 22, November 18, 1939: 12, 20.

"What Do Young Americans Read?" *Publishers Weekly* 138, November 16, 1940: 1895–1896.

"What the Boys Are Reading." *Literary Digest*, October 30, 1920: 35–36.

White, Robb. "Children's Books." *Saturday Review of Literature* 20, August 12, 1939: 9.

Whitney, Phyllis A. "Writing the Juvenile Mystery." *Writer* 76, April 1963: 14–18.

Wiederman, Bernice. "Library Funds Are Too Scarce to Buy Tom Swift." *Wilson Bulletin for Librarians* 3, June 1929: 680.

Wilson, Paul, and Richard Anderson. "Children's Reading Habits: A New Criterion for Literacy." *Book Research Quarterly* 2, Fall 1986: 72–84.

"The Wonderful Career of the Wonderful Wizard." *Publishers Weekly* 179, February 13, 1961: 80–81.

Wright, Ethel C. "Favorite Children's Books of the Past Decade." *Elementary English Review* 12, April 1935: 101–105.

Yost, Edna. "The Fifty-Cent Juvenile." *Publishers Weekly* 121, June 18, 1932: 2405–2408.

———. "Who Writes the Fifty-Cent Juveniles?" *Publishers Weekly* 123, May 20, 1933: 1593–1598.

Young People's Books: Finding List. Chicago: Chicago Public Library, 1912.

Zuckerman, Eileen Goudge. "Nancy Drew vs. Serious Fiction." *Publishers Weekly* 229, March 30, 1986: 74.

THE SERIES

THE FOLLOWING LISTS OF series books used in the writing of this study need some explanation. It seemed desirable to present, if possible, a complete list of the books making up a given series in the order of their publication simply so that these titles might be available somewhere. However, since most of the older series, such as Tom Swift and the Rover Boys, have been out of print, in some cases for as long as half a century, it has sometimes been impossible to find them all. Even when I have had access to individual volumes, many lack title pages or copyright pages and occasionally covers. Furthermore, secondary publishers often issued certain titles in a series giving them dates of publication different from the originals. To be absolutely accurate has been a provoking, if not impossible, task. I have given the dates of the books I have actually used (subject to the difficulties noted). Thus, although the first Bobbsey Twins book appeared in 1904, the earliest edition I could find was dated 1912, and hence I had to use it. Subsequent dates were subject to the same constraint. Moreover, some titles, such as *The Bobbsey Twins in the Great West* (1920?) when reissued in 1966 became *Visit to the Great West*, while *The Play House Secret* (1968) seems to be the *Keeping House* of 1925. In short, one is directed by available information. Individual volumes usually contain titles in the series in order of publication, or, lacking that source, advertisements from which the order may be inferred; both sources omit dates. As far as possible, then, each complete series is accounted for, though I may not have had access to all the books in it. This fact has not proved a liability, since I was concerned with series in general, not with evaluations of particular books.

I have departed from conventional bibliography form in listing these books. The series titles are alphabetized by first word or surname, and are accompanied by author and publisher, if all items in a series were produced by the same publisher under the same author's name; exceptions are noted where necessary. Titles in most series follow a consistent pattern, beginning usually with the name of the chief character or characters, for example, *Tom Swift and His Motorcycle*, *Tom Swift and His Giant Cannon*. In view of this fact and for ease of reference, I have supplied merely the distinguishing part of the title and its date, when available, through 1989.

The A.I. Gang. Signet.
1. Coville, Bruce. *Operation Sherlock.* 1986.
2. Lawrence, Jim. *The Cutlass Clue.* 1986.
3. Coville, Bruce. *Robot Trouble.* 1986.
4. _____. *Forever Begins Tomorrow.* Announced.

The All-of-Kind Family. Sydney Taylor. Dell.
1. *All-of-a-Kind Family.* 1951.
2. *More All-of-a-Kind Family.* 1954.
3. *All-of-a-Kind Family Uptown.*
4. *All-of-a-Kind Family Downtown.* 1972.
5. *Ella of All-of-a-Kind Family.* 1978.

Cherry Ames. The bulk of the series was done by Helen Wells; volumes 10 through 16 were attributed to Julie Tatham. Grosset and Dunlap.
1. *Student Nurse.* 1943.
2. *Senior Nurse.* 1944.
3. *Army Nurse.* 1944.
4. *Chief Nurse.* 1944.
5. *Flight Nurse.* 1945.
6. *Veterans' Nurse.* 1946.
7. *Private Duty Nurse.* 1946.
8. *Visiting Nurse.* 1947.
9. *Cruise Nurse.* 1948.
10. *At Spencer.* 1949.
11. *Night Supervisor.* 1950.
12. *Mountaineer Nurse.* 1951.
13. *Clinic Nurse.* 1952.
14. *Dude Ranch Nurse.* 1953.
15. *Rest Home Nurse.* 1954.
16. *Country Doctor's Nurse.* 1955.
17. *Boarding School Nurse.* 1955.
18. *Department Store Nurse.* 1956.
19. *Camp Nurse.* 1957.
20. *At Hilton Hospital.* 1959.
21. *Island Nurse.* 1960.
22. *Rural Nurse.* 1961.
23. *Staff Nurse.* 1962.
24. *Companion Nurse.* 1964.
25. *Jungle Nurse.* 1965.

Animal Inn. Virginia Vail. Scholastic, Inc.
1. *Pets Are for Keeps.* 1986.

The Series

2. *A Kid's Best Friend.* 1986.
3. *Monkey Business.* 1987.
4. *Scaredy Cat.* 1987.
5. *Adopt-a-Pet.* 1987.
6. *All the Way Home.* 1987.

Arcade Explorers. Seth McEvoy and Laure Smith. Dell.
1. *Save the Venturians.* 1985.
2. *The Electronic Hurricane.* 1985.

The Babysitters Club. Ann H. Martin. Scholastic, Inc.
1. *Kristy's Great Idea.* 1986.
2. *Claudia and the Phantom Phone Call.* 1986.
3. *The Truth About Stacey.* 1986.
4. *Mary Anne Saves the Day.* 1987.
5. *Dawn and the Impossible Three.* 1987.
6. *Kristy's Bad Day.* 1987.
7. *Claudia and Mean Janine.* 1987.
8. *Boy-Crazy Stacey.* 1987.
9. *The Ghost at Dawn's House.* 1988.
10. *Mary Anne Goes Steady.* 1988.
11. *Kristy Meets the Snobs.* 1988.
12. *Claudia and the New Girl.* 1988.
13. *Goodbye Stacey, Goodbye.* 1988.
14. *Hello, Mallory.* 1988.
15. *Little Miss Stoneybrook and Dawn.* 1988.
16. *Jessi's Secret Language.* 1988.
17. *Mary Anne's Bad-Luck Mystery.* 1988.
18. *Stacey's Mistake.* 1988.
19. *Claudia and the Bad Joke.* 1988.
20. *Kristy and the Walking Disaster.* 1989.
21. *Mallory and the Trouble with Twins.* 1989.
22. *Jessi Ramsey, Pet Sitter.* 1989.
23. *Dawn on the Coast.* 1989.
24. *Kristy and the Mother's Day Surprise.* 1989.
25. *Mary Anne and the Search for Tigger.* 1989.
26. *Claudia and the Sad Goodbye.* 1989
27. *Jessi and the Superbrat.* 1989.
28. *Welcome Back, Stacey.* 1989.
29. *Mallory and the Mystery Diary.* 1989.

Sue Barton. Helen Dore Boylston. Little, Brown and Company.
1. *Student Nurse.* 1936.

2. *Senior Nurse.* 1937.
3. *Visiting Nurse.* 1938.
4. *Rural Nurse.* 1939.
5. *Superintendent of Nurses.* 1940.

The Bobbsey Twins. Laura Lee Hope. Grosset and Dunlap.
1. *The Bobbsey Twins—Merry Days Indoors and Out.* 1912 (1904).
2. *In the Country.* 1912 (1904).
3. *At the Seashore.* 1912 (1904).
4. *At School.* 1913.
5. *At Snow Lodge.* 1913.
6. *On a Houseboat.* 1915.
7. *At Meadowbrook.* 1915.
8. *At Home.* 1916.
9. *In a Great City.* 1917.
10. *On Blueberry Island.* 1917.
11. *On the Deep Blue Sea.* 1918.
12. *In Washington.* 1919.
13. *In the Great West.* 1920.
14. *At Cedar Camp.* 1921.
15. *At the Country Fair.* 1922.
16. *Camping Out.* 1923.
17. *And Baby May.* 1924.
18. *Keeping House.* 1925.
19. *At Cloverbank.* 1926.
20. *At Cherry Corners.* 1927.
21. *And Their Schoolmates.* 1928.
22. *Treasure Hunting.* 1929.
23. *At Spruce Lake.* 1930.
24. *Wonderful Secret.* 1931.
25. *At the Circus.* 1932.
26. *On an Airplane Trip.* 1933.
27. *Solve a Mystery.* 1934.
28. *On a Ranch.* 1935.
29. *In Eskimo Land.* 1936.
30. *In a Radio Play.* 1937.
31. *At Windmill Cottage.* 1938.
32. *At Lighthouse Point.* 1939.
33. *At Indian Hollow.* 1940.
34. *At the Ice Carnival.* 1941.
35. *In the Land of Cotton.* 1942.
36. *In Echo Valley.* 1943.

The Series

37. *On the Pony Trail.* 1944.
38. *At Mystery Mansion.* 1945.
39. *At Sugar Maple Hill.* 1946.
40. *In Mexico.* 1947.
41. *Toy Shop.* 1948.
42. *In Tulip Land.* 1949.
43. *In Rainbow Valley.* 1950.
44. *Own Little Railroad.* 1951.
45. *At Whitesail Harbor.* 1952.
46. *And the Horseshoe Riddle.* 1953.
47. *At Big Bear Pond.* 1953.
48. *On a Bicycle Trip.* 1954.
49. *Own Little Ferryboat.* 1956.
50. *At Pilgrim Rock.* 1956.
51. *Forest Adventure.* 1957.
52. *At London Tower.* 1959.
53. *In the Mystery Cave.* 1960.
54. *Of Lakeport.* 1961.
55. *In Volcano Land.* 1961.
56. *And the Goldfish Mystery.* 1962.
57. *And the Big River Mystery.* 1963.
58. *And the Greek Hat Mystery.* 1964.
59. *And the Search for the Green Rooster.* 1965.
60. *Their Camel Adventure.* 1966.
61. *The Mystery of the King's Puppet.* 1967.
62. *The Secret of Candy Castle.* 1968.
63. *Adventures with Baby May.* 1968.
64. *The Doodlebug Mystery.* 1969.
65. *The Talking Fox Mystery.* 1970.
66. *The Red, White and Blue Mystery.* 1971.
67. *Dr. Funnybone's Secret.* 1972.
68. *The Tagalong Giraffe.* 1973.
69. *The Flying Clown.* 1974.
70. *On the Sun-Moon Cruise.* 1975.
71. *The Freedom Bell Mystery.* 1976.
72. *The Smoky Mountain Mystery.* 1977.
73. *In the T.V. Mystery Show.* 1978.
74. *The Coral Turtle Mystery.* 1979.

Subsequent volumes published by Simon and Schuster.

75. *The Blue Poodle Mystery.* 1980.
76. *The Secret of the Pirate's Cave.* 1980.
77. *The Dune Buggy Mystery.* 1981.

78. *The Missing Pony Mystery.* 1981.
79. *The Rose Parade Mystery.* 1981
80. *The Camp Fire Mystery.* 1982.
81. *Double Trouble.* 1982.
82. *Mystery of the Laughing Dinosaur.* 1983.
83. *The Missing Box Mystery.* 1983.
84. *The Ghost in the Computer.* 1984.
85. *The Haunted House Mystery.* 1985.
86. *The Mystery of the Hindu Temple.* 1985.

The New Bobbsey Twins. Laura Lee Hope. Simon and Schuster.
1. *The Secret of Jungle Park.* 1987.
2. *The Case of the Runaway Money.* 1987.
3. *The Clue that Flew Away.* 1987.
4. *The Secret of the Sand Castle.* 1988.
5. *The Case of the Close Encounter.* 1988.
6. *Mystery on the Mississippi.* 1988.
7. *Trouble in Toyland.* 1988.
8. *The Secret of the Stolen Puppies.* 1988.
9. *The Clue in the Classroom.* 1988.
10. *The Chocolate-Covered Clue.* 1989.
11. *The Case of the Crooked Contest.* 1989.
12. *The Secret of the Sunken Treasure.* 1989.
13. *The Case of the Crying Clown.* 1989.
14. *The Mystery of the Missing Mummy.* 1989.
15. *The Secret of the Stolen Clue.* 1989.

The Bobbsey Twins Commemorative Editions. Laura Lee Hope. Wanderer Books.
1. *The Bobbsey Twins—Merry Days Indoors and Out.* 1979.
2. *The Bobbsey Twins in the Country.* 1979.
3. *The Bobbsey Twins at the Seashore.* 1979.

Judy Bolton. Margaret Sutton. Grosset and Dunlap.
1. *The Vanishing Shadow.* 1932.
2. *The Haunted Attic.* 1932.
3. *The Invisible Chimes.* 1932.
4. *Seven Strange Clues.*
5. *The Ghost Parade.* 1933.
6. *The Yellow Phantom.* 1933.
7. *The Mystic Ball.*
8. *The Voice in the Suitcase.*
9. *The Mysterious Half Cat.*
10. *The Riddle of the Double Ring.*

The Series 225

11. *The Unfinished House.*
12. *The Midnight Visitor.* 1939.
13. *The Name on the Bracelet.* 1940.
14. *The Clue in the Patchwork Quilt.* 1941.
15. *The Mark on the Mirror.* 1942.
16. *The Secret of the Barred Window.* 1943.
17. *The Rainbow Riddle.*
18. *The Living Portrait.*
19. *The Secret of the Musical Tree.* 1948.
20. *The Warning on the Window.* 1949.
21. *The Clue of the Stone Lantern.* 1950.
22. *The Spirit of Fog Island.* 1951.
23. *The Black Cat's Clue.* 1952.
24. *The Hidden Chest.* 1953.
25. *The Haunted Road.* 1954.
26. *The Clue of the Ruined Castle.* 1955.
27. *The Trail of the Green Doll.* 1956.
28. *The Haunted Fountain.* 1957.
29. *The Clue of the Broken Wing.* 1958.
30. *The Phantom Friend.* 1959.
31. *The Discovery at the Dragon's Mouth.* 1960.
32. *The Whispered Watchword.* 1961.
33. *The Secret Quest.* 1962.
34. *The Puzzle in the Pond.* 1963.
35. *The Hidden Clue.* 1964.

The Boy Scouts.

Thornton Burgess. Penn Publishing Company.

1. *Of Woodcraft Camp.*
2. *On Swift River.*
3. *On Lost Trail.*
4. *In a Trapper's Camp.* 1922.

Herbert Carter. A. L. Burt Company.

1. *First Camp Fire.* 1913.
2. *In the Blue Ridge.* 1913.
3. *In the Rockies.* 1913.
4. *In the Maine Woods.* 1913.
5. *Through the Big Timber.* 1913.
6. *On Sturgeon Island.*
7. *Down in Dixie.*
8. *At the Battle of Saratoga.*
9. *Along the Susquehanna.*

10. *War Trails in Belgium.* 1917.
11. *Afoot in France.* 1917.

Lieutenant Howard Payson. Hurst and Company.
1. *The Boy Scouts of the Eagle Patrol.*
2. *On the Range.*
3. *And the Army Airship.* 1911.
4. *Mountain Camp.*
5. *For Uncle Sam.*
6. *At the Panama Canal.*
7. *Under Fire in Mexico.*
8. *On Belgian Battlefields.*
9. *With the Allies in France.*
10. *At the Panama-Pacific Exposition.* 1915.
11. *Under Sealed Orders.* 1916.
12. *Campaign for Preparedness.* 1916.

Scoutmaster Robert Shaler. Hurst and Company.
1. *And the Signal Corps.*
2. *Of Pioneer Camp.*
3. *Of the Geological Survey.*
4. *Of the Life Saving Crew.*
5. *And the Prize Pennant.* 1914.

Rick Brant. John Blaine. Grosset and Dunlap.
1. *The Rocket's Shadow.* 1947.
2. *The Lost City.* 1947.
3. *Sea Gold.* 1947.
4. *100 Fathoms Under.* 1947.
5. *The Whispering Box Mystery.* 1948.
6. *The Phantom Shark.* 1949.
7. *Smuggler's Reef.* 1950.
8. *The Caves of Fear.* 1951.
9. *Stairway to Danger.* 1952.
10. *The Golden Skull.* 1954.
11. *The Wailing Octopus.* 1956.
12. *The Electronic Mind Reader.* 1957.
13. *The Scarlet Lake Mystery.* 1958.
14. *The Pirates of Shan.* 1958.
15. *The Blue Ghost Mystery.* 1960.
16. *The Egyptian Cat Mystery.* 1961.
17. *The Flaming Mountain.* 1962.
18. *The Flying Stingaree.* 1963.
19. *The Ruby Ray Mystery.* 1964.

The Series

The Brighton Boys. Lieutenant James R. Driscoll. John C. Winston Company.
1. *With the Flying Corps.* 1918.
2. *In the Trenches.* 1918.
3. *With the Battle Fleet.* 1918.
4. *In the Radio Service.* 1918.
5. *With the Submarine Fleet.* 1918.
6. *With the Engineers at Cantigny.*
7. *At Chateau-Thierry.*
8. *At St. Mihiel.*
9. *In the Argonne Forest.* 1920.
10. *In Transatlantic Flight.*
11. *In the Submarine Treasure Ship.*

Bunny Brown and His Sister Sue. Laura Lee Hope. Grosset and Dunlap.
1. *Bunny Brown and His Sister Sue.*
2. *On Grandpa's Farm.*
3. *Playing Circus.*
4. *At Aunt Lu's City Home.*
5. *At Camp Rest-a-While.*
6. *In the Big Woods.*
7. *On an Auto Tour.*
8. *And Their Shetland Pony.*
9. *Giving a Show.*
10. *At Christmas Tree Cove.* 1920.
11. *In the Sunny South.* 1921.
12. *Keeping Store.* 1921.
13. *And Their Trick Dog.* 1921.
14. *At a Sugar Camp.*
15. *On the Rolling Ocean.*

The Campfire Girls. Margaret Vandercook. John C. Winston Company.
1. *At Sunrise Hill.*
2. *Amid the Snows.*
3. *In the Outside World.*
4. *Across the Sea.*
5. *... Girls' Careers.*
6. *In After Years.* 1915

Dave Dawson: The War Adventure Series. R. Sidney Bowen. Saalfield Publishing Company.
1. *At Dunkirk.* 1941.

2. *With the R.A.F.* 1941.
3. *In Libya.* 1941.
4. *On Convoy Patrol.*
5. *At Singapore.* 1942.
6. *With the Pacific Fleet.* 1942.
7. *With the Air Corps.* 1942.
8. *On the Russian Front.* 1942.
9. *Flight Lieutenant.* 1942.
10. *With the Commandos.* 1942.
11. *With the Flying Tigers.*
12. *On Guadalcanal.* 1943.
13. *At Truk.*
14. *At Casablanca.*
15. *With the Eighth Air Force.* 1944.

Marjorie Dean. Pauline Lester. A. L. Burt Company.
1. *High School Freshman.* 1917.
2. *High School Sophomore.* 1917.
3. *High School Junior.* 1917.
4. *High School Senior.* 1917.

Nancy Drew. Carolyn Keene. Grosset and Dunlap.
1. *The Secret of the Old Clock.* 1930.
2. *The Hidden Staircase.* 1930.
3. *The Bungalow Mystery.* 1930.
4. *The Mystery at Lilac Inn.* 1930.
5. *The Secret at Shadow Ranch.* 1931.
6. *The Secret at Red Gate Farm.* 1931.
7. *The Clue in the Diary.* 1932.
8. *Nancy's Mysterious Letter.* 1932.
9. *The Sign of the Twisted Candles.* 1933.
10. *The Password to Larkspur Lane.* 1933.
11. *The Clue of the Broken Locket.* 1934.
12. *The Message in the Hollow Oak.* 1935.
13. *The Mystery of the Ivory Charm.* 1936.
14. *The Whispering Statue.* 1937.
15. *The Haunted Bridge.* 1937.
16. *The Clue of the Tapping Heels.* 1939.
17. *The Mystery of the Brassbound Trunk.* 1940.
18. *The Mystery of the Moss-Covered Mansion.* 1941.
19. *The Quest of the Missing Map.* 1942.
20. *The Clue in the Jewel Box.* 1943.
21. *The Secret in the Old Attic.* 1944.
22. *The Clue in the Crumbling Wall.* 1945.

The Series

23. *The Mystery of the Tolling Bell.* 1946.
24. *The Clue in the Old Album.* 1947.
25. *The Ghost of Blackwood Hall.* 1948.
26. *The Clue of the Leaning Chimney.* 1949.
27. *The Secret of the Wooden Lady.* 1950.
28. *The Clue of the Black Keys.* 1951.
29. *The Mystery at the Ski Jump.* 1952.
30. *The Clue of the Velvet Mask.* 1953.
31. *The Ringmaster's Secret.* 1953.
32. *The Scarlet Slipper Mystery.* 1954.
33. *The Witch Tree Symbol.* 1955.
34. *The Hidden Window Mystery.* 1956.
35. *The Haunted Showboat.* 1957.
36. *The Secret of the Golden Pavilion.* 1959.
37. *The Clue in the Old Stagecoach.* 1960.
38. *The Mystery of the Fire Dragon.* 1961.
39. *The Clue of the Dancing Puppet.* 1962.
40. *The Moonstone Castle Mystery.* 1963.
41. *The Clue of the Whistling Bagpipes.* 1964.
42. *The Phantom of Pine Hill.* 1965.
43. *The Mystery of the Ninety-nine Steps.* 1966.
44. *The Clue in the Crossword Cypher.* 1967.
45. *The Spider Sapphire Mystery.* 1968.
46. *The Invisible Intruder.* 1969.
47. *The Mysterious Mannequin.* 1970.
48. *The Crooked Bannister.* 1971.
49. *The Secret of Mirror Bay.* 1972.
50. *The Double Jinx Mystery.* 1973.
51. *The Mystery of the Glowing Eye.* 1974.
52. *The Secret of the Forgotten City.* 1975.
53. *The Sky Phantom.* 1976.
54. *The Strange Message in the Parchment.* 1977.
55. *The Mystery of Crocodile Island.* 1978.
56. *The Thirteenth Pearl.* 1979.

Subsequent volumes published by Simon and Schuster.

57. *The Triple Hoax.* 1979.
58. *The Flying Saucer Mystery.* 1980.
59. *The Secret in the Old Lace.* 1980.
60. *The Greek Symbol Mystery.* 1981.
61. *The Swami's Ring.* 1981.
62. *The Kachina Doll Mystery.* 1981.
63. *The Twin Dilemma.* 1981.

64. *The Captive Witness.* 1981.
65. *The Mystery of the Winged Lion.* 1982.
66. *Race Against Time.* 1982.
67. *The Sinister Omen.* 1982.
68. *The Elusive Heiress.* 1982.
69. *The Clue in the Ancient Disguise.* 1982.
70. *The Broken Anchor.* 1983
71. *The Silver Cobweb.* 1983.
72. *The Haunted Carousel.* 1983.
73. *Enemy Match.* 1984.
74. *The Mysterious Image.* 1984.
75. *The Emerald-Eyed Cat Mystery.* 1984.
76. *The Eskimo's Secret.* 1985.
77. *The Bluebeard Room.* 1985.
78. *The Phantom of Venice.* 1985.
79. *The Double Horror of Fenley Place.* 1987.
80. *The Case of the Disappearing Diamonds.* 1987.
81. *The Mardi Gras Mystery.* 1988.
82. *The Clue in the Camera.* 1988.
83. *The Case of the Vanishing Veil.* 1988.
84. *The Joker's Revenge.* 1988.
85. *The Secret of Shady Glen.* 1988.
86. *The Mystery of Misty Canyon.* 1988.
87. *The Case of the Rising Stars.* 1989.
88. *The Search for Cindy Austin.* 1989.
89. *The Case of the Disappearing Dee Jay.* 1989.
90. *The Puzzle of Pineview School.* 1989.
91. *The Girl Who Couldn't Remember.* 1989.

The Nancy Drew Files. Carolyn Keene. Simon and Schuster.
1. *Secret's Can Kill.* 1986.
2. *Deadly Intent.* 1986.
3. *Murder on Ice.* 1986.
4. *Smile and Say Murder.* 1986.
5. *Hit and Run Holiday.* 1986.
6. *White Water Terror.* 1986.
7. *Deadly Doubles.* 1986.
8. *Two Points to Murder.* 1987.
9. *False Moves.* 1987.
10. *Buried Secrets.* 1987.
11. *Heart of Danger.* 1987.
12. *Fatal Ransom.* 1987.
13. *Wings of Fear.* 1987.

14. *This Side of Evil.* 1987.
15. *Trial by Fire.* 1987.
16. *Never Say Die.* 1987.
17. *Stay Tuned for Danger.* 1987.
18. *Circle of Evil.* 1987.
19. *Sisters in Crime.* 1987.
20. *Very Deadly Yours.* 1987.
21. *Recipe for Murder.* 1988.
22. *Fatal Attraction.* 1988.
23. *Sinister Paradise.* 1988.
24. *Till Death Do Us Part.* 1988.
25. *Rich and Dangerous.* 1988.
26. *Playing with Fire.* 1988.
27. *Most Likely to Die.* 1988.
28. *The Black Widow.* 1988.
29. *Pure Poison.* 1988.
30. *Death by Design.* 1988.
31. *Trouble in Tahiti.* 1989.
32. *High Marks for Malice.* 1989.
33. *Danger in Disguise.* 1989.
34. *Vanishing Act.* 1989.
35. *Bad Medicine.* 1989.
36. *Over the Edge.* 1989.
37. *Last Dance.* 1989.
38. *The Final Scene.* 1989.
39. *The Suspect Next Door.* 1989.
40. *Shadow of a Doubt.* 1989.
41. *Something to Hide.* 1989.
42. *The Wrong Chemistry.* 1989.

Doris Fein. T. Ernesto Bethancourt. Holiday House.
1. *Dr. Doom: Superstar.* 1978.
2. *Doris Fein: Superspy.* 1979.
3. *DF: Quartz Boyar.* 1980.
4. *DF: Phantom of the Casino.* 1981.
5. *DF: The Mad Samurai.* 1981.
6. *DF: Deadly Aphrodite.* 1982.
7. *DF: Murder Is No Joke.* 1982.
8. *DF: Dead Heat at Long Beach.* 1983.
9. *DF: Legacy of Terror.* 1984.

Beverly Gray. Clair Blank. Grosset and Dunlap.
1. *Freshman.* 1934.

The Hardy Boys. Franklin W. Dixon. Grosset and Dunlap.
 1. *The Tower Treasure.* 1927.
 2. *The House on the Cliff.* 1927.
 3. *The Secret of the Old Mill.* 1927.
 4. *The Missing Chums.* 1928.
 5. *Hunting for Hidden Gold.* 1928.
 6. *The Shore Road Mystery.* 1928.
 7. *The Secret of the Caves.* 1929.
 8. *The Mystery of Cabin Island.* 1929.
 9. *The Great Airport Mystery.* 1930.
 10. *What Happened at Midnight.* 1931.
 11. *While the Clock Ticked.* 1932.
 12. *Footprints Under the Window.* 1933.
 13. *The Mark on the Door.* 1934.
 14. *The Hidden Harbor Mystery.* 1935.
 15. *The Sinister Sign Post.* 1936.
 16. *A Figure in Hiding.* 1937.
 17. *The Secret Warning.* 1938.
 18. *The Twisted Claw.* 1939.
 19. *The Disappearing Floor.* 1940.
 20. *The Mystery of the Flying Express.* 1941.
 21. *The Clue of the Broken Blade.* 1942.
 22. *The Flickering Torch Mystery.* 1943.
 23. *The Melted Coins.* 1944.
 24. *The Short Wave Mystery.* 1945.
 25. *The Secret Panel.* 1946.
 26. *The Phantom Freighter.* 1947.
 27. *The Secret of Skull Mountain.* 1948.
 28. *The Sign of the Crooked Arrow.* 1949.
 29. *The Secret of the Lost Tunnel.* 1950.
 30. *The Wailing Siren Mystery.* 1951.
 31. *The Secret of Wildcat Swamp.* 1952.
 32. *The Crisscross Shadow.* 1953.
 33. *The Yellow Feather Mystery.* 1953.
 34. *The Hooded Hawk Mystery.* 1954.
 35. *The Clue in the Embers.* 1955.
 36. *The Secret of Pirates' Hill.* 1956.
 37. *The Ghost at Skeleton Rock.* 1957.
 38. *The Mystery at Devil's Paw.* 1959.
 39. *The Mystery of the Chinese Junk.* 1960.
 40. *The Mystery of the Desert Giant.* 1961.
 41. *The Clue of the Screeching Owl.* 1962.
 42. *The Viking Symbol Mystery.* 1963.

43. *The Mystery of the Aztec Warrior.* 1964.
44. *The Haunted Fort.* 1965.
45. *The Mystery of the Spiral Bridge.* 1966.
46. *The Secret Agent of Flight 101.* 1967.
47. *The Mystery of the Whale Tattoo.* 1968.
48. *The Arctic Patrol Mystery.* 1969.
49. *The Bombay Boomerang.* 1970.
50. *Danger on Vampire Trail.* 1971.
51. *The Masked Monkey.* 1972.
52. *The Shattered Helmet.* 1973.
53. *The Clue of the Hissing Serpent.* 1974.
54. *The Mysterious Caravan.* 1975.
55. *The Witchmaster's Key.* 1976.
56. *The Jungle Pyramid.* 1977.
57. *The Firebird Rocket.* 1978.
58. *The Sting of the Scorpion.* 1979.

Subsequent volumes published by Simon and Schuster.

59. *Night of the Werewolf.* 1979.
60. *Mystery of the Samurai Sword.* 1979.
61. *The Pentagon Spy.* 1980.
62. *The Apeman's Secret.* 1980.
63. *The Mummy Case.* 1980.
64. *The Mystery of Smuggler's Cove.* 1980.
65. *The Stone Idol.* 1981.
66. *The Vanishing Thieves.* 1981.
67. *The Outlaw's Silver.* 1981.
68. *Deadly Chase.* 1981.
69. *The Four-Headed Dragon.* 1981.
70. *The Infinity Clue.* 1981.
71. *Track of the Zombie.* 1982.
72. *The Voodoo Plot.* 1982.
73. *The Billion Dollar Ransom.* 1982.
74. *Tic-Tac-Terror.* 1982.
75. *Trapped at Sea.* 1982.
76. *Game Plan for Disaster.* 1982.
77. *The Crimson Flame.* 1983.
78. *Cave-in!* 1983.
79. *Sky Sabotage.* 1983.
80. *The Roaring River Mystery.* 1984.
81. *The Demon's Den.* 1984.
82. *The Blackwing Puzzle.* 1984.
83. *The Swamp Monster.* 1985.

84. *Revenge of the Desert Phantom.* 1985.
85. *The Skyfire Puzzle.* 1985.
86. *The Mystery of the Silver Star.* 1987.
87. *Program for Destruction.* 1987.
88. *Tricky Business.* 1988.
89. *The Sky Blue Frame.* 1988.
90. *Danger on the Diamond.* 1988.
91. *Shield of Fear.* 1988.
92. *The Shadow Killer.* 1988.
93. *The Serpent's Tooth.* 1988.
94. *Breakdown in Axe Blade.* 1989.
95. *Danger on the Air.* 1989.
96. *Wipeout.* 1989.
97. *Cast of Criminals.* 1989.
98. *Spark of Suspicion.* 1989.

The Hardy Boys Casefiles. Franklin W. Dixon. Simon and Schuster.
1. *Dead on Target.* 1987.
2. *Evil, Inc.* 1987.
3. *Cult of Crime.* 1987.
4. *The Lazarus Plot.* 1987.
5. *Edge of Destruction.* 1987.
6. *The Crowning Terror.* 1987.
7. *Death Game.* 1987.
8. *See No Evil.* 1987.
9. *The Genius Thieves.* 1987.
10. *Hostages of Hate.* 1987.
11. *Brother Against Brother.* 1987.
12. *Perfect Getaway.* 1987.
13. *The Borgia Dagger.* 1987.
14. *Too Many Traitors.* 1988.
15. *Blood Relations.* 1988.
16. *Line of Fire.* 1988.
17. *The Number File.* 1988.
18. *A Killing in the Market.* 1988.
19. *Nightmare in Angel City.* 1988.
20. *Witness to Murder.* 1988.
21. *Street Spies.* 1988.
22. *Double Exposure.* 1988.
23. *Disaster for Hire.* 1989.
24. *Scene of the Crime.* 1989.
25. *The Borderline Case.* 1989.
26. *Trouble in the Pipeline.* 1989.

The Series

27. *Nowhere to Run.* 1989.
28. *Countdown to Terror.* 1989.
29. *Thick as Thieves.* 1989.
30. *The Deadliest Dare.* 1989.
31. *Without a Trace.* 1989.
32. *Blood Money.* 1989.
33. *Collision Course.* 1989.
34. *Final Act.* 1989.

Grace Harlowe. Jessie Graham Flower, A.M. Henry Altemus Company.

Grace Harlowe High School and College Series.
1. *Plebe Year at High School.* 1910.
2. *Sophomore Year at High School.* 1911.
3. *Junior Year at High School.* 1911.
4. *Senior Year at High School.* 1911.
5. *First Year at Overton College.* 1913.
6. *Second Year at Overton College.* 1914.
7. *Third Year at Overton College.* 1914.
8. *Fourth Year at Overton College.*
9. *Return to Overton College.*
10. *Problem.* 1916.
11. *Golden Summer.* 1917.

Grace Harlowe Overseas Series.
1. *With the Red Cross in France.*
2. *With the Marines at Chateau Thierry.*
3. *With the U.S. Troops in the Argonne.* 1918.
4. *With the Yankee Shock Troops at San Quentin.* 1918.
5. *With the American Army on the Rhine.* 1919.

Grace Harlowe's Overland Riders Series.
1. *On the Old Apache Trail.* 1921.
2. *On the Great American Desert.* 1921.
3. *Among the Kentucky Mountaineers.* 1921.
4. *In the Great North Woods.*
5. *In the High Sierras.*
6. *In the Yellowstone National Park.*
7. *In the Black Hills.*
8. *At Circle O Ranch.*
9. *And the Border Guerrillas.*
10. *On the Lost River Trail.* 1924.

Chip Hilton. Clair Bee. Grosset and Dunlap.
   1. *Touchdown Pass.* 1948.
   2. *Championship Ball.* 1948.
   3. *Strike Three!* 1949.
   4. *Clutch Hitter.* 1949.
   5. *Hoop Crazy.* 1950.
   6. *Pitchers' Duel.* 1950.
   7. *A Pass and a Prayer.* 1951.
   8. *Dugout Jinx.* 1952.
   9. *Freshman Quarterback.* 1952.
   10. *Backboard Fever.* 1953.
   11. *Fence Busters.* 1953.
   12. *Ten Seconds to Play!* 1955.
   13. *Fourth Down Showdown.* 1956.
   14. *Tournament Crisis.* 1957.
   15. *Hardcourt Upset.* 1957.
   16. *Pay-Off Pitch.* 1958.
   17. *No Hitter.* 1959.
   18. *Triple-Threat Trouble.* 1960.
   19. *Backcourt Ace.* 1961.
   20. *Buzzer Basket.* 1962.
   21. *Comeback Cagers.* 1963.
   22. *Home Run Feud.* 1964.

The Happy Hollisters. Jerry West. Doubleday and Company.
   1. *The Happy Hollisters.* 1953.
   2. *On a River Trip.* 1953.
   3. *At Sea Gull Beach.* 1953.
   4. *And the Indian Treasure.* 1953.
   5. *At Mystery Mountain.* 1954.
   6. *At Snowflake Cave.* 1954.
   7. *And the Trading Post Mystery.* 1954.
   8. *At Circus Island.* 1955.
   9. *And the Secret Fort.* 1955.
   10. *And the Merry-Go-Round Mystery.* 1955.
   11. *At Pony Hill Farm.* 1956.
   12. *And the Old Clipper Ship.* 1956.
   13. *At Lizard Cove.* 1957.
   14. *And the Scarecrow Mystery.* 1957.
   15. *And the Mystery of the Totem Faces.* 1958.
   16. *And the Ice Carnival Mystery.* 1958.
   17. *And the Mystery of Skyscraper City.* 1959.
   18. *And the Mystery of the Little Mermaid.* 1960.
   19. *And the Mystery at Missile Town.* 1961.

The Series

20. *And the Cowboy Mystery.* 1961.
21. *And the Secret of the Lucky Coins.* 1962.
22. *And the Haunted House Mystery.* 1962.
23. *And the Castle Rock Mystery.* 1963.
24. *And the Punch and Judy Mystery.* 1964.
25. *And the Sea Turtle Mystery.* 1964.
26. *And the Swiss Echo Mystery.* 1964.
27. *And the Whistle Pig Mystery.* 1964.
28. *And the Cuckoo Clock Mystery.* 1964.
29. *And the Ghost House Mystery.* 1965.
30. *And the Mystery of the Golden Witch.* 1966.
31. *And the Mystery of the Mexican Idol.* 1967.
32. *And the Monster Mystery.* 1968.
33. *And the Mystery of the Midnight Trolls.* 1969.

Ken Holt. Bruce Campbell. Grosset and Dunlap.
1. *The Secret of Skeleton Island.* 1949.
2. *The Riddle of the Stone Elephant.* 1949.
3. *The Black Thumb Mystery.* 1950.
4. *The Clue of the Marked Claw.* 1950.
5. *The Clue of the Coiled Cobra.* 1951.
6. *The Secret of Hangman's Inn.* 1951.
7. *The Mystery of the Iron Box.* 1952.
8. *The Clue of the Phantom Car.* 1953.
9. *The Mystery of the Galloping Horse.* 1954.
10. *The Mystery of the Green Flame.* 1955.
11. *The Mystery of the Grinning Tiger.* 1956.
12. *The Mystery of the Vanishing Magician.* 1956.
13. *The Mystery of the Shattered Glass.* 1958.
14. *The Mystery of the Invisible Enemy.* 1959
15. *The Mystery of Gallows Cliff.* 1959.
16. *The Clue of the Silver Scorpion.* 1961.
17. *The Mystery of the Sultan's Scimitar.* 1963.

Honey Bunch. Helen Louise Thorndyke. Grosset and Dunlap.
1. *Just a Little Girl.* 1923.
2. *First Visit to the City.* 1923
3. *First Days on the Farm.* 1923.
4. *First Visit to the Seashore.* 1924.
5. *First Little Garden.* 1924.
6. *First Days in Camp.* 1925.
7. *First Auto Tour.* 1926.
8. *First Trip on the Ocean.* 1927.
9. *First Trip West.* 1928.

10. *First Summer on an Island.* 1929.
11. *First Trip on the Great Lakes.* 1930.
12. *First Trip in an Airplane.* 1931.
13. *First Visit to the Zoo.* 1932.
14. *First Big Adventure.* 1933.
15. *First Big Parade.* 1934.
16. *First Little Mystery.* 1935.
17. *First Little Circus.* 1936.
18. *First Little Treasure Hunt.* 1937.
19. *First Little Club.* 1938.
20. *First Little Trip in a Trailer.* 1939.
21. *First Trip to a Big Fair.* 1940.
22. *First Twin Playmates.*
23. *First Costume Party.* 1943.
24. *First Trip on a Houseboat.*
25. *First Winter at Snowtop.* 1946.
26. *First Trip to the Big Woods.*
27. *First Trip to a Lighthouse.* 1949.

Honey Bunch and Norman. Helen Louise Thorndyke. Grosset and Dunlap.
1. *Honey Bunch and Norman.* 1957.
2. *On Lighthouse Island.* 1957.
3. *Tour Toy Town.* 1957.
4. *Play Detective at Niagara Falls.* 1957.
5. *Ride with the Sky Mailman.* 1957.
6. *Visit Beaver Lodge.* 1958.
7. *Visit Reindeer Farm.* 1958.
8. *In the Castle of Magic.* 1959.
9. *Solve the Pinecone Mystery.* 1960.
10. *And the Paper Lantern Mystery.* 1961.
11. *The Painted Pony.* 1962.
12. *The Walnut Tree Mystery.* 1963.

The Lone Ranger. First volume listed Gaylord DuBois as author, with a note that the book was based on a radio program by Fran Striker; thereafter, Fran Striker was given as author of subsequent books. Grosset and Dunlap.
1. *The Lone Ranger.* 1936.
2. *And the Mystery Ranch.* 1938.
3. *And the Gold Robbery.* 1939.
4. *And the Outlaw Stronghold.* 1939.
5. *And Tonto.* 1940.
6. *At the Haunted Gulch.* 1941.

The Series

  7. *Traps the Smugglers.* 1942.
  8. *Rides Again.* 1943.
  9. *Rides North.* 1946.
 10. *And the Silver Bullet.*
 11. *On Powderhorn Trail.*
 12. *In Wild Horse Canyon.*
 13. *West of Maverick Pass.* 1951.
 14. *On Gunsight Mesa.* 1952.
 15. *And the Bitterspring Feud.* 1953.
 16. *And the Code of the West.* 1954.
 17. *Trouble on the Santa Fe.* 1955.
 18. *On Red Butte Trail.* 1956.

Marjorie. Carolyn Wells. Grosset and Dunlap.
  1. *Vacation.* 1907.
  2. *Busy Day.* 1908.
  3. *New Friend.* 1909.
  4. *In Command.* 1910.
  5. *Marjorie's Maytime.* 1911.
  6. *At Seacote.* 1912.

Not Quite Human. Seth McEvoy. Simon and Schuster.
  1. *Batteries Not Included.* 1985.
  2. *All Geared Up.* 1985.
  3. *A Bug in the System.* 1985.
  4. *Reckless Robot.* 1985.
  5. *Terror at Play.* 1986.
  6. *Killer Robot.* 1987.

The Outdoor Girls. Laura Lee Hope. Whitman Publishing Company.
  1. *At Cedar Ridge,*

Race Against Time. J. J. Fortune. Dell.
  1. *Revenge of the Silent Tomb.* 1984.
  2. *Escape from Raven Castle.* 1984.
  3. *Pursuit of the Deadly Diamonds.* 1984.
  4. *Search for Mad Jack's Crown.* 1984.
  5. *Duel for the Samurai Sword.* 1984.
  6. *Evil in Paradise.* 1984.
  7. *The Secret of the Third Watch.* 1984.
  8. *Trapped in the U.S.S.R.* 1984.
  9. *Journey to Atlantis.* 1985.

Red Cross Girls. Margaret Vandercook. John C. Winston Company.
1. *In the British Trenches.* 1916.
2. *On the French Firing Line.* 1916.
3. *In Belgium.* 1916.
4. *With the Russian Army.* 1917.
5. *With the Italian Army.* 1917.
6. *Under the Stars and Stripes.* 1917.
7. *Afloat with the Flag.* 1918.
8. *With Pershing to Victory.* 1919.

Rollo. Jacob Abbott.

First Series. This series, begun before 1840, is very rare. It was published by various houses, among them William Crosby and Company, early in the nineteenth century, and by Thomas Y. Crowell, in the 1890's. Dates of publication are therefore very indefinite and often inconsistent. The order of volumes is known from the Crowell editions.

1. *Rollo Learning to Talk.*
2. *Rollo Learning to Read.*
3. *Rollo at Work.*
4. *Rollo at Play.* 1855/1897.
5. *Rollo at School.* 1855.
6. *Rollo's Vacation.*
7. *Rollo's Experiments.* 1855/1867.
8. *Rollo's Museum.*
9. *Rollo's Travels.* 1840.
10. *Rollo's Correspondence.*
11. *Rollo's Philosophy—Water.*
12. *Rollo's Philosophy—Air.*
13. *Rollo's Philosophy—Fire.*
14. *Rollo's Philosophy—Sky.*

Second Series. Brown, Taggard and Chase Publishers.

1. *On the Atlantic.*
2. *In Paris.*
3. *In Switzerland.*
4. *In London.*
5. *On the Rhine.*
6. *In Scotland.* 1855.
7. *In Geneva.*
8. *In Holland.*
9. *In Naples.*
10. *In Rome.*

The Rover Boys. Arthur M. Winfield. Grosset and Dunlap.
>   First Series
>   1. *At School.* 1899.
>   2. *On the Ocean.* 1899.
>   3. *In the Jungle.* 1899.
>   4. *Out West.* 1900.
>   5. *On the Great Lakes.* 1901.
>   6. *In the Mountains.* 1902.
>   7. *On Land and Sea.* 1903.
>   8. *In Camp.* 1904.
>   9. *On the River.* 1905.
>   10. *On the Plains.* 1906.
>   11. *In Southern Waters.* 1907.
>   12. *On the Farm.* 1908.
>   13. *On Treasure Isle.* 1909.
>   14. *At College.* 1910.
>   15. *Down East.* 1911.
>   16. *In the Air.* 1912.
>   17. *In New York.* 1913.
>   18. *In Alaska.* 1914.
>   19. *In Business.* 1915.
>   20. *On a Tour.* 1916.
>
>   Second Series
>   1. *At Colby Hall.* 1917.
>   2. *On Snowshoe Island.* 1918.
>   3. *Under Canvas.* 1919.
>   4. *On a Hunt.* 1920.
>   5. *In the Land of Luck.* 1921.
>   6. *At Big Horn Ranch.* 1922.
>   7. *At Big Bear Lake.* 1923.
>   8. *Shipwrecked.* 1924.
>   9. *On Sunset Trail.* 1925.
>   10. *Winning a Fortune.* 1926.

Sleepover Friends. Susan Saunders. Scholastic.
>   1. *Patti's Luck.* 1987.
>   2. *Starring Stephanie.* 1987.
>   3. *Kate's Surprise.* 1987.
>   4. *Patti's New Look.* 1988.
>   5. *Lauren's Big Mix-up.* 1988.
>   6. *Kate's Camp Out.* 1988.
>   7. *Stephanie Strikes Back.* 1988.

8. *Lauren's Treasure.* 1988.
9. *No More Sleepover, Patti?* 1988.
10. *Lauren's Sleepover Exchange.* 1989.
11. *Stephanie's Family Secret.* 1989.
12. *Kate's Sleepover Disaster.* 1989.
13. *Patti's Secret Wish.* 1989.

Don Sturdy. Victor Appleton. Grosset and Dunlap.
1. *On the Desert of Mystery.* 1925.
2. *With the Big Snake Hunters.* 1925.
3. *In the Tombs of Gold.* 1925.
4. *Across the North Pole.* 1925.
5. *In the Land of Volcanoes.* 1925.
6. *In the Port of Lost Ships.* 1926.
7. *Among the Gorillas.* 1927.
8. *Captured by Head Hunters.* 1928.
9. *In Lion Land.* 1929.
10. *In the Land of Giants.* 1930.
11. *On the Ocean Bottom.* 1931.
12. *In the Temples of Fear.* 1931.

Sweet Valley High. Written by Kate William. Created by Francine Pascal. Bantam.
1. *Double Love.* 1983.
2. *Secrets.* 1983.
3. *Playing with Fire.* 1983.
4. *Power Play.* 1983.
5. *All Night Long.* 1984.
6. *Dangerous Love.* 1984.
7. *Dear Sister.* 1984.
8. *Heartbreaker.* 1984.
9. *Racing Hearts.* 1984.
10. *Wrong Kind of Girl.* 1984.
11. *Too Good to Be True.* 1984.
12. *When Love Dies.* 1984.
13. *Kidnapped!* 1984.
14. *Deceptions.* 1984.
15. *Promises.* 1985.
16. *Rags to Riches.* 1985.
17. *Love Letters.* 1985.
18. *Head Over Heels.* 1985.
19. *Showdown.* 1985.
20. *Crash Landing!* 1985.
21. *Runaway.* 1985.

The Series

22. *Too Much in Love.* 1985.
23. *Say Goodbye.* 1985.
24. *Memories.* 1985.
25. *Nowhere to Run.* 1986.
26. *Hostage!* 1986.
27. *Lovestruck.* 1986.
28. *Alone in the Crowd.* 1986.
29. *Bitter Rivals.* 1986.
30. *Jealous Lies.* 1986.
31. *Taking Sides.* 1986.
32. *The New Jessica.* 1986.
33. *Starting Over.* 1986.
34. *Forbidden Love.* 1987.
35. *Out of Control.* 1987.
36. *Last Chance.* 1987.
37. *Rumors.* 1987.
38. *Leaving Home.* 1987.
39. *Secret Admirer.* 1987.
40. *On the Edge.* 1987.
41. *Outcast.* 1987.
42. *Caught in the Middle.* 1987.
43. *Hard Choices.* 1988.
44. *Pretenses.* 1988.
45. *Family Secrets.* 1988.
46. *Decisions.* 1988.
47. *Troublemaker.* 1988.
48. *Slam Book Fever.* 1988.
49. *Playing for Keeps.* 1988.
50. *Out of Reach.* 1988.
51. *Against the Odds.* 1988.
52. *White Lies.* 1989.
53. *Second Chance.* 1989.
54. *Two-Boy Weekend.* 1989.
55. *Perfect Shot.* 1989.
56. *Lost at Sea.* 1989.
57. *Teacher Crush.* 1989.
58. *Broken Hearted.* 1989.
59. *In Love Again.* 1989.
60. *That Fatal Night.* 1989.

Sweet Valley Twins. Written by Jamie Suzanne. Created by Francine Pascal. Bantam.
1. *Best Friends.* 1986.

2. *Teacher's Pet.* 1986.
3. *The Haunted House.* 1986.
4. *Choosing Sides.* 1986.
5. *Sneaking Out.* 1987.
6. *The New Girl.* 1987.
7. *Three's a Crowd.* 1987.
8. *First Place.* 1987.
9. *Against the Rules.* 1987.
10. *One of the Gang.* 1987.
11. *Buried Treasure.* 1987.
12. *Keeping Secrets.* 1987.
13. *Stretching the Truth.* 1987.
14. *Tug of War.* 1987.
15. *The Older Boy.* 1987.
16. *Second Best.* 1988.
17. *Boys Against Girls.* 1988.
18. *Center of Attention.* 1988.
19. *The Bully.* 1988.
20. *Playing Hookey.* 1988.
21. *Left Behind.* 1988.
22. *Out of Place.* 1988.
23. *Claim to Fame.* 1988.
24. *Jumping to Conclusions.* 1988.
25. *Standing Out.* 1988.
26. *Taking Charge.* 1989.
27. *Teamwork.* 1989.
28. *April Fool.* 1989.
29. *Jessica and the Brat Attack.* 1989.
30. *Princess Elizabeth.* 1989.
31. *Jessica's Bad Idea.* 1989.
32. *Jessica on Stage.* 1989.
33. *Elizabeth's New Hero.* 1989.
34. *Jessica the Rock Star.* 1989.

Tom and Ricky. Bob Wright. High Noon Books.

1 Series

1. *The Mummy's Crown.* 1982.
2. *The Siamese Turtle Mystery.* 1982.
3. *The Video Game Spy.* 1982.

2 Series

1. *The Gold Coin Robbery.* 1983.
2. *The Silver Buckle Mystery.* 1983.

The Series

3. *The Falling Star Mystery.* 1983.
4. *The Thief in the Brown Van.* 1983.

Tom Swift. Victor Appleton. Grosset and Dunlap.
1. *And His Motor Cycle.* 1910.
2. *And His Motor Boat.* 1910.
3. *And His Airship.* 1910.
4. *And His Submarine Boat.*
5. *And His Electric Runabout.* 1911.
6. *And His Wireless Message.* 1911.
7. *Among the Diamond Makers.* 1911.
8. *In the Caves of Ice.* 1911.
9. *And His Sky Racer.* 1911.
10. *And His Electric Rifle.* 1911.
11. *In the City of Gold.* 1912.
12. *And His Air Glider.* 1912.
13. *In Captivity.* 1912.
14. *And His Wizard Camera.* 1912.
15. *And His Great Searchlight.* 1912.
16. *And His Giant Cannon.* 1912.
17. *And His Photo Telephone.* 1914.
18. *And His Aerial Warship.* 1915.
19. *And His Big Tunnel.* 1916.
20. *In the Land of Wonders.* 1917.
21. *And His War Tank.* 1918.
22. *And His Air Scout.* 1919.
23. *And His Undersea Search.* 1920.
24. *Among the Fire Fighters.* 1921.
25. *And His Electric Locomotive.* 1922.
26. *And His Flying Boat.* 1923.
27. *And His Great Oil Gusher.* 1924.
28. *And His Chest of Secrets.* 1925.
29. *And His Airline Express.* 1926.
30. *Circling the Globe.* 1927.
31. *And His Talking Pictures.* 1928.
32. *And His House on Wheels.* 1929.
33. *And His Big Dirigible.* 1930.
34. *And His Sky Train.*
35. *And His Giant Magnet.*
36. *And His Television Detector.* 1933. Whitman.
37. *And His Ocean Airport.*

Tom Swift, Jr. Victor Appleton, Jr. Grosset and Dunlap
1. *And His Flying Lab.* 1954.

2. *And His Jetmarine.* 1954.
3. *And His Rocket Ship.* 1954.
4. *And His Giant Robot.* 1954.
5. *And His Atomic Earth Blaster.* 1954.
6. *And His Outpost in Space.* 1955.
7. *And His Diving Seacopter.* 1956.
8. *In the Caves of Nuclear Fire.* 1956
9. *And the Phantom Satellite.* 1956.
10. *And His Ultrasonic Cycloplane.* 1957.
11. *And His Deep Sea Hydrodome.* 1958.
12. *In the Race to the Moon.* 1958.
13. *And His Space Solatron.* 1958.
14. *And His Electronic Retroscope.* 1959.
15. *And His Spectromarine Selector.* 1960.
16. *And the Cosmic Astronauts.* 1960.
17. *And the Visitor from Planet X.* 1961.
18. *And His Electronic Hydrolung.* 1961.
19. *And His Triphibian Atomicar.* 1962.
20. *And His Megascope Space Prober.* 1962.
21. *And the Asteroid Pirates.* 1963.
22. *And His Repelatron Skyway.* 1963.
23. *And His Aquatonic Tracker.* 1964.
24. *And His 3-D Telejector.* 1964.
25. *And His Polar Ray Dynasphere.* 1965.

Tom Swift (Third Series). Victor Appleton. Simon and Schuster.
1. *The City in the Stars.* 1981.
2. *Terror on the Moons of Jupiter.* 1981.
3. *The Alien Probe.* 1981.
4. *The War in Outer Space.* 1981.
5. *The Astral Fortress.* 1981.
6. *The Rescue Mission.* 1981.
7. *Ark Two.* 1982.
8. *Crater of Mystery.* 1982.
9. *Gateway to Doom.* 1983.
10. *The Invisible Force.* 1983.
11. *Planet of Nightmares.* Announced.

Uncle Sam's Boys. H. Irving Hancock. Henry Altemus Company.
1. *In the Ranks.* 1910.
2. *On Field Duty.* 1911.
3. *As Sergeants.*
4. *In the Philippines.*
5. *On Their Mettle.*

6. *As Lieutenants.*
   7. *With Pershing's Troops at the Front.* 1919.
   8. *In the Great Marne Drive.* 1919.
   9. *Smash the Germans.* 1919.

The Woodland Gang. Irene Schultz. Black and White and Read All Over Publishing Company.
   1. *The Hidden Jewels.* 1984.
   2. *The Dark Old House.* 1984.
   3. *The Two Lost Boys.* 1984.
   4. *The Missing Will.* 1984.
   5. *The Stolen Animals.* 1984.
   6. *The Old Gold Coins.* 1984.

INDEX

Series titles are printed in capital letters, book and magazine titles in italics, and article titles in quotation marks. Series titles are alphabetized by first word or name, and book titles in series are listed under the series to which they belong.

Abbott, Jacob   6
Academy of Terror   142
Adams, Bess Porter   30
Adams, Harriet   14, 29, 36
Adventure   34
"Adventure Stories Preferred by Boy's Club Readers"   31
AEROPLANE BOYS   12
A. I. GANG   36, 38, 49, 55, 59, 60, 62, 65, 79, 84, 96, 99, 151, 191
  Cutlass Clue   38, 47, 55, 56, 83, 151, 152, 157
  Robot Trouble   55, 56, 60, 95, 152, 154, 157
Alden, Isabella   25
Alger, Horatio   8, 20, 25, 134
ALL-OF-A-KIND FAMILY   76, 77, 79, 81, 84, 86, 129, 162, 163, 165
  All-of-a-Kind Family   71, 89, 129–130, 139, 165
  All-of-a-Kind Family Downtown   72, 165
  More All-of-a-Kind Family   72, 81, 139, 165, 166, 174
Amish   122, 123
ANIMAL INN   40, 175
  A Kid's Best Friend   175
  Monkey Business   175
  Scaredy Cat   175
Animal stories   34, 40
Animals   171–176
Appleton, Victor   13, 14, 21, 25
Arabians   117, 118
Araminta's Goat   105
Arbuthnot, May Hill   30

ARCADE EXPLORERS   38, 39, 57, 151, 152, 154
   Electronic Hurricane   151
   Save the Venturians   151, 153
Arts and humanities   149, 152, 154
AUTOMOBILE BOYS   12
Ayres, Ernest   18, 26

BABYSITTERS CLUB   89, 203
Beckman, Margaret   20, 23, 24, 30
Bellairs, John   37
BEVERLY GRAY   11, 61, 143
   Freshman   191, 198
Biemiller, C. L.   10, 38
Birth   139
Bjorklid, Ase   28
Black persons   37, 104–116, 123, 124
Black Pirate   74
Bloom, Marjorie   31
BOBBSEY TWINS   viii, 9, 10, 13, 14, 21, 24, 25, 30, 33, 37, 38, 40, 49, 50, 51, 52, 61, 76, 77, 79, 82, 86, 88, 101, 107, 134, 144, 166, 171, 176–177, 194
   Adventures with Baby May   176
   And Baby May   176
   At Pilgrim Rock   59, 71, 78, 107
   At School   77, 142, 162, 194
   At the Seashore   60, 89, 90, 92, 105, 109, 116, 129, 131, 144, 162, 198
   Blue Poodle Mystery   176
   Camp Fire Mystery   12, 58, 61, 62, 64, 71, 76, 78, 82, 100, 123, 132, 140–141
   Dr. Funnybone's Secret   115
   Greek Hat Mystery   168
   Haunted House Mystery   37
   Horeshoe Riddle   71, 77, 99, 106, 194
   In Eskimo Land   93
   In London Tower   93
   In New Mexico   93
   In the Country   11, 60, 72, 77, 172, 197
   In the Land of Cotton   107, 108, 189, 194
   In Tulip Land   93
   In Washington   58, 101, 105, 106, 121
   Merry Days Indoors and Out   76, 92, 106, 107, 162, 195, 197
   On a Houseboat   93

Index

   On the Deep Blue Sea 93
   Red, White and Blue Mystery 115
   Tagalong Giraffe 115, 168
   Treasure Hunting 93
BOBBSEY TWINS COMMEMORATIVE EDITIONS 106, 115
BOBBSEY TWINS, NEW. *See* NEW BOBBSEY TWINS
BOMBA 13
Bond, James 184
Bonehill, Ralph 25
Bookman 17
Bowman, Irene 18, 19, 23
BOY ALLIES 25, 159
BOY SCOUTS 12, 22, 34, 75, 158, 159, 177
   Burgess 116, 130
     In a Trapper's Camp 59, 78, 130, 164, 168, 169, 171, 172, 177
   Carter 55, 58, 94, 101
     In the Rockies 12, 25, 94, 102, 124, 125, 170, 172, 198
   Payson 12, 25, 55, 94, 107
     Army Airship 58, 61, 80, 102, 119, 133, 168, 191, 194, 197
     Belgian Battlefields 12
     Panama-Pacific Exposition 80, 94, 97, 102, 109, 117, 118, 143, 167
     Under Sealed Orders 80, 95, 102, 136, 170, 191, 196
   Shaler 61, 63, 95
     Prize Pennant 61, 63, 95, 99, 170
Boys Clubs of America Junior Book Awards Reading Program 31
"Breakfast" (short story) 56
BRIGHTON BOYS 76
   At Chateau-Thierry 158
   At St. Mihiel 158
   In the Argonne Forest 158, 161
Bronson, Charles 184, 186
Brown, Janet 7, 8
Brown, Spencer 116
Bryant, William Cullen 169
Bulletin of the Center for Children's Books 103
BUNNY BROWN AND HIS SISTER SUE 59, 77, 107
   In the Sunny South 77, 105, 108, 109
   On Grandpa's Farm 11, 77
Burgess, Thornton W. 4
Burroughs, John 176
Business 133–134

Cabot, Ella Lyman 199
Caldecott Medal winners 5, 27, 30, 49
Call of the Wild 4
CAMPFIRE GIRLS 25, 158
  In After Years 170
Cariou, Mavis Olive 65
Carringer, M. A. 18, 50
Carter, Nick 19
Castlemon, Harry 8
Chandler, Raymond 182
Characteristics of series readers 35–40
Charlotte Temple 74
Chaucer, Geoffrey 54
CHERRY AMES 49, 75, 91, 94, 99, 191
  Clinic Nurse 61, 64, 94, 99, 100, 131, 189
  Cruise Nurse 50
  Dude Ranch Nurse 40
  Senior Nurse 12, 71, 94, 98, 132
  Student Nurse 11
Childhood of Famous Americans (publisher series) 20
Children of the Damned 203
"Children Want Realism in Books" 32
Children's Library Association 17
Children's literature
  pre-twentieth century 3ff.
  problems of definition 3ff.
Chinese 120–122
CHIP HILTON 5, 51, 52, 54, 55, 59, 76, 84, 87, 92, 98, 99, 118, 131, 143, 178, 195
  Buzzer Basket 162, 195, 199
  Strike Three 118, 128
  Touchdown Pass 65, 133, 164, 195
Class consciousness 128–130
Classical vs. developmental 16, 28, 29
Classics 31–32
Cliffhangers 53
Coincidence 54
COLONIAL SERIES 13
Color of series books 49–50
Commager, Henry Steele 3, 201
Confidence Man 54, 57
Conscientious objectors 160–161
Cooper, James Fenimore 3, 61

Index

Critical History of Children's Literature 3, 6, 9, 11, 12, 17, 18, 116, 201
Criticism of children's literature 16–29
  history 16
  principal objections 21
  qualities and terminology 17
Curwood, James Oliver 169

DAVE DAWSON 76
  At Dunkirk 159
  In Libya 159
  On Guadalcanal 159, 162
DAVE PORTER 13, 25
Deane, Paul 22
Death 145–146
Death Wish 186
Description 57
Dick and Jane 90–91
Dickens, Charles 3, 54
Diction 63
Didacticism 3, 6, 7, 8
Dirty Harry 158
Dodd, Dorothy 22, 24, 26
Dodge, Mary Mapes 6
Dohm, Dorothy 79
DON STURDY 13, 25, 46, 49, 51, 54, 58, 59, 61, 74, 75, 76, 78, 88, 92, 93, 95, 98, 107, 131, 146, 171, 172, 174, 203
  Among the Gorillas 92, 118, 119, 131, 146, 147, 150, 168, 174, 190, 192, 197
  Desert of Mystery 58, 62, 95, 118, 119, 135, 146, 147, 167, 190, 192
  In Lion Land 12, 50, 86, 96, 109, 123, 142, 147, 167, 174, 192, 196
  Land of Volcanoes 59, 117, 128, 133, 166, 168, 177, 188
  On the Ocean Bottom 80, 92, 95, 96, 131, 133, 147, 163
  Port of Lost Ships 58, 95, 131, 146, 147, 155, 190, 192, 194, 196
DORIS FEIN 35, 37, 47, 65, 82, 91, 99, 103, 111, 115, 120, 131, 133, 134, 163, 164, 166, 183, 203
  Dead Heat at Long Beach 85, 132, 135, 165, 179, 183
  Deadly Aphrodite 65, 83, 85, 103, 120, 164, 179, 182
  Dr. Doom: Superstar 65, 103, 123, 181
  Mad Samurai 82
  Murder Is No Joke 85, 120, 135, 179, 182

Phantom of the Casino 85, 120, 138, 164, 165, 182
Dowlin, Edwin 27
Drake, Robert 25
Dreiser, Theodore 174

Eakins, M. 9
Eastwood, Clint 158, 184
Eaton, A. T. 3, 6, 7
Edison, Thomas 148, 149
"Editor Makes Plea for Fantasy and Action Stories" 31
Education 142–145
Elementary School Journal 31
ELSIE DINSMORE 7, 8, 19, 25
Empie, Arthur Guy 159
ENCYCLOPEDIA BROWN 45
Erisman, Fred 146, 148, 167
Evans, Eva Knox 105
"Explain Opposition on Ban in Library of 'Series' Books" 28
Exploits of Elaine 53

Fairbanks, Douglas, Sr. 74
Fairy tales 32, 47
Family life 74–85
Fanfare... 1958–1962 17
Fashion 35, 36
Fat persons 100–104
Fathers 85–92
Fenner, Phyllis 20, 21, 22, 23, 147
Fiction preference 31
Fiction series 33
   definition 33
   overview 33–35
Finley, Martha 7, 8
Finn, Huckleberry 21, 26, 79
Foreigners 37, 116–124
Foreshadowing 54
Frank, Josette 21, 22, 23, 52
Franklin, Benjamin 3
Fruchtman, Susan 28
Fu Manchu 121

Index

Gardner, E., and Ramsey, E.   22, 24
Gardner, Martin   26, 27
Garis, Howard   14
Garis, Roger   14
Gay-Neck   46, 50
Gender issues   85–92
Golumb, Bernard   21
Good life   92–96
Good sportsmanship   194–196
GRACE HARLOWE   11, 55, 75, 79, 85, 98, 109, 139, 143, 163, 171, 177, 199
 Junior Year at High School   75, 81, 83, 118, 136, 143
 Plebe Year at High School   61, 75, 80, 102, 117, 129, 132, 143, 166, 169
 Senior Year at High School   75, 136, 142, 162
 Sophomore Year at High School   64, 94, 129, 143, 144, 188, 192, 194, 195, 196
GRACE HARLOWE'S OVERLAND RIDERS   40, 75, 87, 99, 107
 Among the Kentucky Mountaineers   75, 87, 105, 109
 On the Great American Desert   58, 64, 75, 87, 94, 102, 121, 123, 171, 197
Grahame, Kenneth   9
Grosset and Dunlap   14, 26

Hall, C. Stanley   23
Hanna, G., and McAllister, M.   33
Hannigan, Jane   9, 48
Hans Brinker   79
HAPPY HOLLISTERS   34, 37, 49, 51, 52, 53, 58, 76, 77, 78, 79, 84, 86, 88, 93, 128, 134, 166
 Happy Hollisters   90, 98, 171, 195
 Pony Hill Farm   11
HARDY BOYS   viii, 5, 10, 12, 25, 27, 29, 33, 34, 38, 40, 46, 49, 50, 51, 52, 53, 54, 61, 64, 78, 79, 84, 85, 88, 92, 98, 99, 105, 107, 116, 134, 154, 155, 170, 174, 203
 Crimson Shadow   156
 Footprints Under the Window   92, 120, 133, 137, 155
 Great Airport Mystery   142, 163
 Hidden Harbor Mystery   111–112, 170
 Hooded Hawk Mystery   73
 House on the Cliff   88, 90, 99, 120, 128, 137, 155, 156, 170, 193
 Hunting for Hidden Gold   110, 170, 185

 Melted Coins 137, 155
 Mystery at Devil's Paw 117, 124–125, 131
 Mystery of the Chinese Junk 156
 Night of the Werewolf 37
 Phantom Freighter 63, 97, 155
 Program for Destruction 73, 134, 157, 179, 196
 Revenge of the Desert Phantom 12, 61, 100, 103, 112–113, 121, 137, 141, 144, 178, 191
 Secret of Skull Mountain 39
 Secret of Wildcat Swamp 85
 Short Wave Mystery 185
 Sign of the Crooked Arrow 156, 171
 Swamp Monster 115
 Tower Treasure 71, 95, 102, 122, 137, 185
 Track of the Zombie 37
 Twisted Claw 107
HARDY BOYS CASEFILES ix, 5, 36, 37, 49, 51, 53, 111, 157, 180, 203
 Blood Relations 180
 Cult of Crime 185, 186
 Dead on Target 52, 73, 138, 145, 157, 179, 184, 185, 186
 Death Game 179, 185
 Evil, Inc. 185, 186, 191
 Hostages of Hate 50, 54, 59, 73, 100, 123, 138, 157, 170, 179, 185, 186, 192
 Lazarus Plot 186
Harvey, John 51
Hayes, Charles Wallace 25
Heaton, Mrs. Israel 27, 28
Heidi 79
Heins, Ethel 29
Hess, Fjeril 38
Hollowell, Lillian 20, 22
Home and daily life 34
HONEY BUNCH 53, 77, 78, 86, 93, 98, 103, 107, 203
 Her First Days in Camp 98
 Her First Days on a Farm 11
 Her First Little Trip to the Seashore 58, 59, 71, 88, 102, 142, 197
 Her First Little Trip West 40, 71, 72, 125, 126, 167
HONEY BUNCH AND NORMAN 54, 103
 Play Detective at Niagara Falls 59, 60, 90, 188
Honor 37, 193–194
Hope, Laura Lee 13, 77
Horn Book Magazine 4, 17, 19, 29, 83, 103

Index

Hudson, W. H.   17
Humanities. *See* Arts and Humanities
Humor   47, 59
Hunt, Clara   18, 22, 24

Indians. *See* Westerns and Indian stories
Intruder in the dust   108
Irish   117, 154
Italians   118, 122
Ives, Vernon   158

Jack and Jill   31
James, Henry   57
Japanese   117, 119–120
Jennings, Joe   33
Jews   99, 115, 130, 163
Johnson, Elizabeth   18
Jones, Indiana   184
Jordan, Arthur   30, 32, 33, 34
JUDY BOLTON   55, 76, 99, 154
   Clue of the Broken Wing   55, 90, 130, 155, 162, 196
   Yellow Phantom   55, 57, 60, 90, 94, 137, 142, 193
Justice   188–189
"Juvenile Books During Twenty-eight Years"   8, 12

Kennerly, S. L.   6
Kiefer, Sister Monica   3, 6
Kindness   196–197
Kinlock, Lucy   21, 22, 23, 24
Kipling, Rudyard   4, 9
Korean War   159, 162
Kristensen, Kurt   28, 53

Landmark Books   20
Law enforcement officers   154–158
Lazarus, Emma   124
Lectures   38, 59
Length of series books   48–49
Lewis, C. S.   19

"the list" 25–26
Literary Digest 32, 33
LITTLE COLONEL 25
LITTLE HOUSE 27
Little Men 6
Little Women 6, 19
London, Jack 4, 9, 174
LONE RANGER 51, 53, 54, 62, 98, 124, 154, 189, 193, 194
   Code of the West 121, 189, 193
   Lone Ranger 64, 124–125, 167, 177, 191
   Lone Ranger and Tonto 125, 193, 195
Longlegs the Heron 4, 172
Love stories 34

McCloskey, Robert 58
MacDonald, J. F. viii, 114, 116, 123
Mandel, Richard 90
MARJORIE DEAN 11, 61, 143
Materialism 134–135
Mathiews, Franklin 33, 34, 39
Mechanical errors 54
Meigs, C. 3, 4, 6, 7, 9, 16
Melcher, F. 158
Melville, Herman 54
Mercier, Jean 10
MERRIWELL SERIES (Frank and Dick) 10, 25
Messner Shelf of Biography for Young People (publisher's series) 20
MEXICAN WAR 13
Mitchell, L. H. 18, 19, 23
Moby-Dick 3, 21
Moore, Anne Carroll 17
Moore, Thomas V. 39
Moran, B. 36, 38, 47, 111, 180
Morse, Carleton B. 82
Moses, Montrose 158
Mothers 85–92
Motivation 62
MOTOR BOYS 8, 10, 12, 13, 24
MOVING PICTURE BOYS 25, 146
Muir, John 176
Mysteries 34

Index

NANCY DREW   viii, 5, 10, 14, 20, 25, 27, 29, 33, 34, 36, 37, 52, 54, 57, 62, 63, 76, 79, 85, 87, 89, 91, 98, 99, 103, 105, 107, 131, 134, 136, 144, 154, 170, 171, 176, 178
   Case of the Disappearing Diamonds   33, 54, 64, 72, 76, 131, 134, 138, 156, 178, 190, 191, 195
   Clue in the Diary   156
   Clue of the Black Keys   100, 143
   Clue of the Broken Locket   163
   Haunted Bridge   62, 97, 195
   Hidden Staircase   62, 72, 99, 136, 163, 189
   Mardi Gras Mystery   115
   Mystery at Lilac Inn   14, 80, 95, 99, 108, 128, 154, 189, 194, 197
   Mystery of the Moss-Covered Mansion   58, 63, 72, 80, 83, 117, 154, 193
   Mystery of the Tolling Bell   72, 100, 105, 117
   Secret of the Old Clock   33
   Thirteenth Pearl   14
   Triple Hoax   14
   Witch Tree Symbol   122, 163
NANCY DREW FILES   5, 35, 36, 49, 51, 55, 110, 114, 180, 202
   Deadly Intent   65, 72, 73, 100, 103, 121, 123, 131, 138, 179, 180, 190, 191, 196
   False Moves   138, 184
   Murder on Ice   179, 181
   Never Say Die   179
   Recipe for Murder   50, 179, 181
   Smile and Say Murder   179
   Stay Tuned for Danger   181
   Very Deadly Yours   179
Nature and animals   168–176
"Negro Dialect in Children's Books"   106
Nesbitt, E.   3, 4, 9, 10, 17
NEW BOBBSEY TWINS   5, 34, 37, 49, 53, 110, 131, 203
   Case of the Runaway Money   172
   Secret of Jungle Park   50, 78, 82, 112, 134, 157
New England Primer   3
"New Writers for Girls"   23, 32
New York Times Book Review   17
New Yorker   148
Newbery Medal winners   27, 30, 32, 33, 38, 40–41, 49, 65, 79
Nightmare Session   142
Nolan, Eleanor   116
NOT QUITE HUMAN   37, 39, 49, 59, 150, 152
   Batteries Not Included   150, 152

Terror at Play 37
"Not to Be Circulated" 18, 25, 28

OLD GLORY 13
One Man's Family (radio series) 82
One Summer in Maine 58
Opening page 52
Optic, Oliver 8, 25
Optimism 189–190
"Orange, N.J. Honors Nancy Drew" 10, 29
OUR YOUNG AEROPLANE SCOUTS 159
OUTBOARD BOYS 14
Outdoor Boys in the Blue Ridge Mountains 12
OUTDOOR GIRLS 25, 159
    At Cedar Ridge, or The Mystery of the Old Windmill 170
Over the Top 159

Page, Thomas Nelson 107
Pan-American 13
Paragraph length 51–52
Parents 71–74
Parker, Robert B. 184
Pease, Howard 27, 51, 52
Perils of Pauline 53
Perry, Phyllis 144
Peter Cottontail 27
Peter Pan 93
Philip Lief Group 55
Phillips, Louis 29, 116, 137, 156
Physical appearance as revelation of character 97–100, 104
Physical impairments 139–142
Pierre 54, 57
Plots 22, 46, 61
Pluck, fortitude, and "sissiness" 197–200
Poe, Edgar Allan 3
Popular Mechanics 31
Porgy and Bess 111
Potter, Beatrix 9
Preview endings 53
Prince and the Pauper 79
PRIVATE SCHOOL 145
Proscribed children's reading 25–28

Index

"Provo Library Board Gives Stand" 28
Pyle, Howard 9

RACE AGAINST TIME 51, 74, 76, 111, 180, 203
   Secret of the Third Watch 180, 195
RADIO BOYS 146
RAILROAD BOYS 146
Rankin, Marie 32, 33, 38, 45–46, 49, 50, 51, 52, 57, 65
Reading preferences. *See* Series satisfaction of needs and reading preferences (table)
Realism 34
Reason vs. emotion 190–192
Rebecca of Sunnybrook Farm 79
RED CROSS GIRLS 76, 159
Religion 162–166
Revelation of character. *See* Physical appearance as revelation of character
RICK BRANT 52, 59, 75, 93, 99, 146
   Egyptian Cat 147, 178
   100 Fathoms Under 57, 72, 170, 178, 197
Robinson Crusoe 202
Robots 60, 151–152
Rohmer, Sax 120
ROLLO 4, 6
Romance 35, 135–138
Roosevelt, Theodore 169, 199
Root, Mary E. 25
Rose, Ada Campbell 31
Rosenberg, J. K. vii
ROVER BOYS vii, viii, 8, 10, 12, 13, 21, 25, 38, 46, 50, 51, 52, 54, 55, 62, 75, 76, 78, 87, 101, 104, 107, 109, 131, 139, 170, 173, 177, 203
   In New York 12, 97, 119, 123, 136, 142, 143, 162, 188, 198
   In Southern Waters 105, 109, 119
   In the Jungle 12
   In the Mountains 12, 73, 105, 136, 173, 190, 191, 194
   On Land and Sea 63, 109, 162, 167, 173, 190
   On the Ocean 12
   Shipwrecked 105
Rowell, Adelaide 105
RUTH FIELDING 13

St. Nicholas: A Magazine for Boys and Girls 6, 7
Satisfaction of needs. *See* Series satisfaction of needs and reading preferences (table)
Saturday Review of Literature 17
Sawyer, Tom 21, 26, 79, 148
School life and activities 34
Science fiction 34, 39
Science, scientists, and technology 146–154
Scott, Polly Ann 5, 34, 49, 50
Scott, Sir Walter 3
Sentence length 52
Series Books for the American Girl vii
"Series Library Dispute" 27
Series satisfaction of needs and reading preferences (table) 41–45
Seuss, Dr. 57, 96
Shanklin, Lucille 13, 147
Shepard, John 118
Shibumi 185
Simon and Schuster 14
Sisk, John 21, 22, 23
SIX LITTLE BUNKERS 77
Size of series books 49
SLEEPOVER FRIENDS 79, 132, 203
  Kate's Campout 80
  Patti's Luck 81, 89
Smith, Dora 8, 10, 11
Smyers, R. P. 19
Soderbergh, Peter 10, 15, 16, 28
SOLDIERS OF FORTUNE 13
Sports stories 34
Stang, K. J. vii
Star Trek 150
Star Wars 150
Steinbeck, John 56
Steinfirst, S. 36, 38, 47, 111, 180
Stevenson, R. L. 4
Stockum, Hilda van 145
Stratemeyer, Edward 4, 13, 14, 74, 149, 177, 202
Stratemeyer Syndicate viii, 4, 8, 13, 55, 177
SUBMARINE BOYS 12
SUE BARTON 50, 64, 75, 88, 91, 93–94
  Rural Nurse 64, 74
  Senior Nurse 11, 64, 97, 101, 132
  Student Nurse 11, 63, 101, 118, 188

Index

Visiting Nurse 50, 105, 108, 110, 118, 137, 197
Success 131–134
Summary beginnings 52–53
SWEET VALLEY HIGH   ix, 33, 34, 35, 95, 98, 111, 114, 121, 132, 138, 144, 202, 203
   All Night Long 138
   Dangerous Love 145
   Double Love 99, 138
   Forbidden Love 138
   Love Letters 138
   Out of Control 138
   Out of Reach 121
   Promises 145
   Racing Hearts 50, 138
SWEET VALLEY TWINS   viii, 33, 34, 49, 81, 95, 111, 114, 132, 138, 144, 203
   Choosing Sides 144
   Haunted House 83
   Second Best 81
   Sneaking Out 81, 95, 144
Syndicates for the production of series   viii, 4, 8, 13, 55

Technology. *See* Science, scientists, and technology
Terman, Lewis   5, 20, 21, 22, 23, 24, 31, 33, 48
Thackeray, William M.   3
Things to Come 153
Thirty Twentieth Century Children's Books Every Adult Should Know   4, 5, 19
Thorndill, Christine   177
Titles of series   50
TOM AND RICKY   49, 57, 96
   Thief in the Brown Van 50
TOM SWIFT (first series)   viii, 9, 10, 13, 14, 20, 21, 23, 25, 34, 49, 50, 51, 52, 54, 56, 57, 59, 60, 61, 62, 74, 76, 78, 79, 87, 92, 98, 99, 105, 107, 131, 139, 146, 147–148, 151, 152, 176, 177, 194, 203
   Aerial Warship 147, 148–149
   Airship 12, 74, 109, 131, 144, 147, 171, 195
   Electric Locomotive 147, 149
   Electric Rifle 148
   Electric Runabout 149
   Great Oil Gusher 149
   Motor Cycle 105, 109, 133, 148, 149, 150

    Talking Pictures   105, 110, 133, 136, 148, 152, 163, 188, 189
    Television Detector   147, 167
    Undersea Search   119, 134, 135, 136, 192, 196
    Wireless Message   60, 92, 146, 149, 192
    Wizard Camera   147
TOM SWIFT, JR. (second series)   5, 11, 14, 34, 51, 52, 53, 59, 60, 61, 75, 79, 86, 89, 92, 93, 98, 128, 131, 136, 146, 148, 150
    Caves of Nuclear Fire   71, 72, 93, 98, 170, 175
    Deep Sea Hydrodome   50
    Electronic Retroscope   150
    Flying Lab   88, 100, 125, 150, 167, 191
    Jetmarine   151, 175, 189, 192
    Race to the Moon   25, 71, 83, 150, 151, 167, 189, 191, 192
    Rocket Ship   71, 80, 136, 167, 171
    Spectromarine Selector   150
    Visitor from Planet X   71, 151, 163, 171
TOM SWIFT (third series)   34, 39, 49, 56, 79, 124, 126, 150
    Astral Fortress   56, 126, 140, 150, 151, 152, 183
    City in the Stars   56, 60, 61, 63, 126, 140, 150, 152, 153, 183–184
    Invisible Force   147, 152
Treasure Island   26
Trevanian (author)   184, 185
TV endings   54
Type size   50–51

UNCLE SAM'S BOYS   76
    In the Ranks   90, 98, 159, 173, 198
    On Field Duty   119, 159
    Smash the Germans   159
    With Pershing's Troops at the Front   12, 117, 119, 159, 160
Uncle Wiggily   20, 25
United States vs. travel   166–168

VICKI BARR   75, 91
Vietnam War   159, 162
Viguers, Ruth   3, 9, 10, 11, 12, 17, 18, 19, 22, 24, 116
Violence   159, 176–187

Walden   3
Walker, Joan   32, 33

Index

Wallace, Robert 19, 24
War 34, 46, 158–162
Ward, Pearl 19
Wealth 132–133
Wells, Caroline 25
Westerns and Indian stories 34, 40, 124–127
"What the Boys Are Reading" 31
White, Robb 18
Wiederman, Bernice 21
Wiggin, Kate Douglas 9
Williams, Tennessee 93
Winfield, Arthur 13, 14
Wizard of Oz books 25, 26, 27, 74, 168
WOODLAND GANG 36, 76, 89, 96, 111, 113, 118, 141, 144, 145, 163, 164, 166, 178
   Hidden Jewels 113, 141
   Missing Will 50, 113, 114, 138, 144, 157, 174
   Old Gold Coins 89
   Stolen Animals 113, 157
Wright, Harold Bell 169

Yost, Edna 14
Young Adult Services of the Public Library, A.L.A. 23
Young People's Literature in Series vii

OHIO UNIVERSITY LIBRARY

Please return this book as soon as you have finished with it. In order to avoid a fine it must be returned by the latest date stamped below.

RETURN BY

MAR 15 1993   MAY 1 1 2002

MAR 04 1993
                APR 2 1 2002

DEC 0 1 2009

RECEIVED
SEP 0 4 2009

CL   JUN 5 1992